The First
American Grand Prix

The First American Grand Prix

The Savannah Auto Races, 1908–1911

Tanya A. Bailey

McFarland & Company, Inc., Publishers
Jefferson, North Carolina

Unless otherwise indicated, all photographs
are from the author's collection.

LIBRARY OF CONGRESS CATALOGUING-IN-PUBLICATION DATA

Bailey, Tanya A., 1969–
The First American Grand Prix : the Savannah auto races, 1908–1911 / Tanya A. Bailey.
    p.   cm.
Includes bibliographical references and index.

ISBN 978-0-7864-7697-8 (softcover : acid free paper) ∞
ISBN 978-1-4766-1522-6 (ebook)

1. United States Grand Prix Race—History—20th century.
2. Automobile racing—Georgia—Savannah—History—20th century.   I. Title.
GV1034.12.U54B35 2014   796.7209758'724—dc23   2014013790

BRITISH LIBRARY CATALOGUING DATA ARE AVAILABLE

© 2014 Tanya A. Bailey. All rights reserved

*No part of this book may be reproduced or transmitted in any form
or by any means, electronic or mechanical, including photocopying
or recording, or by any information storage and retrieval system,
without permission in writing from the publisher.*

On the cover: Fiat taking a corner (FIAT and FIAT USA,
Great Savannah Races Museum); Trophy cup for
Auto Club's Savannah Race (Library of Congress)

Printed in the United States of America

McFarland & Company, Inc., Publishers
Box 611, Jefferson, North Carolina 28640
www.mcfarlandpub.com

To my parents John and Val Bailey and my brother Johnny:
thank you for taking me to the races and teaching me to love cars!

To my husband Martyn, my children J.T. and Elisabeth,
who I adore. Thank you for your love and support.

To all the drivers, owners and organizers of the early
Savannah Races, thank you for giving your hearts and minds
to the auto racing world and for making Savannah
the City of the Golden Era of Road Racing.

Contents

Acknowledgments	ix
Preface	1
Prologue: Early Racing in Savannah	5
1. The Automobile Club of America and the American Automobile Association	15
2. Early Racing in the South	25
3. America's Finest Course, of Course!	31
4. March 1908 Drivers	47
5. From Triumph to Tragedy in Savannah	61
6. Drivers of the International Light Car and American Grand Prize Races of 1908	80
7. International Light Car Race of 1908	112
8. American Grand Prize of 1908	120
9. Drivers of the 1910 and 1911 Races	135
10. Cars and Races of 1910	147
11. The November 27, 1911, Races: The Tiedeman Trophy, the Savannah Challenge, and the Vanderbilt Cup	167
12. American Grand Prix of 1911	179
13. What Happened to the Great Savannah Races After 1911?	197
Epilogue	205
Appendix: Specifications and Race Results	
SPECIFICATIONS: CARS OF 1911	206
RACE RESULTS, 1908	208

Race Results, 1910	209
Race Results, 1911	210
Notes	212
Bibliography	220
Index	222

Acknowledgments

Special thanks go to Elisabeth Smith for assisting with research at the Great Savannah Races Museum and providing input on the engineering aspects of the early race cars. Thank you to Martyn and J.T. Smith for encouragement, unending patience and inspiration. I would like to thank the following people for their support and advice: Dr. Rick Timms, Dr. Konrad Eisenbichler, Maldwyn Jenkins, Brian and Paula Palmer, and Mr. Bill Shira, who is a great mentor to the business community and an avid race fan.

I must point out that this book could not have been written without Dr. Julian K. Quattlebaum having documented this history from a firsthand account of the races, and his nephew Robyn Quattlebaum, whom I am very proud to count among my friends. Thank you, Robyn, for working with me on the Great Races Centennial in 2008 and for the wonderful photos and images of the races that have contributed to this book and the Great Savannah Races Museum. Thank you to John and Ginger Duncan, who have been wonderful neighbors, supporters and contributors to the Great Savannah Races Museum Collection. I would like to thank Paul Tracy, Doug Nye, Jerry Helck, Horace Davies, and Don Cherry for inspiring me from afar. Thank you to David Malsher, editor of *Racer* magazine, for listening to my stories about Savannah's prominent place in auto racing history and inviting me to assist on the David Bruce-Brown story.

Thank you to the Horseless Carriage Foundation and the Georgia Historical Society for providing excellent reference materials and keeping early automobile history alive. Thank you to Fiat and Mercedes Benz for sending information, photographs and materials pertaining to the Savannah races and for the roles they played in making these races such a success. Thank you to the beautiful people of Savannah, who have embraced me as their own.

Preface

I was very fortunate to grow up in a family that had a great interest in racing. Early in life, I was introduced to antique vehicles by my Papa, who along with my brother, restored a 1940s model International pickup truck. My interest was piqued, even though I was too small to do much. I watched their progress very closely and tried to help by holding a wrench or an oil can as they worked. I wanted to be around that old truck—and my brother and Papa as they worked—as often as I could. That love of antique cars never went away.

My first job out of high school was working for Rothmans, Benson and Hedges, which sponsored the Rothmans Porsche Series. The young employees and summer interns were invited to volunteer to help the marketing department prepare for the events. In turn, we received tickets and, if we were very lucky, perhaps a short ride around the parking lot in the company's Porsche. A few years passed and I completed a diploma program in creative writing and started freelancing. My first piece, an article about my childhood friend, Paul Tracy, was published in *World of Wheels* magazine. Paul was kind enough to let me interview him when he was starting out with Roger Penske's team in Indycar and later the CART and Champcar series. He was a tremendous influence on my early writing on racing.

A few years after I began freelance writing for racing magazines such as *On Track*, I returned to school to study English, Renaissance studies and biology at University of Toronto. As soon as I finished my degree, I moved to Savannah, Georgia, with my husband, who is an engineer. My two worlds—history and racing—collided when I learned Savannah held some very large road races during the pioneering era—also known as the Golden Era of Racing—beginning in 1908. I inquired of City of Savannah officials as to whether they would be holding a centennial and offered my assistance if they were. At that time, they said they weren't very well informed about the history of the races. They suggested that I spearhead an event and offered to put me in touch with several people to help accomplish that.

I began collecting items to bring home to Savannah, which I hoped would reveal to the local community how the world saw these significant races. While I was researching, I was also planning the centennial event for the First American Grand Prix—the Grand Prize—along with a talented and dedicated group of people from all walks of life in Savannah, including Dr. Rick Timms, who built the Hutchinson Island race course now named Grand Prize of America Avenue. Rick was one of the promoters of the Indy Lights Race on Hutchinson Island in downtown Savannah in 1997 and worked tirelessly to bring professional racing to the city. His job was not an easy one, but he did pull it off. He was extremely encouraging when I contacted him about the Centennial events and became a friend and mentor to me. Rick also worked as a trackside trauma physician and surgeon and was very knowledgeable about race course safety. I was very fortunate to have such an expert to consult with from time to time and felt Savannah was also extremely fortunate to have him.

I began collecting items from all over the world and came to realize how very significant and sadly overlooked these races were. However, the Centennial was a vastly successful event and allowed me to kick-start local interest in the races. I thought very highly of the fabulous track on Hutchinson Island. It would be wonderful to have professional racing return to Savannah at this venue, which could be much like a Monaco of the South, as Savannah was from 1908 to 1911. I started traveling and volunteering in the media centers of Champcar races in Houston, San Jose, and Las Vegas, at my own expense, hoping to learn more about the racing industry from the inside rather than through the journalist's perspective. These were great experiences and I had the opportunity to meet many wonderful people from the Champcar and ALMS series as well as many highly revered journalists such as Chris Economaki and David Malsher.

Malsher, editor of *Racer* magazine, was an excellent person to talk to. I told him about the Savannah races of the past and he showed a genuine interest in Savannah's place in the Grand Prix history of America. In 2009, he contacted me about assisting with finding information and photographs for an article on David Bruce-Brown, who won a double championship in Savannah in 1910 and 1911. The article ran in the February 2010 issue of *Racer* and I was very excited to see the Savannah history being noticed by the motorsports media.

Over the next few years, my interest in the Savannah races deepened. It seemed that not only was this a forgotten chapter in what should be America's most celebrated motorsports event of all time, but the connection to Grand Prix racing and the prehistory of Formula One became apparent in the connection with teams such as Fiat, Mercedes-Benz and Renault. It seemed that very few realized that Grand Prize was simply the English moniker for Grand Prix and that Savannah had, in fact, held the first American Grand Prix in 1908. No less impressive was the fact that the track was the most cutting-edge road racing course of its time and the races' success has never been replicated in the United States in terms of attendance, technology and significance.

I have covered the building of this course, which utilized Macadam road-building techniques, in depth, as well as provided a look at the personalities behind the races: the car or team owners, drivers, and organizers. Many of the ties forged among these people complete the picture in a way that only a spectator would have experienced at that time. They also offer the opportunity to look at how the races affected the lives of everyone involved for years to come, including Savannah's racing and newer racing venues.

I strove to show what was so unique about Savannah's races and how the city was a Southern mecca of racing in ways that go far beyond the auto races of 1908–1911. The history is very rich, from the bicycle racing which preceded the auto races, to the motorcycle racing that took place after. I explore the theories of why the races came about, and the factors or events that effected the demise of road racing and Savannah's races, in particular. I have tried to objectively compare these events and look at how they fit with the contemporary races, such as the French Grand Prix, the Vanderbilt Cup and the Coppa Florio.

Primary resources have been a great key to finding deeper answers to the questions that spurred my writing, including some of the rare items found in the Great Savannah Races Museum, which I founded in 2012. While I do rely on secondary resources, they are few. Among the most significant resources are Julian Quattlebaum's *The Great Savannah Races* and Peter Helck's *Great Auto Races* and *The Checkered Flag* books. Both of these authors were actual witnesses to auto racing events of this period, and their works are invaluable references to the early history of the sport. Dr. Quattlebaum left his collection to the Georgia Historical Society, which is a treasure trove for research. This gentleman offered a look at Savannah's races from the perspective of a well-educated native of the city who was there, and who had an understanding of the cars and their significance. Most importantly, he was someone who conveyed his love for racing. His work could never be duplicated, but I hope that this book offers the other side of the coin in a way: a look at the races from an outside perspective, from the drivers who came here to how the world viewed the races when they occurred.

I also add some technical information on the cars and industry to help the reader look at the race results with a more critical eye. In addition, I have enjoyed *Thunder at Sunrise,* by John M. Burns, which pulled the Vanderbilt Cup races and Grand Prize races into one place very well and offered the setting of the Indianapolis 500 in contrast. My focus is different, in that I try to show how the Savannah races stood apart and were not as strongly connected to the Indianapolis races as some might assume.

After years of objective research, I am convinced that Savannah was the most suitable venue for America's most significant early races and I hope readers will see why this is so. My book also explores Savannah's races in the context of the great city it was at that time: a city that was poised to become as large and prominent as Chicago or New York and could have been a mecca for the automobile industry, as Detroit became. I try to answer the how, why, where and when questions that historians and race fans are often left wondering about.

I hope you will enjoy my work. Please come to visit Savannah, where you can see many relics of these early races for yourself all around the city. I would be remiss not to add my personal hope that by presenting Savannah's great history in auto racing, perhaps the professional racing world will take notice and find its way back to racing in Savannah!

Prologue: Early Racing in Savannah

How did a small Southern city, barely known in today's world of motorsports, ever come to host the first American Grand Prix—known in English as "Grand Prize"? This race, which is strongly related to the prehistory of Formula One, was held in Savannah in 1908. It was not a fluke that Savannah was chosen as its site. Various forms of racing had taken the city by storm in the decades before auto racing arrived. Racing was an exciting new pastime which began shortly before the turn of the century and Savannahians had truly caught the bug. They enjoyed watching any type of race: yacht racing, foot racing, bicycle racing, motorcycle racing, horse racing—even bicycles racing horses! The earliest locations for racing events in Savannah were Doyle's Race Track alongside the Warsaw River and Wheelmen's Park, which was located on the northeast corner of Victory Drive and Skidaway Road. The Savannah Electric Company was one of the city's prominent patrons of sporting events; it even partnered with the Thunderbolt Casino to put on a bicycle "race" of sorts where the cycles traveled across a high wire, 90 feet in the air above a man-made lake, while acrobats hung on to them from below.[1]

The bicycle and racing craze was a crucial factor in the origins of auto racing in Savannah and in America. Several very important automobile inventors and racers of the pioneering days came directly from the bicycle industry. Among these were the famous Duryea Brothers; Edgar Apperson, who raced in Savannah's first automobile races in March 1908; and Alexander Pope, who entered the Pope-Hummer in Savannah's Vanderbilt Cup race in 1911. The lessons learned from early bicycle technology also led to aviation inventions by Orville and Wilbur Wright in Dayton, Ohio, where the brothers built and repaired bicycles.

A club for bicycle enthusiasts in America was formed in 1880. Known as the League of American Wheelmen (L.A.W.), it was the premier group for bicycle development, racing and related sports. Like many early automobile clubs, the group worked with the government to enact changes to bicycling laws and encouraged the Good Roads Movement. The League of American Wheelmen was heavily involved in providing financial and intellectual support to Congress for the appropriation of $10,000 to launch an inquiry regarding roads. This led to the formation of a new government department: the U.S. Office of Road Inquiry, which later became the Federal Highway Administration.[2]

National bicycle racing events were held on the east side of Savannah, in a town called Warsaw, also known as Thunderbolt, in 1893. Savannah had a population of 61,000 at that time, so the attendance of 1,500 spectators was a very good turnout from the locals. The

League of American Wheelmen at their national meeting in Hartford, Connecticut. The L.A.W. was the organization responsible for financially supporting the establishment of the U.S. Office of Road Inquiry, which later became the Federal Highway Administration.

Savannah Electric Company owned and ran the streetcar service out to Thunderbolt. It was thrilled with the high turnout, but unfortunately, put too many cable cars on the tracks to transport spectators to the event and inadvertently overloaded the circuit. The transportation breakdown lowered the number of spectators who could travel to the events, as hundreds of people were unable to make the trip to the east side by other means. The Savannah Electric Company was very involved in sponsoring these events because its revenues came from the fares it charged to use the electric streetcars or subway lines of the early period. One of its most popular routes was out to Thunderbolt along what is now Victory Drive.

Bicycle races were extremely profitable for the organizers. One of the favorite entertainments for the crowds was the bicycle "trick riding" by Charles L. Williams. His ability to get his bicycle airborne on jumps and to seemingly twist the bicycle into a pretzel astounded the crowds. There were also a lot of eyes on the panel of celebrity judges, who were housed in a special box near the grandstands. The celebrities were a mix of men from the local community and the bicycle racing world. They included Jack Prince, H.C. Wheeler and Whitaker. Members of Savannah's own local cycling club, known as the Savannah Wheelmen, were quite a presence at the events they helped to organize. The Savannah Wheelmen had a bicycle race of their own during the events, which was won by R.V. Connerat in 2 minutes and 51 seconds. He was closely followed by F.W. Williams at a time of 2 minutes and 52 seconds.

Two Charleston brothers, John and Isaac Baird, did very well at the Savannah races, with Isaac breaking records in the one-mile handicap race with a time of 2 minutes and 37 seconds. This set the bar high for the Southern riders in the sport that year. Isaac Baird raced

The Thunderbolt Casino in 1908 on the Wilmington River was the place where many of the drivers and teams held celebratory dinners during the racing events of 1908–1911.

in the exhibition with the renowned August Zimmerman to open the events, then entered two one-mile races and the quarter-mile open. Both brothers entered the three-mile handicap and the one-mile handicap. John Baird won the three-mile handicap race with a time of 8 minutes and 9.5 seconds.

Thunderbolt was called Warsaw at that time, after the Warsaw River. This was the place where curiosity seekers and high society alike went to play. The Thunderbolt area had multiple music venues situated on the banks of the river in band shells, formal gardens, restaurants, recreational facilities and sporting venues. Entertainment from the mid–1800s to the turn of the century included many forms of racing, most of which began alongside the river, which is now named the Wilmington River and is part of the intracoastal waterway. A yacht club played a prominent role in the early events; with its location between the salt marsh and a picturesque bend of the river, it was the perfect spot for regattas and sailboat races, especially as Doyles' Race Track was located right next to it and offered horse racing. The Thunderbolt Casino was also located in this early recreation district and drew people from all over the country. In the heart of this entertainment and sports lover's mecca was Mechanic's Road, a very unassuming street in Thunderbolt, today housing the Thunderbolt Museum. However, it was one of the earliest roads in the area from the mid–1800s through to America's first Grand Prix auto race of 1908. Mechanic's Road was the heart of racing in Savannah. It would become part of the excellent hairpin turn used in the Grand Prize Race of 1908 and backed onto Doyles' Race Track, which was the camp for the Fiat team that won the Grand Prix in 1908.

The Coliseum at Wheelmen's Park was the first racing venue in Savannah to receive significant national attention. It began as a simple oval-shaped bicycle racing track and was located directly on the Thunderbolt streetcar line. This track was significant to bicycle racing

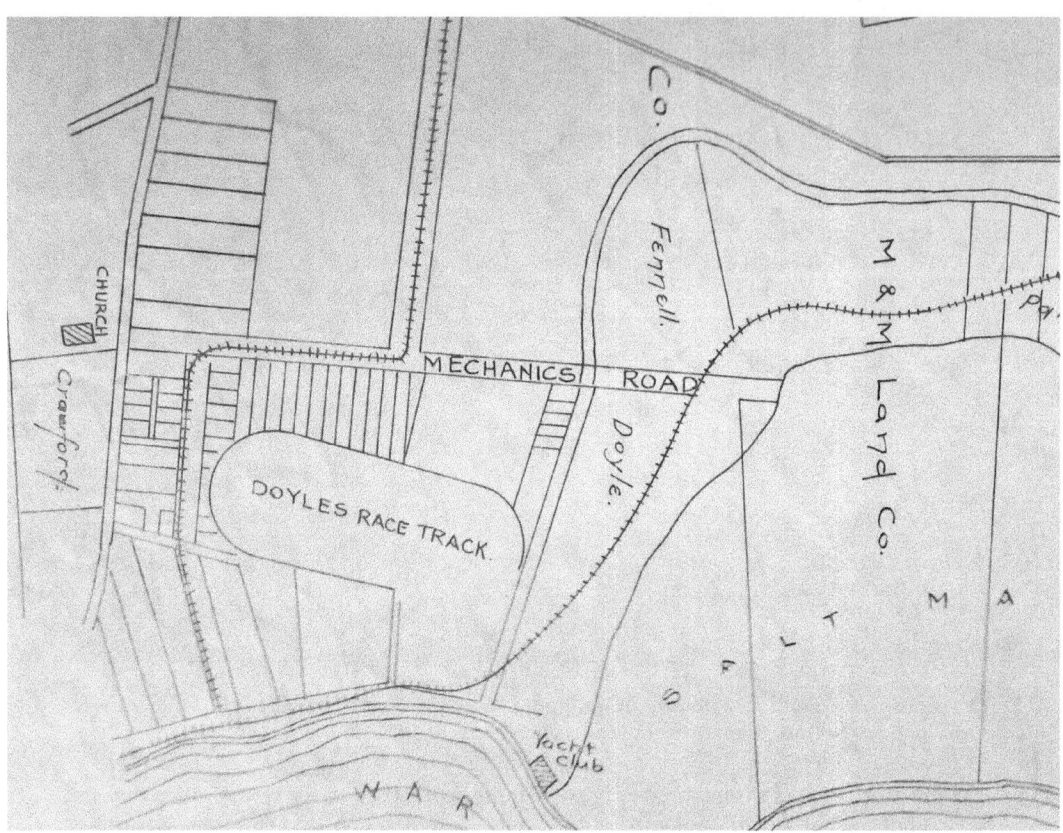

Doyles' Race Track in Thunderbolt, Georgia, was the center of the racing world in Savannah at the turn of the century. Horses, and later cars, were raced on the track, which was located close to the banks of the Wilmington River, where yacht races were held from the late 1850s onward. Teams such as Fiat made their camp at Doyles' Race Track during the Grand Prize races (courtesy City of Savannah, Research Library and Municipal Archives, 3121–007).

due to its modern construction and the fact that champion racers came from all over America to race on it in the earliest days of the sport. The track, which was the first paved cement bicycle track in America, opened in February 1893. It quickly attracted the attention of the League of American Wheelmen, the organization that comprised the top riders in the country in that time who competed at the national and international level. The Savannah race was the first League of American Wheelmen race to be held in Georgia.[3]

Savannah's Wheelmen's Park was unique because the only other cement course in the world at that time was the famous "Buffalo Velodrome" in Paris, France. The Savannah track was part of a larger complex on the Thunderbolt Shell Road. It contained a pit complete with telephones, grandstands and bleachers seating 3,500 people. Within the track was an athletic field for baseball, football and a 200-yard rifle range alongside the grandstand. The track itself was a four-lap track with banked curves measuring 1 foot in 5 feet. The front stretch of the track was 30 feet wide and the back stretch narrowed to 15 feet. Several prominent men in Savannah were responsible for building the $10,000 track, including C.S. Richmond, S.M. Whitesides, R.H. Polk, W.J. Lindsay, and Henry MacAlpin.[4]

World champions of the era such as Zimmerman, Smith and Johnson raced on the

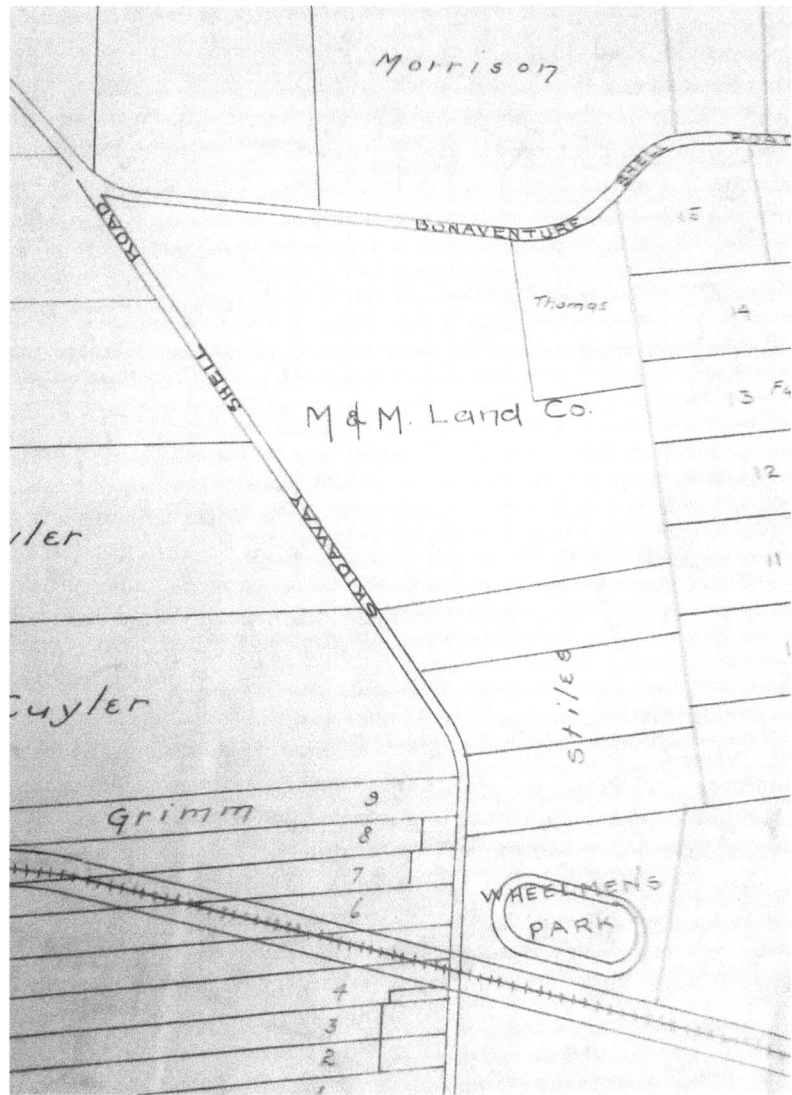

Wheelmen's Park was located at Skidaway and Victory Drive in Thunderbolt, Georgia. The park was first built in 1866 as a sod track by Abraham Beasley, a well-known black businessman in Savannah. It later became home to the Savannah Electrics baseball team and the Bicycle Racing Coliseum (courtesy City of Savannah, Research Library and Municipal Archives, 3121–007).

track, and famous trainer T. Eck arrived to survey the track and winter events.[5] August Zimmerman of Camden, New Jersey, was famous for his graceful riding and many victories. He was the first hero among American cyclists, winning acclaim from the press everywhere he went. Many believed he was the greatest cyclist of all time—and the fact that he could draw up to 30,000 spectators went far in supporting the claim. A typical racing weekend would offer purses of $500 and up to the riders.

Although few words have been published about the Savannah track, it was well known among the national pioneering circuits in bicycle racing. As soon as it was built, the experts in the sport touted its speed and excellent location as making it a superior venue for bicycle racing. Four thousand spectators showed up to witness the first events. More than 26 electric rail cars took people directly to the course, and people also arrived on foot and by carriage. Hundreds of Savannah's ladies showed up with the male spectators, wearing the colors of the Savannah Wheelmen. They enjoyed the racing and the live music provided at the grandstand and bleacher areas. The sport was new and exciting to the people of Savannah, but the world champions Zimmerman and Isaac Baird truly captured their attention and catapulted bicycle racing into a phenomenon in the region. The novelty of seeing a state-of-the-art concrete track—which was built at a time when many had never seen concrete on a road, let alone a race track—drew thousands to see this wondrous technology over the next few years.[6]

Several races were held on the course over the cool, windy days of February 22 and 23, 1893. The first race was at three o'clock in the afternoon. More than 200 riders attended the meet. All of the racers met at the DeSoto Hotel on Liberty Street in downtown Savannah and were transported to the track in Thunderbolt by carriage. The day began with a quarter-mile exhibition race between the popular champion Zimmerman and H.C. Wheeler of New York. Wheeler was given a handicap of 20 yards.

The first day of racing was primarily made up of local matches and short sprints to warm up the crowd for the big events on the second day. As was customary for the bicycle races, the first race held was a novice race for local cyclists from Savannah and Brunswick, Georgia, and from Charleston, South Carolina. The men who raced included Charles Williams, T.P. Whaley and J.L. Johnson of Charleston; W.C. O'Byrne, W. Gross, and R.V. Conneras of Savannah; and R.E. Schuman of Brunswick. It was a close race, won by J.L. Johnson, who finished the quarter mile in 3 minutes and 12.5 seconds. He was very closely followed by W.W. Gross, who came in second with a time of 3 minutes and 14 seconds.[7] The local cyclist races were thought to have the twin benefits of attracting local spectators and finding talent in the sport that might be undiscovered.

The second race was the one-mile open featuring M. Ed Wilson of Savannah; Isaac Baird and Steve Welsh of Charleston, H.R. Steensen of Rockaway, New Jersey; and H.C. Wheeler of New York. Baird won the race in 2 minutes and 46 seconds, 8 seconds ahead of the second-place winner Welsh, who completed the mile in 2 minutes, 54 seconds.[8]

Several unusual events were also included in the first day's events. One was an egg race, although not as we know such races today. For these races, the egg had to be carried by the bicycle riders back and forth to designated locations and switched for other eggs. The other event involved a "diminutive rider" who was apparently teased about his speed and the 10-inch-wheel bicycle he rode in a sort of clownish comedy routine. As in many races, one of the day's biggest talking points was a collision which occurred during the novice race. Each moment could bring awe, fear, excitement and despair to the crowds. Bicycle racing was an instant hit! Savannahians could not wait for the bicycle races to return to their beautiful new Coliseum.

One infamous event occurred in later years. Marshal Major Taylor, a black world champion racer who had raced bicycles around the world, arrived in Savannah to race at Wheelmen's Park in 1898. He encountered some hostility due to his race and, immediately upon arriving, had to change rooming houses in order to reside with a black family on Lincoln Street during his visit. His time in Savannah was very unfortunate. The owners of Wheelmen's Park did not permit black racers to ride and he was turned away. Taylor turned to the roads to train, most notably on the Louisville Road. However, even on the public roads he encountered criticism. A group known as "The White Riders" were not happy to share the road with Taylor as he trained. One day, they chased him from the outskirts of town where

The Savannah Automobile Club Car was used on the course after work was completed each year, to test it out before any drivers or teams arrived for the races. The occupants are unknown (courtesy Pratt Matthews family).

Louisville Road is located, back into the city. The following day he received a letter from the group telling him to leave town.

Over time, the earlier bicycle racing began to change in form. If you lived in America at the turn of the century and you hadn't heard of the motor-paced bicycle racing craze, then you didn't know Jack—Jack Prince, that is. Jack was born John Shillington Prince in Coventry, England, in 1859. Prince was a world champion bicycle racer who had assisted with the organization of the earlier Savannah races. He was one of the leading promoters in America for the sport by the late 1890s. Prince oversaw the building and management of circular wooden bicycle racing tracks, also known as velodromes. Several of these were coliseums located in Southern cities such as Atlanta and Jacksonville, Florida. Prince's tracks were usually sketched out hastily, rather than being designed via formal architectural plans. Their creator seemed very well-to-do and was famous for wearing a Derby hat. Prince was described in the Savannah newspapers as "a hustler" who could get things done quickly and efficiently.[9] Prince would simply scope out the potential for spectators in a city, visit a promising site and get to work driving wooden stakes into the ground for the new coliseum— that is, an open-air race track. In a matter of days or weeks, dozens of carpenters would arrive, along with railroad cars full of lumber and steel spikes. The coliseums would take shape quickly, within a month or so, and grandstands and boxes for officials would be built last.[10] It was a slightly different setup in Savannah, however, with its cement course.

Motor-paced racing was almost a mixed genre falling somewhere between motorcycle races and bicycle races. The bicycle riders were paced for time by a motorized bike that rode with them. These events were among the earliest type of motor racing seen in most places in the world. Savannah was no exception. The motor-paced races of 1902 and onward were, in a way, a restructuring of the bicycle racing sport. They provided excitement, new technology and a heightened level of danger to the riders and spectators. Bicycle tires often had difficulty keeping up with the pacer speed and were known to burst at such high speeds, especially in longer races. It is also quite important to note that it was during this time of high popularity for motor-paced racing in America that the first major road race took place: the Vanderbilt Cup, which was held on Long Island in 1902. The Vanderbilts, who were already familiar with the Georgia coast, would likely have followed the racing in Savannah. It was no coincidence that the city had such a significant reputation in racing that the AAA and ACA might vie to hold races here. Some of the finest racing courses of their time had been built for the bicycle races at Wheelmen's Park and for yacht races and horse races in Thunderbolt. At the turn of the century, Savannah was already a racing mecca, far ahead of cities that rose in prominence relative to racing much later such as Indianapolis and Daytona.

The racers who came to the Coliseum were generally the top men in the industry. They raced a circuit each fall from September to December. Dominating the sports headlines of the newspapers on an almost daily basis, the feats of the racers were enjoyed all over America and especially in Savannah, where the baseball season was just finished. Beginning September 10, 1902, the "motor-bicycles" raced in the Coliseum in Savannah under Prince's direction. Prince arrived in the city at the start of the new season with three of the sports' top racers, motors for the bicycles, and safety equipment for the track.[11]

The racers were famous across America: Jay Eaton; Gus Lawson, also known as "the Terrible Swede"; Charles Turville; and Dare-Devil Callahan, of Philadelphia. To begin the season, a six-night event took place at the Coliseum, where each of the men would ride beginning at 9 p.m. and continue for 30 minutes. The racer who had completed the most miles in that time was the winner. However, the long-distance events were preceded each evening by short sprints between the racers. There were also opportunities for amateur racers to try their hand at racing in the velodrome. Prince structured the races this way both to heighten community support and as a way of discovering new talent. When a new racer emerged from the amateur ranks, Prince would train and work with him, as he did with Atlanta's Bobby Walthour. Walthour himself became well known in Savannah, most especially after he rode against a racehorse in November 1902. A street on Wilmington Island, just east of downtown Savannah, is named after him.

Interest in the Savannah series spread well beyond the region and the results were reported in cities as far away as New York. Notably, Jay Eaton was a world champion who not only raced bicycles, but also participated in foot races and long-distance walking events, such New York's Six Day Walk in 1902.[12] He raced in the American circuit organized by Jack Prince.

The only other sports to compete with turn-of-the-century bicycle racing for widespread public attention were baseball and boxing (prize-fighting). The automobile and auto racing were introduced briefly to the people of Savannah as early as 1901, although formal races were not held. Race cars owned by the Rainey Brothers and a Mr. Baxter of New York came to Savannah in the spring and winter of that year, visiting T.A. Bryson. Bryson owned the bicycle shop and garage at Bull Street and persuaded the men to return with their race cars in the winter of 1902 for a racing festival to be held in December.

Savannah had made its start with bicycle racing, and it had built one of the premier coliseums in the world. Soon, automobile racing would evolve out of the bicycle races. The city had positioned itself very well to become a contender for top auto racing events in the pioneering days of the sport. Savannah had successfully established a strong record for excellence by building a top-notch racing facility at the Coliseum. The local clubs and city leaders were very capable of drawing one of the world's best bicycle racing organizers and world champion racers to the city. It was natural, then, that Savannah would soon become the focus of top automobile clubs in America and host the biggest auto races in the world. The stage was almost set for America's first Grand Prix to begin in the southern port city.

1

The Automobile Club of America and the American Automobile Association

British philosopher Roger Bacon, writing in the 13th century, may have been the first person to predict the development of a horseless carriage. Like Nostradamus, Bacon prophesized about the future. Yet, Bacon's prophesies were unlike the vague notions of events that Nostradamus was famous for. Most revolved around scientific inventions, such as the airplane and the automobile. Bacon described the coming of "chariots that shall move with unspeakable force, without any living creature to stir them."[1] He was not alone in his beliefs. Two centuries later, during the Renaissance, Leonardo da Vinci drew his famous spring-powered car (which was never built); German sculptor and painter Albrecht Dürer subsequently carved *The Great Triumphal Carriage*, which looks remarkably like the big touring cars of the 1920s.[2]

These men were not only great artists, but also theorists and mathematicians. They held the most progressive of beliefs regarding technology, and in so many of their predictions, they were correct. Unfortunately, none of them was a project manager or manufacturer. We would have to wait several hundred years for others to turn these automotive drawings and ideas into physical objects.

This finally occurred in 1769, when the first steam-powered vehicles were developed. These tractors were built by the French manufacturer Cugnot.[3] As the technology developed through the mid–1800s, electric vehicles joined in the mix. Finally, by 1869, gasoline-fueled internal combustion engines were invented in Germany and quickly spread to France. Although these earliest models were not initially a reliable technology, all three types of vehicles would continue to be refined.[4] By the 1880s, the automobile had become a firmer reality. The electric and steam-powered "horseless carriages" of this era dominated the early automobile market.[5]

It didn't take long for these new beasts to reach the shores of America. The automobile experienced a state of rapid evolution over the next 20 years, becoming faster, safer, and better handling. The industry grew as quickly as the technological advances emerged. This can be seen in the value of the automobile inventory in America. In 1895, the total value of manufactured automobiles in the country was a mere $157,000. By 1899, this number grew to $1.29 million. By 1910, the value of cars manufactured in America reached a whopping $237 million.[6]

An early cartoon depiction of the fear of the automobile from France around the turn of the century, when people believed drivers were out of control and dangerous.

How did the idea of racing cars come about after the automobile was developed? In the mid–1800s, racing was a brand-new concept to early transportation technology, and it began with bicycles. On May 31, 1868, the first bicycle race was contested in St. Cloud, Paris.[7] The race was attended by the European aristocracy. An Englishman named James Moore won the event, riding a wooden bicycle with iron tires. Like automobiles, bicycles were raced both for sport and for development purposes.[8] However, auto racing acted more as a propellant for growth of the industry itself than bicycle races did. Auto manufacturers used racing and competitive events to develop speed, endurance, and hill-climbing capabilities. It was a way to test their technology, and to get people excited about their products. And they succeeded beyond their wildest dreams!

Racing had begun shortly after the automobile was invented in Europe. In fact, it was the French who gave the world its first auto race: the Paris–Rouen race held in June 1894. This race was 124 kilometers in length and took 6 hours and 48 minutes to complete. *Le Petit Journal*, the newspaper that sponsored the event, received entries from 102 vehicles of various types. The participants included electric, steam, hydraulic, and liquid models—even an engine that claimed to work by gravity![9]

Unfortunately, the qualifying was fairly grueling and knocked many of the competitors out of the race. Vehicles had to complete 30.5 miles in four hours. Only 19 cars passed the qualifying and went on to race, including five Peugeots and four Panhard-Levassors. Despite a brief off-course excursion through a potato field, Count Jules De Dion finished first in his steam-powered tractor, averaging 11.6 mph. However, he was disqualified because his vehicle required a stoker in addition to the driver. A three-horsepower, petrol-powered Peugeot driven by Alain Lemaître officially won the race.[10]

In 1895, Italy joined the racing world and staged its first race. Automobile racing leagues began forming rapidly in the East and West. In America, the American Motor League was formed in Chicago, Illinois, while the famous Auto Club de France was formed that same year at De Dion's home.[11] Not to be outdone by the Italians or the French, the *Chicago Times Herald* owner, H.H. Kohlsaat, organized the first race in America. It was held November 28, 1895, only two years after the first race in France. The race was 54 miles and ran from downtown Chicago to Evanston, Illinois. The entrants included two electric and four gasoline-powered vehicles.[12]

Winter weather conditions marred a great deal of the Chicago race, as the drivers had to contend with icy, snow-covered roads and most spectators had left by dusk due to the cold. The Duryea and Benz cars were the favorites. The winner of the race was the Duryea, but it was a bittersweet victory because most spectators had moved indoors before the race's end.[13] Notably, a Sturges electric-powered motorcycle also entered the race, which helped to encourage the first motorcycle race; it was held one year later in 1896 and spanned from Paris to Marseilles.[14]

When the year 1899 dawned, it brought the world's first female driver to auto racing: Madame Labrousse, who raced the Paris to Spa event on July 1.[15] That same year, another very significant event occurred which would eventually bring international road racing to Savannah, Georgia: The Automobile Club of America (ACA) was formed. This organization was created to act as the official representative of the United States at international racing events. The organization included members of the Vanderbilt and Astor families, along with Winthrop E. Scarritt, who would eventually become its president.[16] These families and individuals played a key role in bringing the first American Grand Prize race to Savannah in 1908.

Members of the Automobile Club of America were among the most significant pioneers of American auto

The headquarters of the Automobile Club of America was located at 54th Street and Broadway in New York City in 1907.

racing. They included Willie K. Vanderbilt, Jr., and his cousins Cornelius Vanderbilt III and David Morris. These men had been attending some of the most spectacular and significant Grand Prix races of Europe. The Grand Prix de France and Targa Florio in the mountains of Sicily were two such examples. Both races had high attendance and the courses themselves were considered to be the best examples of auto course development. The auto course built in Savannah for the first American Grand Prize race would strive for and succeed in reaching this level of excellence.

Willie K. Vanderbilt's sister, Consuelo, had married into the British aristocracy. However, her husband, the Duke of Marlborough, was in love with another woman. Eventually, the two were estranged and divorced, but during the period of her estrangement from her husband, Consuelo spent a great deal of time with her father and brother, Willie K. and Willie K., Jr., in Paris, attending races. They were quite a sight to see, with the men dressed in formal tails and ladies in the finest Parisian fashions. This was standard racing attire for the wealthy and the nobility who attended the larger racing events of Europe.[17] Willie K. was a driver himself and had established a number of records in Europe and America. Racing ignited a passion in the Harvard graduate, who wanted to bring these large cup races to America and encourage American auto manufacturing.

These developments would soon come about, spurred by the formation of another club: the American Automobile Association (AAA) in 1902.[18] The club was determined to rival the powerful ACA, to which Willie K. had belonged and for which he served as vice president at one time. His cousin through marriage, Dave Hennen Morris, was president of the ACA; another cousin, Cornelius Vanderbilt III, also served in some of the highest positions of the club. After the AAA formed, many members of the ACA joined the new club or remained members of both.

Automobile clubs were forming all over the nation. In some places, they were small and unassuming. In others, they wielded great power. For example, some members of the Chicago Automobile Club felt that belonging to a club put them above the law. While speeding through the suburb of Glencoe near Chicago, one member was shot at by police for excessive speeding. The club banded together, hoping to prosecute the policeman for enforcing the speeding laws. However, an enraged populace supported their civic leaders and police force. Even more laws governing automobile driving were enacted. Another troubling incident occurred later that year, again involving a Chicago Club motorist. When he

William K. Vanderbilt was an automobile racer at the turn of the century in both America and Europe. Vanderbilt broke many early records, and was a patron in the Daytona Beach races and founder of the Vanderbilt Cup race and Long Island Parkway.

was stopped in Glencoe and given a speeding ticket, the motorist kidnapped the police officer. He was later released unharmed, and the driver was fined $50.[19]

It was a time of both growth and turmoil for the automobile clubs. During a banquet in 1904 held by the Automobile Club of America, several AAA members attended and approached Willie K. Vanderbilt to discuss the future of the automobile and racing in particular. Despite the amount of time he had spent in Europe attending or participating in races, he had grown apart from the ACA. The AAA members proposed Vanderbilt sponsor a big cup race in America and join the AAA. Willie K. agreed and sponsored a silver cup valued at $2,500 to be raced for on Long Island; he also undertook the process of building the Long Island Parkway where the event would be held. Willie K. was very committed to developing the American automobile industry, but he remained a member of the ACA as well as the AAA. For its part, the ACA had remained steadfastly loyal to its European counterparts and the European rules on racing. It is important to note that it was the ACA that organized and sanctioned the original time trials for Grand Prix cars on Long Island in December 1902, which preceded the Vanderbilt Cup Race in that location. These time trials prepared the American entries for international events such as the Gordon Bennett Cup.[20]

The Vanderbilt Cup became a very popular event in American racing. It gave birth to many smaller races, mostly put on by other automobile clubs. However, as the AAA grew in popularity, the organization kept a close eye on larger clubs which might hold races. In many cases, it would oppose races, such as a proposal by the Chicago Automobile Club to start a race in 1908. AAA members were concerned that a larger race would detract from the Vanderbilt Cup. Their greatest rival, however, was the ACA, with its strong bonds to the international automobile clubs which contested the great Grand Prix races of Europe.

Despite the early successes of 1904 and 1905, the AAA had a great deal of trouble with the Vanderbilt Cup race in 1906 and 1907. Multiple problems occurred because of the lack of track safety and sustaining local and state support of the event proved difficult. A boy had his legs cut off when one of the cars accidentally ran over him, a spectator was killed, and multiple injuries occurred both on and off the track that were related to automobiles and the races. Newspaper reports after the 1906 race were brutally harsh, with headlines saying things like "Trail of Blood is Course of Auto Race."[21]

The race planners were unsuccessful in finding a way to create effective crowd control around the track. This left spectators wandering on and off the track at will, causing injuries and even deaths during practices and race days. The AAA Racing and Technical Board members were unable to convince the state of New York to supply soldiers to guard the course during events to ensure the safety of participants and spectators. This unwillingness stemmed from the growing unpopularity of the race with locals who shared the roads, villages and fields where the race was contested.[22]

Sadly, it seemed to become more difficult each year to capture the hearts and minds of the local inhabitants. The Long Island Parkway passed through several towns and the race was received very differently by inhabitants from one place to the next. In some locales, it was embraced with enthusiasm. In others, the inhabitants resented the race, which inconvenienced them during the weeks of practice and on race day. Some did not enjoy the crowds of revelers who filled every farmer's field days before the race, camping out and creating noise in areas that were normally quiet and peaceful. Others were so upset with the race that they wrote long letters to the newspapers complaining of its associated problems.[23] Often, these people expressed anger at automobile drivers in general.

During that period, Judge Chase of the New York Court of Appeals gave a statement during a judgment of an automobile related case. He said, "Automobiles have but recently come into use.... Good judgment has not always been exercised in their use, and the rights of others have sometimes been overlooked by their owners and drivers.... Opposition has arisen to their unrestricted use upon the public streets and highways."[24]

Much of this ill will toward the races was misplaced anger toward the autoist in general. It was still a very new concept for people to be sharing the roads with drivers; until recent times, such venues had been the domain of horses, buggies, bicycles and pedestrians. Some felt their rights to use the road for these purposes were being usurped. Others were angered by automobile-related deaths in their communities. The general perception of the autoist can be seen in many forms in this period, such as a cartoon that ran in the *San Francisco Chronicle* on July 24, 1904. It showed a man with an automobile being approached by an automobile insurance agent offering him accident insurance. The man laughingly replies that it is the pedestrians who need an insurance policy because he will be safe in his car.[25] The newspapers were filled with accounts of accidents and often fistfights between drivers and farmers or pedestrians.[26] In Oshkosh, Wisconsin, the state proposed an auto bill that would sentence speeding drivers to prison.[27] Across the country, complaints about automobiles poured into local governments and autoists were increasingly threatened with heavy fines or jail for driving, or not having lights at night.

On Long Island, many people believed that drivers were "speed freaks" who were influenced to speed by the races. Like many cities and towns across America, Long Island had its fair share of problems with pedestrians, drivers and other road users being injured or killed by drivers who refused to heed the speed limits. Things reached a head in 1906 and 1907. After the injuries and fatality in 1906, several residents of Long Island towns, which had began launching petitions as early as 1904, filed lawsuits against the AAA in an attempt to stop the Vanderbilt Cup from being contested on Long Island.[28]

One solution that presented itself was to move the race to New Jersey temporarily, and build the Long Island Parkway into a longer, safer course. This idea was championed by Willie K. Vanderbilt, Jr. New Jersey seemed at first to like the idea of having the race. Unfortunately, the local support was short-lived. A bill was proposed in Congress that would change how autoists registered their vehicles. Until that point, vehicles had to acquire a registration in every state they passed through; New Jersey did not even allow a one-day grace period for a traveling autoist to obtain one. The new law would give autoists the right to drive through any state in their vehicle as long as they held a valid registration in their home state. The rights being granted to automobile drivers outraged the New Jersey populace and support for the Vanderbilt Cup race being contested there evaporated.[29]

In addition to these issues, the requests to local and state governments to provide troops or police to guard the course and help ensure a safe event were denied. It seemed the state and local authorities did not wish to rile up the already angry populace by doing anything that would help promote racing or speeding. This must have been a significantly difficult decision for lawmakers to make, due to the fact that many of the AAA members were high-ranking politicians or worked in government positions themselves. As such, they would have had close ties with the decision makers, but apparently this did not help their case.

On top of that, dire economic issues struck the Northeast through the late summer and early fall of 1907. The New York Stock Exchange fell by 50 percent that year, starting an event known as "the Panic of 1907" or "the Knickerbocker Crisis" that peaked in October 1907—the same month the race was normally run. Many members of the AAA were tied to the banks and investments affected, and their interest in the race at a time of financial crisis naturally waned.

With all of these issues mounting in 1907, the Vanderbilt Cup was doomed. The AAA cancelled the event entirely, unsure of when or if the race would return to Long Island. However, this great race still had a champion and hero in Willie K. Vanderbilt. He was not about to give up, nor would the members of the AAA who had fought hard to establish and organize the event. In early 1908, Willie K. himself proposed to return the Vanderbilt Cup race to America. Immediately, the AAA received proposals from two cities: St. Louis, Missouri, and Savannah, Georgia.[30] Both clubs offered military protection for the course and events—something that had not yet been seen at an American race. However, Savannah went a step further and organized a two-day stock car racing event. This gave the city a significant edge over St. Louis because it enabled Jefferson De Mont Thompson and other members of the AAA to travel to Savannah, see the local course-building skills, and witness how well organized city officials were in handling such an event.[31]

Almost immediately after proposing the return of the Vanderbilt Cup, Willie K. found he had a new set of problems to deal with. His two automobile clubs were getting ready to go to war with each other. In early 1908, Willie K. was still a member of both the ACA and the AAA. An affiliation through a third automobile club, the New York State Automobile Association, actually joined the two feuding organizations for better or for worse. This third club fell under the umbrella of the AAA, as did many car clubs of the time.

Trouble had been brewing between the AAA and ACA since 1907, regarding the ACA's right to sanction international auto racing events in America. The Vanderbilt Cup was just such an event that used the "international race event" designator. When the ACA decided to cut ties with the New York State Automobile Association in the spring of 1908, mere weeks before the first Savannah races of March 18 and 19, it signaled that more trouble was on the horizon regarding the international sanctioning issue. Willie K. was not pleased about his club's withdrawal from the New York State group. Since he was a director of the AAA, the break meant he would have to choose a side. He did so with apparent reluctance.[32]

This is an official gold seal of the Automobile Club of America from 1909. The seal depicts a turn-of-the-century automobile tire with wings on either side of it. The organization's official motto was "Velocitas Sine Periculo," which means "Speed Without Danger."

Some within the AAA questioned Vanderbilt's loyalty to them and felt he had misgivings about the club and the Vanderbilt Cup race. He responded by setting up a meeting with President Hotchkiss, where he explained that he would not be retiring from his position as a director of the AAA. This assured his colleagues in the AAA that he was not in complete agreement with the ACA for cutting ties to them.[33] However, his family members, such as cousins Cornelius Vanderbilt, Jr., and David Hennen Morris, who was being touted to become a leader in the ACA, remained firmly on the other side of the conflict. For its part, the ACA was looking

The original Eighth Annual Automobile Club of America Show Program from 1907 sold for only 10 cents and was a beautiful collection of scenes of New York City at night. The cover depicts a common image from this era: a lady driving a small car with the initials ACA just under her right hand. The show was held at the Grand Central Palace from October 24 to 31, 1907, and the events were a precursor to the ACA's involvement in auto racing. Exhibits included balloons, dirigibles, aeronautical motors, full-size gasless flying machines with and without engines, life-size airplane models, kites, parts and accessories for automobiles and early automobile art and photography.

for bolder direction, stronger ties to racing and new blood in its leadership that could accomplish these things.[34]

The ACA was working on several initiatives to lower automobile costs for its members and hoped this would eventually lead to lower costs for all drivers. These initiatives were among the reasons for the sudden split from the New York Automobile Association. Since that group belonged to the AAA and a bill had been proposed that would raise car licensing fees for drivers, it seemed as though the two clubs had opposing missions.[35] The fact that the licensing fees would fatten the coffers of the AAA, and in turn likely increase its power over car clubs in the nation, did not help to quell the rivalry between the clubs. Nor did the intention of putting the fees toward safer road construction and maintenance soften the blow. The ACA members felt they were the true leaders in that respect as well, and were particularly dedicated to making safer road transitions at areas such as train track crossings.

In early March 1908, only weeks before the Savannah stock car races were held, the ACA was making bold moves to acquire more power and protect its position as sole sanctioning body for international racing in America. An anonymous ACA member stated to *The New York Times* that the club recognized the authority of the AAA as it related to racing and automobile contests. However, only three days before the race, the group also insisted that the ACA "will continue to give automobile events of a practical nature and plans are already underway so that these will appeal with greater force and popularity to the members of the club as well as to all motorists generally."[36]

The timing of this statement—right before the Savannah races—along with the split occurring almost simultaneously that removed the link between the ACA and the AAA was no coincidence. While the general consensus of the time was that Savannah was a contender for the Vanderbilt Cup, it must be noted that only two weeks after the Savannah races were held, Jefferson De Mont Thompson, president of the AAA, publicly stated that the races were likely to stay in New York if the Long Island Parkway could be completed by October.[37]

As the weeks and months passed, the AAA also began to encounter more trouble with international automobile clubs, which threatened that any foreign teams that participated in a race in America not sanctioned by the Automobile Club of America, the official sanctioning body for international competitions, would be disqualified from all foreign races. That effectively meant that the Benz, Mercedes, Fiat, Renault and other European cars that competed internationally would not be able to race in the Vanderbilt Cup. Although the AAA's mission was focused more on promoting American automobile manufacturing with its race, the international teams were quite famous and certainly were a great attraction for spectators. The Vanderbilt Cup owed a great deal of its cache to the participation of the iconic drivers and cars of Europe. The argument moved oversees at the request of the AAA.

On July 6, 1908, a tense meeting occurred in Dieppe, France. Willie K. Vanderbilt and A.E. Batchelder, who led the Foreign Affairs Committee of the AAA, sought to reverse a decision made by the Automobile Club de France (ACF), which had vowed to disqualify French manufacturers that entered the Vanderbilt Cup, according to the rules of the International Recognized Clubs at Ostend. Willie K. and Batchelder were not allowed to be present for the proceedings due to a very terse letter the AAA had sent to the ACF. However, they submitted a statement that they had not received the rules of Ostend.[38]

Willie K.'s cousin, Dave Hennen Morris of the ACA, was admitted to the meeting. The ACF and the Automobile Club of Germany (ACG) confirmed that they did not wish to recognize more than one club in each country and that the ACA had prior claim to being the recognized club for America.[39] Willie K. Vanderbilt, who had once been closely involved with the ACF, must have felt stung by the refusal. At the very least, he would have been disappointed that the ACF and ACG did not recognize the AAA, or the Vanderbilt Cup as an equal to the Grand Prix races of Europe.

Meanwhile, the ACA held very successful auto shows in New York that showcased the glowing metropolis which was the home of their headquarters. In contrast, the racing contests the group had held were not nearly as successful. The races ended very poorly in some cases due to difficulties with the insurance for the events and at other times with inclement weather marring the proceedings. Despite these problems, by the summer of 1908, the ACA decided to contest its own Grand Prix race, following the ACF rules for international auto racing competition.[40]

In a statement issued in mid–July, the ACA set out its reasons for organizing the upcoming Grand Prize Race in Savannah, Georgia. Along with this statement, the ACA produced a copy of a receipt dated September 23, 1907, from the AAA acknowledging that it had indeed received the rules of the International Recognized Clubs at Ostend in the prior year. In mid–August 1908, the ACA went a step further and published a formal statement of its sole right to sanction American interests in international competitions:

> Pursuant to the agreement adopted at Dieppe by the International Association of Recognized Automobile Clubs it has been resolved that all participants, including the manufacturer, agent, private owner, driver, and mechanician, taking part in any international race in America not sanctioned by the Automobile Club of America will be disqualified from any competition in any future races held in this country or abroad.

That successfully ended the argument about which organization was recognized as the promoter of American racing interests that wished to affiliate with international racing. It was also seen as a ban of the Vanderbilt Cup race.[41]

Savannah had long desired to host the Vanderbilt Cup, and in early 1908 it would have the chance to prove the city could put together an excellent contest. One key factor in Savannah being a possible contender for the race was that it was well known to many of the high-ranking members of the auto clubs. Just southeast of Savannah, the beautiful Jekyll Island Club was a winter resort frequented by the most prominent families in America.[42] *Munsey* magazine called it "the richest, the most exclusive, the most inaccessible" of all clubs of the super wealthy. This winter resort was built by the Rockefellers, Vanderbilts, Astors, and Pulitzer, among others.

Once ensconced on the island for the winter months, the men (and sometimes the ladies) ventured into the city of Savannah for business and pleasure. Savannah had, therefore, been a very familiar and welcome part of the Vanderbilt family winter vacation for over 20 years. It was only natural that after the Vanderbilt Cup race held annually in Long Island was cancelled in 1907, a city in the vicinity of the Vanderbilts' winter playground would be considered as its new home.

For their part, the members of a small auto club called the Savannah Automobile Club knew they had a chance to host the crown jewel of American motorsports—the Vanderbilt Cup. They would go to great lengths to achieve this goal.

2

Early Racing in the South

The earliest auto races in the Southern United States began on the northeast beaches of Florida. Auto racing was very quick to spread to other Southern cities after the turn of the century, including New Orleans, Louisiana; Birmingham, Alabama; and, of course, Savannah. Texas had several automobile racing venues, including races at San Antonio, Dallas, Taylor, Amarillo, Wichita Falls and Waco. The most famous of all the Texas races was in Galveston, which held the largest automobile race in America in 1912, an event even more highly attended than the Indianapolis 500 that year.

The Florida Beach Races

The beginning of beach racing in Florida started with an idea from a northern tourist, J.F. Hathaway. Hathaway reportedly was a guest at the famous Ormond Beach Hotel, a high-class resort built by Henry Flagler for the rich and powerful who enjoyed wintering in the area. Automobile and transportation magnates were definitely among the list of regular guests at the resort, including Henry Ford, Harvey Firestone and J.D. Rockefeller. Hathaway took photos of the area and wrote up the details of his idea for auto races on the perfect racing surface: the beach. He sent this proposal to the editor at a popular publication of the time, *The Automobile*. Ormond, now known as the "Birthplace of Speed," and Daytona would bring motorsports to the South. It didn't take long for Hathaway's idea to take hold. Within weeks, an early racing promoter and contributor to *The Automobile*, William Morgan, had taken up the cause and found his way to Ormond Beach to see if the idea had merit. Immediately, he met with John Anderson and Joseph Price, who managed the hotel. Together, they began working on plans to hold beach races that they hoped would become an annual event beginning in March 1903.

The races at Ormond and Daytona Beach were casual affairs at first, with just two or three drivers. On March 26, 1903, the first drivers to race at the beach were Alexander Winton; H.T Thomas, driving the Bullet; and Frank X. Mudd, in an Olds Pirate. Mudd spoke glowingly of the course when he returned north, saying, "That beach is the greatest thing of its kind in the world."[1] The initial race was primarily attended by regional spectators and hotel guests, who gathered around the dunes at low tide to watch the cars race across the hard-packed sand. One key to the success of this type of racing was shared with Savannah's races: It was safer to race on the smooth surface of the beach, away from traffic, potholes and other dangers of the average dirt track. It also required little cost, since the ocean itself did the labor in repacking the sand in place during high tide.

One of the major developers in Florida, Henry Flagler was instrumental in getting the Florida beach races going. It did require some effort to gain AAA sanctioning. Since the AAA was dependent on the growth of local automobile groups, new clubs would have to be formed in the area. Three cities in the immediate vicinity were happy to comply: Jacksonville, Daytona and Ormond Beach, with Pablo Beach in Jacksonville eventually building its own race course. Together, the clubs could do the normal work of a local organizer and present their plans to the AAA for sanctioning of the events. Drivers in the events were not just local daredevils, either. Some of the famous and wealthy drivers of the time such as Willie K. Vanderbilt and Walter Christie got behind the Florida beach races very quickly, entering cars and eventually sponsoring other drivers in their cars at the events.

The 1903 races offered a $2,000 purse for the winners of the race, including three cups valued at $500 each. This large sum of money attracted many of America's finest drivers of the times and heightened the excitement of the events for the crowd. The races would grow even larger when they were held January 26, 1904, in the cold and misty days of winter. On January 29, clouds hovered overhead and the teams were certain it would rain. But the rain held off as two elimination races were held before the final race. Bowden led W. Gould Brokaw, but neither could match Willie K. Vanderbilt, who won the final heat of the day in 48 seconds.[2] His best time during the meet occurred in a one-mile race that he completed in 39 seconds, sending the crowd into thundering cheers. Vanderbilt would offer a cup for a 100-mile race the following year. Sir Thomas R. Dewar, of Dewar's Scotch-Whiskey fame, would offer another cup for a one-mile race.

The Ormond–Daytona Beach races were called "the leading automobile races of the year" by the *Chicago Daily Tribune* in 1904 after only two years of racing and proclaimed to be second to no other race in the country.[3] Several Europeans would travel over on ships for the event, including some who drove in the Vanderbilt Cup and American Grand Prize races.

In 1905, the races began a bit unusually. Racers had arrived weeks early to practice and test their cars on the beach. This was almost unprecedented in the racing world, as was noted in automobile literature of the time. Walter Christie was the first driver to arrive with his 90-horsepower car. Soon after came others, including Barney Oldfield and the famous Green Dragon. A Napier entered one event, with its driver McDonald breaking a world record. There was a steam class in which 20 cars entered, including a Renault, a Darracq, two Pope-Toledos, a Stanley Steamer, a Columbia and a Decauville. The European Fiat and Mercedes were prominent in the events. The Loxley Trophy for a 50-mile race was also awarded. Only American cars could enter the race for the Loxley, so it was a favorite event for the American spectators. The events of 1905 were somewhat marred by a disagreement over whether the Dewar Cup could be awarded. Those who opposed its bestowal said not enough limits were placed on car and engine size. The conflict became the subject of a special meeting one evening during the races and perhaps foreshadowed the trouble ahead. The classes of cars at the races were highly segregated based on brand, size, and country of origin, with the exception of Willie K. Vanderbilt's International Trophy. In addition to the divisions cropping up among various parties involved in the racing events, the death of Frank Croker of New York and his riding mechanic cast a pall over the races.

A new foreign champion was crowned at Daytona–Ormond in 1906. Victor Demogeot, a French chauffeur, who was the riding mechanic to Victor Hemery, was able to maintain a speed of 123 mph in a two-mile event, making a time of 58.45 seconds. On the previous days, cars such as the De Dietrich, Darracq, Stanley Steamer and Napier had drawn crowds into the clubhouse. However, this year's events had some problems, such as delaying of the two-mile race until Monday, which disappointed spectators who traveled by train for the day to see the event. The beach was also reported not to be in very good condition. Many of the drivers were already preparing to depart for Cuba, which was hosting its first race in February, after the Florida events ended.[4]

Many of the favorites returned in 1907: Louis Wagner in a Darracq, Fred Marriott with his Stanley Steamer, and Ray Harroun, who would one day win the inaugural Indianapolis 500. Marriott would wreck while racing at a top speed of 125 mph and suffer serious injuries that would take years to heal. Plans for a new course came into shape. Having not held the Vanderbilt Cup on Long Island in this year, the AAA met with the automobile clubs of Florida to discuss expansion of the events. They proposed a 300-mile race, with 150 miles run each day. However, the proposal would rely on improvements being made to the course, including constructing loops for the cars to go back and forth. There was a great deal of excitement initially, but the idea would begin to lose steam as other cities, including Savannah, began proposing to host the Vanderbilt Cup race or start other major races.[5]

By 1908, the European cars were competing in full force at the Daytona–Ormond races. Philadelphia millionaire Louis Bergdoll won the main 125-mile event in a Benz in 1 hour, 53 minutes and 30 seconds. The Fiat Cyclone almost beat the Benz. Unfortunately, this year was a bad one for accidents, which had a negative effect on future events; similar misfortunes had earlier occurred in places like Long Island, which cancelled its 1907 Vanderbilt Cup race after multiple tragedies in 1906. It was also reported that the beach was not in as good a condition as it was in prior years. Samuel Stevens led most of the event in the Fiat Cyclone, and a Christie car driven by R.G. Kelsey entered but encountered mechanical difficulties after just 50 miles. A fire in the Packard garage also put that car out of contention before the race even started. Another fire involving Harry Levey's Hotchkiss car blazed up by the Judges Stand.[6] All in all, the fires seemed to capture more interest than the actual racing event. The beach races were at their end. The number of entrants had declined, it was impossible to control the tides which determined what shape the beach would be in for racing, and there was less interest from spectators. Throughout the racing industry, everyone knew that the great beach races were finished.

New Orleans Mardi Gras Races

A city similar to Savannah that also had early races in the same period was New Orleans, Louisiana. From 1909 through 1911, New Orleans had some very well-attended and popular auto racing events. The races were first announced in December 1908 for the upcoming Mardi Gras carnival in 1909 on a one-mile course located at the Fairgrounds. These competitions were usually held in conjunction with Mardi Gras and were attended by some of the big-name drivers. More than 7,000 people attended the 1909 race. Ralph De Palma drove a Fiat Cyclone and won a 10-mile handicap event, breaking Barney Oldfield's 1904 record for the event. One of the first females on the auto racing scene, Joan Cuneo, had a very successful race in New Orleans. Cuneo had famously been the only female to drive in the prestigious Glidden Tours in 1907 and 1908. She was also the owner of seven automobiles of her own and, like Alice Potter, who famously drove from coast to coast across America, Cuneo drew a great crowd of admirers for her participation in the sport.

In 1909 at New Orleans, Cuneo broke her own record at the five-mile event of the Mardi Gras exhibition races with a time of 5 minutes and 5 seconds, which improved on her previous time of 6 minutes and 4 seconds in the five-mile event. Somewhat unusually, she was also permitted to drive in the 50-mile race with the men and led the field, which included Ralph De Palma, for 19 miles. "She negotiated the turns with ease, and made them sharper than most of the men."[7] Cuneo placed second in the race, which was quite a feat for women everywhere and attracted a great deal of interest, especially given the suffragettes' ongoing fight for women's rights in the midst of her rising career. Only De Palma could beat her time. Cuneo also won some of the other events, including the Klaxton Trophy and the Klaw and Erlanger Trophy. But Cuneo's joy and success in motorsports would not be permitted to continue for long. Within a month, the racing authorities put a stop to the female driver's career by instituting a new rule that women could not compete in sanctioned auto racing events.

The 1910 events in New Orleans brought even more well-known drivers and cars for six races. Oldfield would return with the "fastest car in the world"—a 200-horsepower Benz touted to be capable of speeds up to 127 mph. The Fiats would return, as well as Simplex, Knox, Jackson, Packard, Isotta-Fraschini, Buick and Darracq models. Many of the same drivers and cars that normally entered the Vanderbilt Cup and American Grand Prize races were in attendance, such as Bob Burman, Louis Strang and George Robertson. However, it was considered a run-of-the-mill year for the New Orleans Carnival Races with no records broken, despite Oldfield's sensational Benz being present and winning the five-mile race in 4 minutes and 33 seconds. De Palma won the ten-mile race in his Fiat, with Oldfield driving a Knox and placing second in the event and Kirscher being third in the Darracq. Caleb Bragg, a newcomer who would make quite a name for himself in Savannah, won the amateur stock car race in a Fiat.[8]

In 1911, the Model T driven by Frank Kulick was attracting a lot of attention. Kulick would drive the car in Savannah's Tiedman Trophy Race on November 27, 1911. The Model T was only 20 horsepower, yet Kulick had five first-place finishes at New Orleans, much to the delight of his fellow Detroitians. Bob Burman brought in the Buick "Bug," which won four of the opening events. He spoke at length of the Dorian remountable rims that he used, attributing his success to the new part and declaring that detachable rims were the way of the future for auto racing.[9]

The Carnival Races had achieved much, but experienced the same problem after 1911 that other races like Savannah had: the emergence of races where big corporate money and fat local coffers had come together and begun dominating the sport. The AAA also worked to squelch races by suspending even its biggest-name drivers, like Barney Oldfield, for participating in unsanctioned races at Ascot and San Antonio. Organizations that were under sanction of the AAA, including the Vanderbilt Cup and Indianapolis 500, began to worry about the existence of other events which might overshadow their own. Some of the most fun and interesting auto racing events, like the New Orleans Mardi Gras races, became the unfortunate victims of their insecurity and rising quest for power. The major AAA events had one thing in common: They strove to be exclusive and famous in their own right. They did not want to be just one race among a string of races around the country; they wanted to be *The Race*.

Galveston Beach Cotton Carnival

The Galveston Beach Cotton Carnival provided one of the earliest major races in the South. The Galveston Automobile Club organized the first race in 1906, which was attended by approximately 3,000 spectators. The races grew in stature and size from 1909 through 1914 and were held as part of the Cotton Carnival each summer. It was vitally important to Galveston to ramp up efforts to rebuild the area after the Galveston Hurricane of 1900. This hurricane was the costliest storm ever to occur in the United States, even when compared with Hurricane Katrina, and was a Category 4 storm. More than 20 percent of the island's population—8,000 people were killed during the storm and the entire city of Galveston was destroyed. In the years that followed, the devastated area badly needed to find ways to bring people back to the area, and fund the rebuilding of the entire town, with special emphasis on the Galveston Beach area, approximately 1,000 yards from East Denver beach. Racing was seen as an excellent tool for rebuilding efforts.[10]

Both motorcycles and automobiles raced in the AAA-sanctioned event. There were many drivers and cars from the big races and a large variety of categories, ranging from big 50-mile races to shorter 10-, 5-, 2-, and 1.5-mile races. The purses were not quite as spectacular as those offered by the Vanderbilt Cup or American Grand Prize. In 1909, a first-place winner could expect to receive $75, with $50 going to the second-place finisher and $25 to third place. However, that did not stop a deep talent field from showing up to race at the Texas beach. Some of the most famous drivers of the time were there: Barney Oldfield, Len Zengle, Harry Endicott, Ralph Mulford, Joe Horan and Eddie Rickenbacker (who later became a famous fighter pilot). The cars were equally impressive, with Studebaker, Buick, Peugeot, Chadwick, National and Duesenberg vehicles entered.[11]

The Daytona Beach races had ceased at this time and Galveston aspired to be their successor—in fact, it wanted to become the largest beach racing event in the country. Captain J.W. Munn, president of the Galveston Automobile Club, traveled to New York to meet with the AAA, just as the Savannah Automobile Club members had done while bidding for the Vanderbilt Cup. By 1912, the Galveston Club and the Texas State Automobile Association were raising over $6,000 in prizes for participants. This was the year that Galveston took over the honor of holding the biggest race in the South, as the Grand Prize and Vanderbilt Cup races were not contested, despite an agreement for them to be held in Savannah.

In 1914, the Galveston races were still attracting some of the country's finest drivers, including America's champion, Ralph Mulford. Mulford entered 16 out of 17 events over the four days of racing starting July 30, 1914, at Galveston Beach. He won ten of those events in a Peugeot driving an average speed of 74.65 mph in the longer events, such as the 50-mile race. He even beat Tom Alley, the former mechanic of Ralph De Palma. The 50-mile race may have been one of the most spectacular races of the year, with an extremely close finish. Eddie Rickenbacker lost to Mulford in the event by just one second[12] and Peugeot became quite a hit in America.

Unfortunately, in 1915 the Cotton Carnival races were abandoned. *The Horseless Age* described it best: "The last of the once respectable automobile beach racing contests has been discontinued." It was reported that the Cotton Carnival Committee felt the automobile racing events had lost their prestige. The complaints reported in the media seemed to come from "out-of-towners,"[13] similar to one of the concerns raised after Savannah's races ended in 1911. The specter rising in the shadows may again have been the newer, monopolistic business model of racing events such as the Indianapolis 500. Monopolies were still going strong at this time period in America, but were most prevalent in the North. A famous example occurred in an industry related to the automobile. Standard Oil, an Ohio firm, was broken up by the government in 1911, while U.S. Steel was hit with an antitrust suit. "Cornering the market" by reducing competition whenever possible was a major part of business strategy in many industries, despite the Sherman Antitrust Act of 1890. Perhaps the practice was kept quiet as much as possible, but there is no reason to believe that any major U.S. business—let alone the early racing industry—would not be touched by monopolistic business practices. They were occurring regularly in this period and became particularly strong in the automobile-related industries.

In fact, Standard Oil was owned by the Rockefellers and Henry Flagler, who was a major supporter of the early beach races in Florida. Did Carl Fisher, the brilliant, wealthy inventor and cofounder of the Indianapolis 500, have any connection to a business with a monopolistic business strategy? The answer is yes. Fisher and Allison owned Prest-O-Lite, the dominant manufacturer of headlamps used on American automobiles. Theoretically, the tendency to want to be the only game in town—or at least the largest—may have leaked over from their business model to become part of Fisher's plans for the Indianapolis 500. Although the 500 is a much-loved and highly revered event in motorsports and has produced some of open wheel racing's most exciting racing moments and drivers, it is possible that its earliest survival depended on other races' demise.

However, it was not a singular effort, but most likely the efforts of many players in the industry, which helped some races rise while squelching others, road racing in particular. The chase for supremacy in motorsports was certainly a detriment to some races, along with other issues that cropped up locally. It served to remove or reduce the importance and success of Southern races—especially the more popular venues—in the pioneering days of the sport. Galveston, a coastal city and port where cotton was king, had many similarities to Savannah. Unfortunately, cotton and shipping could not stand up to oil and auto parts as these industries grew. Auto racing was pulled back up into the north and west, where these industries were based.

3

America's Finest Course, of Course!

If you have ever been to a race track, you will most likely have arrived and taken your seat before the cars ever come onto the track to practice or race. During that interlude, your eyes will have subconsciously traveled over the circuit and assessed what you saw. Most likely, either you will have felt impressed by the design and flawless look of a cutting-edge course, or you will have noted imperfections in design or rough surfaces and thought the track needed work.

Spectators, drivers, team owners and organizers of the Savannah races did exactly the same thing more than 100 years ago. However, the unexpected occurred when people arrived for the races in March and November of 1908: They found a course that was a whole new style of circuit built to a level that was unsurpassed in America and, some claimed, the world. The quotes of multiple drivers who had tested out the finished product over the year landed on the postcards for the November race, proclaiming Savannah's course to be "America's Greatest Automobile Course."[1]

The course built in Savannah was unique for several reasons. First, it was a tremendous challenge to build in the area. Savannah is situated approximately halfway between Jacksonville, Florida, and Charleston, South Carolina. The heart of the city is on a high bluff approximately 12 miles from the Atlantic Ocean on the Savannah River. Salt marshes created from tributaries of the river lead out from the downtown area to the beaches of Tybee Island and other coastal areas. The geological term for this type soil and rock is "coastal plain" and Savannah is situated on the area known as the Pamlico Formation. This formation runs along the southeast Atlantic coastline and consists of very low-lying areas with mixtures of salt marshes, flood plains surrounding river tributaries, and pine–oak forests or stands. The magnificent views of salt marshes, palmetto trees and live oaks would have rivaled the views we see today at racing venues like Monaco or Spa.

The original race course was located at the south end of the city, beginning at what is now Victory Drive and extending farther south and east over oak-lined avenues, across newly built bridges and through the heart of the tidal salt marsh. The clayey muds and loamy sand were the predominant soils to be built upon. These are some of the most challenging types of soil to work with, and a high water table makes road construction even more complex.

During this era, road building was a very new science. Engineers and geologists often worked together to gather data about the exact makeup of soil to customize the mix of soil and possibly rock or concrete substance needed to build a road surface. A road surface needed to be porous to drain water properly. This could not have been more important than on a race track where cars might be traveling in excess of 100 mph, and most especially in a salt marsh area where minor flooding could occur from tides. In addition to having excellent drainage, the desired road surface was a well-compacted, smooth surface that was as free of dust as possible.[2] Drivers would require the best visibility possible to race safely at high speeds and see the track and objects around them. The organizers, for their part, would hope to have the highest possible visibility so spectators could view the racing clearly. In wet areas, such as the salt marshes, extra care would need to be taken to ensure that race cars did not hit ruts or have their wheels get stuck in mud.

The answer for Savannah was to invest in the most cutting-edge road construction technique available at the time. The mayor of Savannah and members of the Savannah Automobile Club had a vision for road building and were thinking very much like the world's leader in road construction at the time: the French. Since the time of Trésaguet, the French engineer who defined the principles of road and bridge construction in 1775, France had been the undisputed world leader in road development. During the period of the Savannah races, France had invested approximately $625 million in roads; however, the earlier roads were built for the iron tires found on horse and buggies and were built to withstand loads of less than half a ton.[3]

One technique that was used in America from the early 1900s was Macadam road building. This style was reserved mainly for rural highways that connected cities and was rarely

Above: Original Foltz postcard (the first of two styles produced) from the November 26, 1908, races depicting scenes of Savannah and the new race course. The quote "America's Greatest Automobile Course!" came from the drivers who attended the races held in March 1908, such as Louis Strang. *Opposite:* The second version of the "America's Greatest Automobile Course" postcard by Foltz showing different scenes of Savannah and the race course.

used on city streets due to its cost and complexity. Savannah took the small rural trails that had been used to that point and built Macadam roads using the highest-quality materials available, such as Augusta gravel for the trap rock. No other venue in America, and possibly none in the world, had yet gone to such an expensive and high-level undertaking—and certainly not for a race course. The "mile of dirt" was ordinarily the standard for racing in America.[4] Savannah was a lot of things, but "ordinary" was not one of them. If something was going to be done at all, it would be done to the highest achievable standards. The track built for the November races was over 25 miles in length—25 miles of the finest roads that could be found in the entire country.

In 1907, when plans were developed to build the March stock car track for Savannah, the Long Island Parkway had not yet been built. When it was, it was designed primarily as a highway connecting Long Island to New York, with much less emphasis on use for racing. In fact, towns along the race route created havoc for the AAA when it began planning for the first Vanderbilt Cup races. The idea of racing on the road was vehemently opposed by many local citizens, who wanted to stop its construction because of the annual race.[5] This put quite a damper on the building of the parkway during its construction and several hurdles had to be overcome to gain the locals' cooperation.

It was just the opposite in Savannah. The thought of the races, the crowds and taking on the challenges of beautiful avenues and bridges through the marshes and Spanish moss–laden oaks that would allow people to travel easily into the "countryside" pulled the entire community together into a whirlwind of excitement. Although Savannah was a prosperous port city and well known to many, once news of the 1908 races began to circulate, the eyes of the world were focused on the Southern locale. In turn, the Good Roads Movement capitalized on the races as a place to showcase an excellent example of road construction.

This Vanderbilt Cup Long Island moving postcard depicts a scene from the Long Island race of 1906 featuring the Le Blon Thomas Car, taking the "hairpin" turn. These items were designed and made by the Winthrop Press. Measuring 3 × 4.5 inches, it contains 31 pages with a still shot of the car going around the bend so that when it is flipped, you are watching the scene in motion.

The Good Roads Movement was very important to highway and road construction as well as automobile development during this period. The automobile had been introduced to the American population less than 20 years before, so roads were still primarily made of compacted dirt—not the best surface for automobiles, which had to consider getting wheels stuck and engine parts filled with dust and mud. America was a world leader in building railroads, but for every mile of railway tracks there were ten miles of highways.[6] It was vitally important to build roads, as pointed out in 1909 by a spokesman for the Association of Licensed Automobile Manufacturers, Coker F. Smith:

> A nation's reputation for enterprise, progress, and all that goes to make it worth living in is determined very largely by the character of its roads, the great arteries through which flow the business and pleasure of the nation.[7]

Despite many financial and technical impediments to developing higher-level road construction, there was a strong movement for progress in this area, which grew from 1905 onward. One of the pioneers of road construction was a 19th-century engineer from England, whose name was John L. Macadam. Macadam discovered that small pieces of broken stone—what we known today as gravel—could be mixed with a concrete-like substance and layered over a well-compacted and prepared soil surface to create a hard dust-free surface that would deflect and repel water to maintain a homogenous top.[8]

Macadam's method was chosen for 15 of the 25 miles of the course built in Savannah in 1908. It was considered the best road construction of its time, most especially when coupled with dust-free surfacing techniques. This method reduced wear and tear on tires significantly, which allowed for race cars to be on the track for longer periods than was possible on dirt.[9] Dirt roads which were barely more than country trails were transformed into Macadam roads with widths of 60 feet. In addition, the corners were professionally banked to challenge and test car and driver.

However magnificent the course, the cost was exorbitant. The average cost to build a Macadam road was $9,000 per mile.[10] A 15-mile portion of Macadam road course could cost in excess of $135,000 unless ways were found to control the costs. On top of that was the cost of building solid bridges that would be ideal for racing on and the high costs of building sound embankments. All of these costs would have been at the highest end of the scale in Savannah due to the added complexity of building with the high water table and in wet soils. However, the use of convict labor brought those numbers down and an excellent county engineer, Mr. Blandford, ensured the road would be built to the best standards with costs kept to a minimum.

In comparison, the first course used for the Vanderbilt Cup races consisted of 28.44 miles of roadways that were already built for commercial and residential use. It was expanded over several years and a portion of it raced upon in 1908, following a hiatus in 1907. Considerable efforts were made by A.R. Pardington, with the highest level of support from Willie K. Vanderbilt, to build the Long Island Parkway. The highest point of the rolling hills could be 200–300 feet above sea level, but not many areas of the roadway would go through these elevations. The vegetation they built through was primarily an oak scrub, with some areas consisting of sea sand and gravel. Some of the views of the ocean would be magnificent, matching the picturesque areas found on the Savannah track. These tracks were like sisters, both built using Macadam in many areas.[11]

The Savannah course may indeed have served as an early model to the AAA for building methods to use on the Long Island Parkway. Both were close to the Atlantic, with high water tables that posed similar challenges to builders. While the Long Island Parkway was being planned and before the material makeup of the course was decided upon, its top leaders made several visits to look over the Savannah course, built for the March stock car races. They declared:

> The course appears to be the best of its kind on this side of the Atlantic and it is for this reason that the AAA have sent its most representative members to personally investigate. They are more than pleased.[12]

Even after the Long Island Parkway construction began, many were still lauding the Savannah track as the finest in the country and the new roads as having tremendous influence on road building:

> Savannah offers one of the best illustrations of the growth of road building in the South. The advancement in highway construction has been such as to enable the local authorities to lay out a seventeen mile track for the [1911] races over the best roads to be found in the United States. In some parts of the track the road bed is superior to many specially constructed dirt tracks. The roads were not built for racing but as part of the great chain of public highways that are encircling the entire country.[13]

De Mont Thompson of the AAA was also interested in the construction of the Brooklands Autodrome, which he visited in early fall 1907. In addition to the excellent banking, Thompson was particularly impressed by the tarring process used in Paris. After seeing this, he would recommend this material to his club when he returned to America (13). The 1908 Vanderbilt Cup course was 23.45 miles, of which 9 miles was newly built with a concrete surface and 14.45 miles was public roads. A grandstand was built to seat 5,000 people. The Long Island Parkway had 300 feet of pits with water service. Wire fencing was installed prior to the 1908 Vanderbilt Cup race, but these fences were torn out by unruly spectators before any guard even arrived for the start of the race.[14] In 1909 and 1910, the course was shortened and only 5.5 miles of the Long Island Motor Parkway was used for racing.

At the time the Long Island Parkway was being planned, locating a source of revenue to pay for the roadway was complex. As the project kicked off, the plan was to raise the money through four sources:

1. Toll charges for use of the road, which started out at $2 per vehicle (approximately $50 today)
2. Admission from the Vanderbilt Cup race event
3. Fees for manufacturers to test cars
4. Other racing and automobile events and contests[15]

Savannah's course differed from the Long Island Parkway in that it was the longest course built for racing. There would be no toll, and convict labor would be employed to bring down the costs. Like the Long Island course, Savannah's course had different sections made of different materials; unlike the parkway, it would not become a throughway, but rather would allow expansion into the Southern area of the city for residential and commercial purposes. The other uses would take a back seat and be an added bonus, as the area where Savannah's course was built was very rural and thinly populated at the time of its inception. Savannah was also very fortunate that the residents in the course area were avid supporters of the races.

The famous Indianapolis Speedway was also being built in this time. Carl Fisher had grand plans to build what he felt would be the best race track in America. Initial plans were for a two-mile oval and a three-mile inner loop for a total course of five miles. Grandstands were expected to seat 35,000 people and a budget of $500,000 was proposed for the entire venue, including clubhouse grandstands, tracks and other buildings.[16] Fisher felt that the road courses were dangerous, and pointed to the Vanderbilt Cup tragedies on Long Island as proof. However, he would have had little fault to find at Savannah, which had policed the course extremely well and built the finest racing surface ever found in America. Fisher also believed that road racing was not suitable for testing cars and drivers, with a smaller speedway being a better option for this purpose.

Many disagreed with Fisher at the time, and simple scientific method would later prove his theory inaccurate. Scientific method in any discipline relies heavily on recreating the environment and conditions closest to what a subject will operate under in normal circumstances. Therefore, the road races, which were held on roads that would actually be used for automobiles, with the addition of banking to simulate elevation changes and offer greater challenges for racing, as well as the benefit of distance, which cars and drivers would be required to deal with, were actually the most suitable environment for testing automobiles. The road courses could give manufacturers a wealth of deeper research and development opportunities.

Eventually, the cars used for racing were not developed for the road, but rather specifically for the race course and most especially for the speedways. There was a great deal of controversy from the manufacturers about this trend. Some were in favor of it, some were not. Fisher also felt more people would attend races at a speedway, which is inaccurate due to simple space constraints. A road course such as the Long Island Parkway and Savannah's Grand Prize course could accommodate hundreds of thousands of spectators, with many vantage points and a chance to see the cars turn a lot of laps up close. Entire villages and cities surrounded the big road courses, which offered more than ample infrastructure to suit the large variety of socioeconomic preferences of racing fans. This meant the fan base was very diverse, with the spectators ranging from the wealthiest businessman to the most modest stable boy. People also had a variety of choices in how to get to the races: by car, by boat, by foot, and by bicycle. In any case, Fisher, along with partners Allison, Newby and Wheeler, incorporated the Indianapolis Speedway in 1909 and started out by holding non-auto racing events such as aviation events and (later) motorcycle races.

Like many new ventures, the first Indianapolis Speedway did not achieve the resounding success that would be experienced later. This early type of track was a poor choice for the automobile and the first cars to try racing there had several problems. In August 1909, drivers and their cars were covered in oil, dirt and tar. Louis Chevrolet was blinded temporarily when a rock flew up and hit his goggles. The dirt surface was not a good option in terms of visibility, and it was definitely not good for the participants to get dirt and oil into their cars' engine parts. The course had many ruts and there were deep holes in the turns. Safety became a major issue and the AAA eventually boycotted the auto racing events until the track could be made safer. Improvements were undertaken immediately to build concrete walls around the course and pave portions of the course with brick. A new meet was held December 17 and 18 of that year under sanction of the AAA The final total expenditure for the new venue was $700,000 and the owners did not expect to make a profit in the first events.[17]

The race course in Bologna, Italy, was considered to be the best course ever constructed by most people in the industry during this period. It had four stretches, the longest of which was 12 miles, which allowed drivers to pass one another easily. Savannah's roads were considered to be just as good as the race course in Bologna.[18]

Most of the revenue in Savannah went to the militia who guarded the course or back into the public funds to pay for construction of the roads. In fact, a tremendous amount of money was needed to fund such large efforts. During the November 1908 races, 14 companies of soldiers guarded the track, numbering 18,000 over the month during practice and racing events. Approximately 600 rounds of ammunition was given to each of the companies as "riot ammunition" in the event that the crowds grew unruly. Fortunately, that did not occur.[19]

Macadam road building was the cutting-edge technology of the time; its only equal was the new asphalt technique. Savannah used both methods to build the course and pave the main street of Savannah. In 1907, Bull Street, which runs from East Bay Street, where City Hall is located, was paved with Trinidad Lake asphalt, one of the finest grades of asphalt available. Bull Street eventually became White Bluff Drive, one of the primary roads for the 1908 race course, which is now the home of Hunter Army Airfield.

Macadam was a very interesting process to build a road with. The mixture of materials used could be customized in different areas based on amount of rainfall, temperature and topography. "Macadam" is defined as follows:

> A surface composed of broken stones of small dimensions, the largest not exceeding 2.5 inches in diameter, suitably bound together into a compact mass so as to be substantially a sort of concrete but with no matrix other than stone dust or screenings.[20]

Macadam can be difficult to differentiate from gravel in historical photos because it bears a striking resemblance to a gravel surface; however, it did contain a binding material more like concrete. Regular Macadam roads were built to form rural highways which connected cities to one another. The regular width for this use was approximately 12–15 feet. At 12 feet, two cars could pass each other; at 15 feet and with a shoulder built, a third car or horse and buggy could pull off the road without impeding two lanes of traffic.

In the earliest days, the Macadam road surface was built to a depth of 8–12 inches. This was thought to provide more strength to the road. In areas where the ground contained clayey soils, a thicker surface was also more desirable. However, it was important to keep clays out of the foundation. The Macadam technique required a more porous soil foundation that would not hold water. By 1908, Macadam surfaces were reduced in thickness from three to six inches in depth and were deeper in the center than at the sides. A typical road might be six inches deep in the center and four inches

Photographs of (left) W.F. Brown, Chatham County engineer, and (right) T. Newell West, the superintendent of public works and roads, as they were featured in *How the Race Was Run and Won*, a promotional booklet produced by the Indian Refining Co. Inc. in 1911 depicting the 1910 Savannah races.

at the sides. The traprock could consist of igneous rock, granites, felsites or harder forms of limestone.[21] Igneous rock was considered the best of these choices. In Savannah, Augusta gravel was selected, which was the very highest grade of traprock available.

The traprock could be broken by hand or machine. The tools required for building a road were primarily hand tools such as picks, shovels, and rakes. Most localities in America used a crusher to break the rock. In Savannah, the use of convict labor meant the rock could be broken by hand. This was a common practice to help make road building more affordable. Portable crushing machines might be purchased for $1,600 to $2,500 by cities that would use them seasonally to repair or expand roads. These machines consisted of a traprock crusher with an engine and boiler, a number of portable bins to carry the rock, and a screening elevator which revolved and lifted out the crushed traprock.[22] Another option was to have the gravel shipped in, already crushed.

A steamroller could be used at this point, although some localities still used a roller pulled by a team of horses. Steamrollers were made by companies such as J.I. Case, which also manufactured the famous Case cars entered in the Savannah races of 1911. A large number of companies manufactured these machines, with as many as 600 types available. Most steamrollers weighed about 10 tons and cost from $2,500 to $3,500 to purchase.[23] Water carts with very broad tires (to avoid adding ruts to the road) were also used in the process. A drag scraper was used to prepare the road foundation for the Macadam. From there, spreader machines could deliver the crushed stone to the surface, where laborers could spread it to the planned specifications.

The foundation was typically constructed at about 5 percent grade and most localities would build the road so that it

This postcard is part of a collection of over 40 images that were produced for the 1911 American Grand Prize and Vanderbilt Cup races. It is entitled "Convicts Building Race Course—1911." Convict labor was used to build the Savannah race course, which allowed the city to fund the cutting-edge Macadam roads that were built to European Grand Prix standards.

This postcard is part of the collection produced for the 1911 Savannah races and is entitled "Convicts Resurfacing Roads—1911." By 1911, the race course had evolved from the first course built in March 1908 and the course that was enlarged in November 1908. In 1910 and 1911, the course was shortened and the roads were resurfaced, especially in areas where the banking needed to be heightened or reduced.

sloped off on both sides to allow for sufficient water runoff. This was especially important in Savannah, which has a subtropical climate and, therefore, heavy rainfall and heavy flooding at certain times of the year. With the low elevation and tides, water could cover roads easily at times.

Once the competition rules were established, work began on the track in Savannah. As noted earlier, the course designers used convicts for general labor duties to keep the cost of building the course to a minimum for taxpayers. Notably, the convicts who assisted in building the track would be permitted to watch the races from beside the Judges Stand.

Many private landowners in Savannah allowed the banked turns to be constructed on their property. In fact, 10 out of the 12 banked turns were on private property. The turns were built on a 140-yard radius. The course was 30–60 feet wide, with some paved portions. Those portions that were paved were constructed with Augusta gravel, which was well known at the time to be the highest-quality road surface in the region. The paved sections were narrower, with widths ranging from 15 to 24 feet. The main straightaway was 3.5 miles in length and 50 feet wide. A large grandstand was built near Estill (now Victory Drive) and Abercorn Street. The judges stand was located along Estill adjacent to the start–finish line.

The final step in preparing the course for use was to oil the surface to keep dust down. This allowed the drivers and spectators to see better. Horses and buggies carried a large drum of oil punctured with holes to spread the oil evenly in widths of approximately 10–12 feet.

3. *America's Finest Course, of Course!* 41

This postcard is part of the collection produced for the 1911 Savannah races and is entitled "Convict Labor—Widening the Course—1911." By 1911, Savannah had realized that having wider areas in premium viewing areas would allow for more passing of cars, which the crowd loved. The city undertook widening of several key locations to heighten the experience of spectators.

In two areas on the course where trolleys normally passed, the tracks were pulled up. Two footbridges were built where spectators arriving in cars could pull up, cross the bridge on foot and be met on the other side by another car to take them to viewing areas inside the track.

The track was made up of a mixture of well-packed Augusta gravel, with some portions of the track paved and some areas fenced. The width ranged from 30 to 60 feet over the 18-mile course. Prior to a new day of practice or a race, the course was freshly oiled. This could be tricky for ordinary drivers and racers alike. Tom Barber, a chauffeur who was crossing the course on March 17, 1908, after it was freshly oiled, skidded off the road due to the slippery surface. Barber was thrown from the car and suffered a broken leg.

The March 1908 track was only 17 miles, but by November 1908 the track had been enlarged to the full 25 miles for the American Grand Prize race. Much of the same surface techniques were used for the extension, with increases in materials. The amount of oil ordered for the course in November rose to 180,000 gallons.[24] The widths, which had ranged from 30 to 60 feet for the March races, were now primarily 60 feet, with banks as high as the Brooklands track at Surrey, England.

More than 1,000 convicts assisted in building the course. The course also contained a ten-mile International Light Car Race course for the support races that would be held in the days preceding the big race. The grandstands and start–finish line were located along Estill Avenue, and Habersham Street with the actual start–finish and judges stand very close to Atlantic. The corners, which were one of the most amazing feats of road construction

This postcard is part of the collection produced for the 1911 Savannah races and is entitled "Oiling the Road." Companies such as Indian Refining provided oil to help keep dust down. This step, which was a key part of the road building and maintenance process, allowed increased visibility for the drivers and spectators during the race.

and set the Savannah course apart from every other race track in America, were built with a radius of 140 yards to maximize speed coming into and leaving the bend.[25]

As the cars started the race and crossed the line in front of spectators in the grandstands, they would have come to a well-banked left turn onto what was White Bluff and is now Bull Street. A five-mile straightaway took the drivers south to Montgomery Crossroads. As they traveled east on Montgomery Crossroads, they would find an abrupt right turn, also well banked at Waters Avenue. The International Light Car Race drivers would have continued straight into the ten-mile loop, while the Grand Prize drivers would have taken the right turn onto the additional 15-mile course, crossing through the beautiful salt marshes, past cabbage palm trees, and over the beautiful Vernon River. After passing over Meridian and Whitefield, the driver would head for Montgomery Road, where the newer section of the course commenced.[26]

At this point the course fully widened to 60 feet, enough for five cars to drive side by side. Two sweeping turns took the driver to Ferguson Avenue, where drivers could reach speeds of up to 95 mph. This stretch of the course was considered to be the finest stretch of road ever built in America and possibly the world at that time. As they proceeded onto Isle of Hope Road and then La Roche Avenue, there were six heavily banked turns to challenge the drivers. The driver would veer right onto Skidaway Road, then make a sharp right to pass through Warsaw, now known as Thunderbolt. Next the driver approached the Wilmington River along Thunderbolt Road, then made a hairpin turn. The cars would end up returning 180 degrees to head back over Dale Avenue, which adjoined Estill, where the start–finish line would complete the lap.[27]

Savannah Automobile Club Members in 1910 as they were featured in *How the Race Was Run and Won*, a promotional booklet produced by the Indian Refining Co. Inc. in 1911 depicting the 1910 Savannah races. From left (top) to right: Mayor George W. Tiedeman, Judge Oliver T. Bacon, Harvey Granger, Arthur W. Solomon, and Frank C. Battey.

While the duties of receiving entries, deciding on rules and managing the racing aspects of the event fell to the Automobile Club of America, the Savannah Automobile Club and City of Savannah were responsible for building the course, arranging accommodations, advertising and handling the grandstand construction and management. The arrangements for the course and timing would be the most complex and expensive of any race in history. Mayor Tiedeman, along with the members of the Savannah Automobile Club, promised a magnificent course in 1908:

> Every hole the size of a pinhead will be filled and rolled so as to not only make the course absolutely safe and free from jars, but to render it the greatest speedway and record-breaking course the world has ever known.[28]

This was a monumental task, yet with their minds set on achieving greatness, coupled with the talent of the club members who built the Savannah track, they achieved their goal. The course committee for Savannah consisted of Harvey Granger, the committee chairman; Frank C. Battey; George W. Tiedeman, mayor of Savannah; George J. Baldwin; J. Ward Motte; and N.H. Van Sicklen. The Grandstand and Parking was headed by Chairman R.M. Hull.[29]

Harvey Granger may have been the linchpin in the races for several reasons. First, Granger was a visionary in road construction and transportation. In his lifetime, he paved the first concrete road in the state of Georgia; finished construction of the Atlantic Coast

Highway, which connected Jacksonville, Florida, to cities all along the East Coast; and was a vice president-at-large on the Dixie Overland Highway project, a highway that was planned to start in Savannah and lead to California.

Granger was a well-known landowner who shaped much of the southside of Savannah. He owned a large parcel of land known as the Granger Tract, which was deeded to the City of Savannah on November 13, 1906. This land was donated to the city to build four lanes between the roads of Estill (now Victory Drive) and 44th Street, 44th and 45th Streets, 45th and 46th Streets, and 46th and 47th Streets. In addition, three public parks were to be built in this parcel: one at 45th and Habersham, one at 45th and Harmon, and a third at 44th and Atlantic. The third at Atlantic still contains a parcel of parkland known as Atlantic Mills Park.[30]

A very civic-minded gentleman, Granger was a leader on many projects and committees that helped Savannah to become one of the most advanced cities in the country. Although he was officially a member of the Race Committee of the Savannah Automobile Club, Granger was truly the lead architect of the course and many roads around Savannah. He also adored the automobile, which explains in part why he gifted his tract of land for laneways to be built which would allow for parking behind the houses on the streets in those neighborhoods. Yet, he clearly understood that pedestrians needed to be accommodated as well and allowed for parks where people could walk and meet in the community.

Granger had been one of the Savannah Automobile Club members who had traveled to New York for several years to watch the Vanderbilt Cup race on Long Island. He was entranced with the races and ended up being one of the primary spokesmen for Savannah alongside Frank Battey and Mayor Tiedeman. In mid–December 1908, Granger was among the group of men who traveled to New York to see the Grand Prize Cup presented to Fiat, whose headquarters was at 57th and Broadway. The group was treated to rides on the Long Island Parkway in a Lancia roadster. Granger loved the car so much that he purchased it and brought it home to Savannah.[31]

Granger was known to be a man who was very modest about his accomplishments. Upon completion of Coastal Highway 17, many speeches of thanks were given to honor him. He was gifted a silver loving cup from the cities of Savannah and Brunswick and Chatham County for his work on October 13, 1927.[32] However, Granger's work was not easy and he fought for what he believed in, even when it went against city leaders.

In 1910, Granger was appointed as an associate member of the AAA contest board, undoubtedly a boon for Savannah in trying to attract the Vanderbilt Cup Race for 1911.[33] That year, he also took on the city of Savannah for imposing an ordinance stating that automobiles utilizing the public roads must be registered with the city. Granger was vehemently against this measure and took his case against the mayor and aldermen all the way to the Supreme Court on August 15, 1916, claiming the required registration was unconstitutional and invalid. The Supreme Court did not agree with Granger and the city prevailed, keeping its registration ordinance.[34]

There is no way to know exactly how this lawsuit and potential negative feelings that would naturally have come up between Granger, a key player in bringing the races to Savannah, and the city leaders, such as Mayor Tiedeman and later Mayor Pierpont, would have affected the races. It is also difficult to ascertain whether Granger's appointment to the AAA would have had any negative impact on the relations between the Savannah Automobile Club and the ACA when Granger became associated with its fierce rival. The reasons for the races' demise are somewhat hazy, with various theories being proposed and a number of circumstances coming into play. However, one thing is clear: Harvey Granger was the last person to visit New York (alone) in 1912 in the hopes of persuading the racing teams to return to Savannah, and he sailed home in October of that year without being able to accomplish that feat.

Mayor and Judge George Washington Tiedeman

Mayor George W. Tiedeman was one of Savannah's greatest champions and advocates for bringing the big auto races to Savannah and building the road course to the finest standards possible in 1908. Tiedeman was born September 11, 1861, in Charleston, South Carolina. He was the son of merchant Otto Tiedeman, a highly respected grocer who had emigrated from Germany to South Carolina in 1840. He learned English and became a partner in the grocery business where he worked after only one year of U.S. residence. Otto had three sons and a daughter, and one of his sons became one of the most influential men in Georgia and a very well-known leader in America—George W. Tiedeman.[35]

In 1887, the 26-year-old George moved to Savannah to begin work with his brother Irvin, who owned a wholesale grocery business. From that point on, he quickly became part of Savannah's business community. Well known in the community for his financial acumen, Tiedeman became interested in applying his skills as a political leader. He was known to be a man of few words, yet was very well liked and considered to be highly intelligent, with a superb grasp of how to build the community and ensure the city would prosper. Tiedeman was extremely dedicated to this cause, joining the boards of the Chamber of Commerce and Board of Trade during his tenure as president of Georgia State Savings Association.[36]

Most Savannahians

George W. Tiedeman was mayor of Savannah from January 21, 1907, to January 27, 1913. Tiedeman was one of Savannah's most forward-thinking mayors. He loved automobiles and was the father-in-law of the Hudson Motor Car Company founder, Roy Chapin (courtesy Horace Davies).

thought of Tiedeman as being very community minded and loyal to the interests of the people above all else. He was a great believer in new technology and worked hard to bring many cutting-edge improvements to Savannah. Tiedeman was elected first as alderman for the city and later as a three-time mayor of Savannah, beginning in his forties and serving six years as mayor. The city of Savannah had fallen into a state of disrepair before Tiedeman arrived on the scene. His vision and administration of Savannah changed that situation, and he became very popular with the people and business owners alike. He had a clear understanding of the need for continuous improvement in many areas of the city.[37] As his election was taking place, Savannahians looked to Tiedeman for his strong business acumen, conservative and economical values, and progressiveness. He won the mayoral election by 2,538 votes, a significant number for that time.

In 1890, Tiedeman married Floride Shivers of Savannah. They had three children: Carsten, Inez and George. Carsten would follow in his father's footsteps to a large degree, becoming an alderman for the city of Savannah while running Tiedeman Mortgage and Finance. Later, he would leave this position to move to Detroit, where he was offered a position as head of the Guardian Detroit Trust Company. Inez also lived in Detroit after marrying Roy Chapin, founder of the Hudson Motor Car Company.[38] Tiedeman's son George passed away at only seven years of age from meningitis.[39] In 1961, Carsten and Inez Tiedeman had the famous fountain in Forsythe Park renovated after it had fallen into disrepair. They undertook this project as a memorial to their mother and father.[40] This fountain has become very famous in Savannah and is seen in several movies, being featured prominently in Clint Eastwood's *Midnight in the Garden of Good and Evil*.

Among his accomplishments, Tiedeman brought the American Grand Prize races to Savannah and championed the building of the esteemed road course. He also brought electric lights to the city, motorized the fire department vehicles (which were the first in the United States), established Daffin Park and facilitated the purchase of Bonaventure Cemetery. In 1917, Tiedeman retired from his grocery business and focused on financing other business projects.

The Tiedeman home was an architectural wonder, set in the Victorian District of Savannah. It is located at 226 and 228 East Huntingdon Street and stands in contrast to the many gingerbread-style wood frame homes in the area. It consists of two semi-detached houses that were built for brothers George and Irvin. The red brick stands in contrast to the more common Savannah gray brick buildings. However, it is also the style itself, with terracotta tiles, steep arches and a turret, that makes the home unique. Tiedeman also had a beautiful summer home on the Isle of Hope known as Carsten Hall.

Tiedeman was very involved with the Savannah Automobile Club and its efforts to bring a major race, such as the Vanderbilt Cup, to the city. He attended the Vanderbilt Cup races in Long Island and did a great deal of traveling to New York while discussions were under way about bringing the race to Savannah. He was a leader and city spokesperson to both the AAA and ACA. Mayor Tiedeman was also a very generous man who believed in the racing efforts so much that he sponsored the Tiedeman Trophy. If not for his efforts and his progressive ideas as mayor, the first American Grand Prize and Vanderbilt Cup races would not have occurred in Savannah. Mayor Tiedeman passed away June 30, 1935.

4

March 1908 Drivers

The earliest drivers who came to Savannah were true pioneers. They were fearless, driving untested equipment at times, not knowing whether they would live or die while they raced. The development of technology meant a great deal to them. Although for some, the thrill of going fast and competing with others was a large part of why they raced, it was different for others. Some wanted to develop automobiles; others wanted to build the sport itself. Louis Strang, who raced in the March 1908 races in Savannah, may have been the most famous of the drivers who entered those events. It is his words, along with Len Zengle and George Robertson's, that echo down through the generations about the high quality of the course and organization that first brought the racing to Savannah. Some of these drivers had some very wild experiences, both on track and off. They were fantastic and daring and they reflect the same qualities in America's earliest major races.

FRANK W. LELAND

1908 • Savannah Challenge: First Race of Six-Cylinder Cars

Leland's racing career was fairly short, owing to the fact that he was primarily a mechanic and test driver for Stearns. The Stearns Company capitalized on his flashes of brilliance when he did compete in motorsports by widely promoting his name and accomplishments in the six-cylinder Stearns from 1907 to 1909. One of Leland's early successes in competition came in August 1907 when he entered and won the Class A division of the Fort George, New York, Hill Climb. Leland was driving the number 3 Stearns on the 1,900-foot course, which included a grade of 10 to 15 percent. The course was described as winding, dangerous and very steep. The Stearns had a 45-horsepower engine which made the climb easily, putting Leland in first place and breaking a record with 28 seconds.[1]

Leland was entered in two races in Savannah, Georgia, in March 1908. Arriving several weeks early, he was very impressed with the new course and tested the Stearns over it for several weeks, proclaiming it was simply wonderful. Leland would race George Salzman in a short two-car race on March 18, 1908, and then enter the larger competition on March 19, 1908. His luck was not very good in either race. The race against George Salsman in the six-cylinder Thomas ended on lap 2 when the Stearns engine broke through the crankcase. Unfortunately, Leland's luck was not much better the next day in the big race. The Stearns could not match the big Isottas, Apperson, Acme and Loziers. Like Fred Tone in the American, Leland was forced to withdraw by lap 16.[2]

Leland tried his hand at racing again, in a Hill Climb back at Fort George. He was less successful this time. The Stearns Company advertisements claimed problems with rims plagued the driver and car and "spring conditions" were an issue. Later that year, Leland traveled to Algonquin, Illinois, for the Chicago Motor Club's climb at Perry Hill and Phillips Hill. Leland had better luck here, winning the Algonquin Cup on Phillips Hill in his six-cylinder Stearns in a time of 29 seconds, in front of 8,000 spectators.[3] Yet, he did not seem bitten by the racing bug so much as he was driven to push and test the cars in order to tweak them for production. At the end of the 1908 racing season, Leland went out west with Stearns to help with the expansion of the western markets. He acted primarily as a demonstration driver, but also gathered information on the cars' performance on the trip from the East Coast to the West.[4]

The trip was a great success to the Stearns Company and Leland was promoted to chief tester, in charge of testing chassis for the company. He set up a farm 60 miles from Cleveland which the company would use to drive cars back and forth, weighting them down with wet sand and putting them through their paces to build a tougher car for their customers. Leland continued in testing roles after his racing career ended.

J.B. LORIMER

1908 • Southern High-Powered Cup

Lorimer drove the Blue Bird Thomas-Detroit against George Salzman at the Southern High-Powered Cup event on March 18, 1908, in Savannah. The next day, he entered the Savannah Challenge. Lorimer worked for Hugh Chalmers as a chauffeur on and off. On one special occasion, Chalmers had a celebrity guest visiting him: the world-famous and internationally renowned Polish pianist and composer, Ignacy Jan Paderewski, who later went on to become the second Prime Minister of Poland. Paderewski's "Minuet in G" was extremely popular in the classical music world and he was known to be particularly protective of his hands, insuring them for what would amount to tens of millions of dollars today.

Having just competed in Savannah a couple of months before Paderewski's visit, Lorimer was asked to take him for a spin in the big Thomas. Lorimer, of course, decided to give the musician quite a ride and put the pedal down all the way, making the car fly. Paderewski was fine for a few minutes, then suddenly began shouting at Lorimer in a mix of Polish, French and English. The pianist complained that his hands were getting too cold and he might be so badly chilled that he would be unable to perform that evening. Lorimer obligingly pulled over and made arrangements for a limousine to pick up the musician.[5]

HERBERT H. LYTLE

1908 • Southern High-Powered Cup

Herbert H. Lytle was one of America's earliest and most daring drivers. He was born July 9, 1874, in Malone, New York. Lytle raced in 1904 at Harlem in a Pope-Toledo, impressing the crowd with a spectacular win during the five-mile race. The car weighed between 1,432 and 2,204 pounds. His teammate was Billy Knipper, whom he would compete against and team up with at many meets, including Savannah's races. Placing third was L.D. Sheppard of the Sheppard Auto Company, who drove an 18-horsepower car. Lytle placed second in the ten-mile race, where he had a handicap of seven minutes which he was unable to make up. The race ended with a 25-mile timed event in which Lytle participated. He impressed the spectators and media alike with a time of 30 minutes and 30 seconds.[6]

It was August 14, 1905, when Herbert Lytle raced a Pope-Toledo in Glenville, New York, just southeast of Buffalo. Lytle was highly acclaimed for his performance and finished second. However, only days later, a very sobering event occurred in Buffalo. An accident involving Jay Webb occurred on August 18 and Jay was thrown from the track and into the water. He was unconscious. The driver sustained a crushed skull among other injuries and doctors immediately said he would not survive. The remaining drivers in the race, Lytle and Salzman, called off the race a lap or two later when they were informed that Jay had been badly injured.

Lytle would carry this awareness of the dangers of racing with him for the rest of his life. The accident was so grisly that William Hotchkiss, of the Hotchkiss Automobile Company and AAA, stated that "he would go before a court and ask for an injunction against further auto racing in this state." Ironically enough, Hotchkiss belonged to the upper echelons of the AAA; he served and organized racing events, including the largest in New York: the Vanderbilt Cup. Only a year later, one of Hotchkiss's cars was involved in a fatal accident where the driver Elliott Shepherd struck and killed his own best friend, who was a spectator at the races.[7]

Lytle seemed to stay away from racing after the tragic events of August 1905. However, in 1908 he was gearing up to return to auto racing with Edgar Apperson's 40-horsepower red "Jack Rabbit." Lytle was substituting for driver George Robertson for the Southern Runabout Cup Race on March 18, 1908. Robertson had an argument with owner Edgar Apperson and was released from the competition. Lytle would take the wheel, racing against J.B. Lorimer in a Thomas-Detroit Bluebird and Len Zengle in a Pennsylvania. Lytle won the race in 3 hours, 35 minutes and 41 seconds. His friend and rival Salzman was also racing in Savannah in the Southern High-Powered Cup race. Salzman would drive the Thomas-Detroit "Flyer," the same car that won the famous New York to Paris race the same year. Salzman also won his race, when the Stearns broke down. Racing was back in their blood and the two drivers would put behind them the tragedies of Buffalo.[8]

Lytle was one of the sport's earliest strategic planners for winning a race. He had formed a method for Savannah, which he shared with the media, stating that he would drive each lap in 20 minutes. To stick to his plan, the driver strapped a watch to the steering wheel of his car and he remained very close to his word on the timing. Lytle was asked if he would write a short piece for the *Savannah Evening Press* during the March 1908 races and he was happy to oblige. He wrote:

> It was the car that won the race. The engine could not have worked better, the other mechanism was in as good shape when we finished as at the start, and I guess I was lucky to keep the machine and the tires together all the way through. The engine never missed once. I had to stop once to change the spark plugs, as one of them did not seem to work well. Again I stopped to take on gasoline and oil. The Apperson was the best car in the race and came in first.[9]

Lytle had a very tough year in 1909, beginning with a 14-week battle with typhoid fever to start the year that would keep him away from early racing events. As soon as he began to recover, he started to consider racing, perhaps in Daytona if he was strong enough. Although he did not make it for those races in the end, Lytle would continue racing for the Apperson team through 1909. However, his luck had changed drastically. On June 6, 1909, at Crown Point, he suffered a broken spring. At the Lowell Road Race of September 8, he had a broken camshaft. In Riverhead, in the Long Island Automobile Derby on September 29, he wrecked the car and was badly injured when it flipped over. Lytle's riding mechanic, James Bates, was killed and the local media went ballistic. They were already up in arms over the fatalities at the Vanderbilt Cup and the Derby did nothing to help assuage their fears.[10] Lytle was replaced as driver for the year-end race at Philadelphia, and his seat taken by Harding.

The year 1910 started out slightly better for Lytle. He was now driving the American Underslung car. He raced in Atlanta on May 6 and 7 that year and finished first in a 50-mile free-for-all race with a time of 40 minutes, 20.02 seconds and second in the 10-mile free-for-all in 7 minutes, 43.46 seconds. These stellar performances would unfortunately be the last high points of Lytle's racing career. Later that month, Lytle raced at Indianapolis. The race would leave Lytle with a broken knee and another injured mechanic, William Clifton, when their rear tire blew and sent them off of the track.[11] Lytle's last major race would be back in the seat of an Apperson, where his bad luck returned: he wrecked the car in the pits on May 30, 1911. His son Herbert Lytle, Jr., would also become a racer and entered youth races in several cities, including Indianapolis in June 1911, where he placed second and third.[12]

Lytle did not enter any other major races. In February 1912, he became manager of the Apperson Brothers Agency in Kokomo, Indiana.[13] He died March 7, 1932.

WILLIAM R. McCULLA

1908 • Savannah Challenge

McCulla was a race car driver and later an engineer of automobile and airplane engines in America. He raced in England, Australia, Ireland and Scotland. He began his racing career early, in small events around the turn of the century. Prior to the Savannah races of March 1908, McCulla had eight years' driving experience with many of the big European race cars, including Mercedes, Renault and Fiat. One of his earliest wins was the 874-mile Lands-End to John D. Groats race, which traversed the entire length of Great Britain from north to south in 1905. He went on to another major victory in 1906, when he drove a Fiat in the Sydney–Melbourne Cup and won the Manchester Hill Climb over a field of 48 drivers. He was particularly good at the endurance races and broke some impressive records in 1907. In England he held the one- and five-mile race records and in America he held the record for 50 miles after his run in Pittsburgh, Pennsylvania.[14]

In September 1907, the Morris Park 24-hour race was held in the Bronx, New York. McCulla was hired to drive the 80-horsepower Darracq. The race started with five-car relays of 5 seconds' separation. McCulla participated in the Mile Trials during the events and went up against George Robertson in a 120-horsepower Hotchkiss; William Wallace, who also drove a Darracq; and two motorcycles—a 7-horsepower Indian driven by Stanley Kellogg and a 3-horsepower NSU driven by A.G. Chapple. It was a time when motorcycle racing was also popular. Mixed races with automobile and motorcycles competing against one another had been occurring since the late 1800s. McCulla placed third in the Mile Trials.[15]

In 1908, McCulla was signed to drive the Apperson on March 18, 1908, in Savannah, Georgia. He would drive in the Savannah Challenge, replacing George Robertson after Robertson and Edgar Apperson had a falling out over an incident which occurred during practice. There was almost as much excitement for McCulla to be racing in Savannah as there was dismay that George Robertson lost his ride. Unfortunately, with little practice time in the car and on the course, McCulla was doomed. He was out of the race after just a couple of laps when he turned the car over. Fortunately, no one was hurt. McCulla was humble and accountable for his part in the accident when he spoke to race reporters after the incident, stating: "I misjudged the speed of my car while attempting to pass the Isotta, and took a sharp left-hand turn too fast. As a result, my car turned over.... The only damage done to the car was to the steering wheel. A temporary repair was made, and the car was driven to the garage under its own power."[16]

By 1910, McCulla was still racing, but also working in research and development engineering. In May, he participated in the long-distance Harrisburg to Atlantic City Race put on by the Motor Club of Harrisburg. He drove a six-cylinder Kline Kar. The Kline Kar was an American-made automobile of very high luxury, built first in York, Pennsylvania, in the Baily Carriage Company warehouse. The operation moved in 1912 to Richmond, Virginia. The company was immediately involved in the auto racing industry with its cars and named their 6–50 roadsters Jimmy and Jimmy Jr., after the designer. The company went into mass production for a few years, much to the chagrin of Kline, who reported being relieved when it went out of business in 1924. McCulla considered the mass-production method of building automobiles to be cheap and inferior. McCulla did well in the Kline during the three-day race, although his performance was marred when he received a 3-point penalty for adding oil between noon and sunset. The race began on May 10, 1910, in Harrisburg, Pennsylvania, then moved on to Philadelphia and Atlantic City.[17]

Later in 1910, McCulla participated in *Cleveland News*–Cleveland Automobile Club Reliability Run. This was a small event to test the endurance of automobiles. McCulla was beginning to move his career into more of a test driver mode. He received a perfect score at the event driving a Hudson, which helped him secure work in the automobile engineering field.[18] By 1913, McCulla was well into his engineering career. He was working for Packard and by February 26, he had worked his way up to an appointment as assistant research engineer at the Detroit facility. He continued to test the cars for Packard in various endurance events. In one such test, McCulla was reported to have "set the fastest record for sustained road driving under unfavorable conditions."[19]

McCulla had started the endurance run in winter weather on icy roads in Chicago and driven straight through to Detroit, a distance of 284 miles, in 6 hours and 54 minutes. He was also an advocate for racing engineering and spoke often about his experiences in foreign and domestic race cars. When many in the industry began to praise the choice of putting the gearbox up front, McCulla wrote about his disagreement with the practice, referencing his experience in the Darracq.[20]

In 1915, McCulla took a break from working for Packard and went to work for Knox Motors in Springfield, Massachusetts. However, the experience was short lived and he spent a great deal of the time in Europe learning more about trucks used for war purposes. In 1916, he returned to Packard, bringing his newly gained experience and an avid interest in aviation with him. In February of that year, he was appointed as head of the Aeroplane Motor Division in the Engineering Department of Packard.[21] He spent the remainder of his career primarily working in aviation, although he always had an interest in motorsports.

Harry Michener

1908 • Savannah Challenge

Driving for Lozier early in his career, Michener began racing in a handful of smaller events, including the Savannah Challenge Race of March 19, 1908. He held his own against the big Isottas driven by Strang and Lytle and brought the 545-cubic-inch Lozier into fourth place during the first ever stock car road race in America. It would be a very big year for Michener, full of highs and lows. Michener was a great favorite with the crowds, especially at the long-distance events. He was closely watched by racing fans. So in October 1908 when he raced at Philadelphia in front of a crowd of 400,000 race fans, there was shock and fear when he suddenly flipped the six-cylinder Lozier only a mile and a half from the end. Michener was pinned underneath the car. He was knocked unconscious, but eventually recovered.[22]

It would not be the only time the driver showed the dangerous signs of fatigue from a long-distance race. As recounted in *A Speedway Is Born*, Michener was once driving the Brighton Beach track with his riding mechanic, Lynch. Suddenly, he turned to Lynch and asked him a strange question out of the blue: "What is that house? I never saw it before." When Lynch asked him what he was talking about, Michener waved at the grandstand and said, "That house right there." Lynch recommended he pit on the next go-around. When he did, Michener slumped over in a dead faint over the wheel.[23]

The year 1908 was a very busy year for the young driver, as he traveled to Savannah to race twice. His first trip was for the Savannah Challenge in March 1908, but his successes in that year earned him a second trip back to race with the Grand Prize drivers. Wearing his traditional white sweater, driver's hood and goggles, Michener joined the ranks of the Grand Prix elite, driving alongside the champions of Europe: Louis Wagner and Felice Nazzaro in their Fiats, Ferenc Szisz in a Renault, and Victory Hemery and René Hanriot in the big Benz cars. Michener was determined to compete with the Europeans in his Lozier and make a name for himself at America's first Grand Prix race. He was favored as much as Ralph Mulford and George Robertson by the crowds. Sadly, before the famous Grand Prix race, Michener was injured during practice. He was replaced by Ralph Mulford, who would use the opportunity to his best advantage to make a name for himself among the racing elite when Michener was unable to race.[24]

Disappointment at the end of 1908 led to brighter skies in 1909 for Michener. He was signed to drive the Lozier at the Portola Road Race in Alameda County in California and he placed third in the event. He also raced another endurance race of 800 miles in San Francisco in a four-cylinder regular stock Lozier known as the Briarcliffe model. Other cars participating included the Stearns, a Thomas, a Packard and a Stevens-Duryea. Michener won the September event and made a name for himself in the annals of motorsports, proving the smaller engine could outrace some of the bigger models.[25]

Michener's final major race came at Portola on February 22, 1911. The course had been shortened and was very roughly surfaced this time. Additionally, the excellent guard for the course that was enjoyed in 1909 was not in place. The new governor of California, Hiram Johnson, refused to call up the State Guard. Some of the guards showed up anyway, although they were out of uniform and crowds would not listen to them. Many injuries ensued. Michener did not race a Lozier this time; instead, he was at the wheel of an Inter-State for the nine-mile Light Car Race. This may have been planned at the last minute when Lozier, Speedwell and Buick pulled out of the race because of abandonment of the stock car classification. Michener was entered along with an EMF, a Mercer, a Maxwell, and a Ford, with the Mercer winning the event.[26] Unfortunately, it would be a sad final event for Michener.

MALCOLM A. NEWSTETTER
1908 • Savannah Challenge

Newstetter was born in 1886 and was virtually unknown in the auto racing world when he piloted a 45-horsepower Acme Sextuplet and placed third in the Savannah Challenge

Race of March 19, 1908. However, Newstetter was not unknown in the technology field. He was the inventor of an automatic electric generating system. This system allowed engines to be started or stopped by the charge of a battery. The U.S. Patent Office had a suit filed by another party claiming they had invented it, but Newstetter was able to prove he had the prior claim and won the right to the patent. He founded the Newstetter Electric System Company in Reading, Pennsylvania. He was also an importer of automobiles. Sadly, Newstetter died of appendicitis around November 1909 at the age of 23.

AL POOLE

1908 • Savannah Challenge

Poole raced a 40-horsepower Mercedes against Joe Tracey in a five-mile race in 1903. Shortly thereafter, Poole began his career as Tracey's riding mechanic for the Vanderbilt Cup winner. The two were great friends and in 1905, they made the trek with the Locomobile to France for the Gordon Bennett Cup Race. This was the last year of the Gordon Bennett competition, as it would be replaced by the French Grand Prix.[27] By 1908, Poole had made the jump from riding mechanic to driver. He was chosen by Isotta Import Company President C.M. Hamilton to race the company's 50-horsepower car at a variety of events. These included the Savannah Challenge on March 18, 1908, with mechanic Pepparday. Prior to the race, Poole received a telegram from Joe Tracey, offering some advice: "Keep cool; slow on the corners; good luck." He was considered to have a conservative style in his driving, especially in the first half of a race. In the second half, he would drive more aggressively.

Poole also raced at Lowell Road and Elkwood Park in Long Branch, New Jersey, where he won the 100-mile race for the Guggenheim Trophy with a time of 2 minutes and 10.26 seconds. Poole also held the record with Cyrus Patschke for 24-hour races. Poole was very adept at the Hill Climbs and was hired by Isotta to participate in the Bridgeport Hill Climb. It was a one-mile "free-for-all" race with an attendance of 12,000 spectators. Poole set the record for the event and took home the trophy.

Poole was truly a master at the endurance racing and easily trounced some of America's best-known drivers of the pioneering days, such as Ralph Mulford, Louis Chevrolet, Bob Burman and Ralph DePalma. On July 31, 1909, he was partnered with Vanderbilt Cup Champion George Robertson for the Brighton Beach 24-hour race at the motordrome. The race would begin on a Friday night at 9 p.m. and end Saturday evening. Robertson started the race, with Poole taking over in the middle and Robertson finishing. They drove the 885 miles and won.[28]

GEORGE SALZMAN

1908 • Southern High-Powered Cup

George Salzman entered the automobile industry at the turn of the century and in 1902 was hired by E.R. Thomas as assistant superintendent of the company. He began in the Sales and Mechanical Department working on the 60-horsepower Thomas cars. However, within a few years he was testing and driving the cars in racing events.

In 1905, Salzman was starting his racing career, entering events in the northeastern United States. The Buffalo Derby was one of the earliest events he participated in. It was a sobering experience for a young driver, as Salzman witnessed the dangerous reality that race car drivers had to contend with when they entered events in those early days. A friend and fellow driver, Jay Webb, veered off the road during the race and plunged down an embankment, landing unconscious in a pond. Spectators who were standing nearby jumped into the pond to pull Webb out as the race continued. Webb sustained many injuries, including nine broken ribs and a broken right femur, and it was feared he would catch pneumonia or pleurisy and die. When the race finished, Salzman was in second place behind Herbert Lytle and ahead of Fred Tone, both of whom he would meet a few years later in Savannah.[29]

In 1906 and 1907, Salzman joined the Glidden Tour with the 60-horsepower Thomas Flyer. The Glidden Tour was an 875-mile tour of cars organized by Charles Jasper Glidden. In 1906, the Glidden Tour began on July 9. In addition to the roads of New Hampshire and New York, it included a portion across the northern border at Buffalo and into Canada. The roads of New York State were extremely rough and difficult to navigate for the drivers, particularly from Utica to Saratoga. At Plattsburg, the tour crossed again into Canada, heading for Montreal and Trois Rivieres and then Quebec City to the northeast.[30] In 1907, Salzman drove the same car in the Tour, which was shortened to one day. Salzman made a perfect score in the tour this year, giving him another good preparation for the long road races he would encounter in his career in the next few years.

In early March 1908, Salzman came to Savannah to enter the Southern High-Powered Cup race, reserved for six-cylinder cars. The Matheson car did not make it to Savannah to race, leaving a small field of only two cars. Salzman's only competition was Frank W. Leland driving the Stearns. From the outset, Salzman had an advantage on the Stearns. His competitor's car suffered a mechanical failure after just one lap. Salzman continued racing, reaching 85 mph at times, and completed the race in 3 hours, 2 minutes and 25 seconds in the "Flyer." Salzman also raced in the Fairmount Park Motor races that year, but only completed six laps before a crankshaft malfunction.[31]

Salzman, still based out of Buffalo, New York, drove again in the Buffalo Derby in 1908. He became treasurer and general manager of the American Motor Car company. A sales branch of the company was opened in Atlanta that year. It placed a $65,000 order with the company with the stipulation that Salzman be relocated to oversee the branch's sales and manage the business. Savannah was still hoping for the Vanderbilt Cup to come to the city in 1908 and the American company promised that if it should happen, it would enter Salzman in the race.[32]

In October 1908, Salzman did enter the Vanderbilt Cup race in a 110-horsepower Thomas car, but it was held back in Long Island, not in Savannah. He had a fair race, often challenging at the beginning, but in the end, he had fallen behind and was flagged down on lap 11 as the race ended.[33]

Salzman went through a bizarre event in 1910. A man had begun impersonating Salzman, taking jobs and even entering a race from New York to Seattle under his name. Unfortunately, the man also racked up a rather large hotel bill at a high-class hotel in Philadelphia and left without paying. The man even produced a forged letter of recommendation from E. Thomas, which Thomas denied all knowledge of. Advertisements and notices were taken out in several publications such as *The Motor* and *The Horseless Age* to warn people that the man who drove an Acme in the New York to Seattle race was not George Salzman of the Thomas Company. It took Salzman a considerable amount of time and energy to clear up the case of mistaken identity and the impersonator was never found.[34]

In his later years, Salzman became a leader in engine manufacturing with Walker in Cleveland. He was elected to the company's Board of Directors on February 14, 1921.

Louis Putnam Strang

1908 • Savannah Challenge (March) and American Grand Prize (November)

The nephew of Walter Christie, Strang went by several names and nicknames in his lifetime—Lewis P. Strang, Louis Strang, Christie Strang and Louis Christie—and was referred to in Europe once as William Strang. He was called Mile-a-Minute-Man by the mainstream press in 1910, when his personal life became a thing of tabloid-like news. The place of Strang's birth is a source of much controversy. Some of his family members claim that he was born August 7, 1884, in Atlanta, Georgia, and the newspapers of the period report his birth in Amsterdam, New York. He spent most of his childhood and adult life in upstate New York.[35] He was the son of Estella Loranie Putnam Strang and Le Grand S. Strang, a jeweler in Amsterdam. His racing career and life are fascinating and well documented. Strang learned a great deal about engines and became a mechanic and driver shortly after the turn of the century. He was good friends with the Chevrolet brothers, particularly with Louis Chevrolet, who also raced for Buick early in his career. The cars Strang raced were both imports and domestic and included Isotta-Fraschini, Renault, Fiat, Buick and Marion.

Strang was entering races by 1905. However, it was his uncle, Walter Christie, who gave Strang his greatest start in the racing industry, taking him overseas to France as mechanic. Christie may have been sorry two years later when Strang began taking the car to races without permission. Indeed, the vehicle had to be tracked down by private detectives when the Christie car went missing during a shipment from Birmingham, Alabama, to New Orleans, where it was supposed to be shipped to New York. In fact, the car had never been shipped. Strang was entering races in the South, such as in Birmingham, Alabama, and St. Paul, Minnesota. Unfortunately, the car was under a purchasing agreement at the time and Christie found out after the fact that the cylinder was cracked from use of the wrong grade of fuel. Strang, fearing that his uncle would have him charged, sent him a telegram asking what steps he was going to take against him. Although Christie did not have his nephew charged, the two were estranged thereafter. Strang stopped using "Christie" as part of his name and simply went by Louis or Lewis Strang for the remainder of his life.[36]

Strang also began racing for other wealthy car owners by 1908. On March 19, 1908, he drove the 50-horsepower Isotta-Fraschini belonging to another controversial figure, John H. Tyson. He won the Savannah Challenge Trophy, which was staged in March as a major showcase for the AAA put on by the City of Savannah, which wanted the Vanderbilt Cup to be raced there in October 1908. It was an excellent start to the year for the driver. A month after his win in Savannah, Strang had a fantastic performance in the Briarcliffe Trophy race of April 1908. The course was 32 miles long and located in Westchester County. The race went 240 miles and Strang won in 5 hours, 14

Louis Strang was a very famous driver in the bigger races in Europe and American shortly after the turn of the century. He had a very colorful life and personality and was the nephew of Walter Christie. He won the first race in Savannah.

minutes and 13 seconds. A buzz had really begun about the driver and his romance with a beautiful actress. After Briarcliffe, the newspapers were full of praise, including *The New York Times*, which stated, "How much of the triumph was due to the machine and how much to Strang's wonderful handling of the car.... Strang gave a most surprising exhibition of skill."[37]

Strang would win so many races that year that he became a household name. If his racing career was moving at lightning speed, Strang's personal life was shaping up to be a super roller coaster. He had married a beautiful actress and dancer named Jeanne Spaulding (stage name: Louise Alexander). He returned to Savannah in November 1908 driving a 737-cid, 12.07-liter Renault with European teammate Ferenc Szisz. With a sixth-place finish in the race, Strang became the first American driver to finish an American Grand Prix race.[38]

Strang seemed to be poised for superstardom in the racing world in 1908, despite having bad luck at Briarcliffe on October 5 in the Renault. He had done an amazing job leading the 880-mile race for 18 hours and held a substantial lead when the rod suddenly broke and tore open the crankcase on his car. Strang's race was finished, and he would not make the podium in the Savannah Grand Prize in November. However, his luck would change even more significantly in the coming year or two. He was having great difficulties at the races, he fell out of an airplane and his pretty wife of only one year would change her mind about her career and decide to return to the stage. She took on a starring role in a bizarre production about vampires. Strang hoped she would have a change of heart and the two would reunite. He realized this was not likely when he learned that she was personally involved with her partner, Julian Mitchell, and was named in his divorce proceedings as his mistress. Strang, having just recently had the airplane accident, said, "Two knockouts together, this is the limit," and gave up on the marriage for good.[39]

By 1910, Strang had been hired by the J.I. Case tractor firm, which was also building racing cars. He was given the position of manager of its racing team and airplane division. Strang was still an excellent mechanic who knew the engines thoroughly. He devoted most of his time that year to building the "Miss Case" car, which was to be the first car for the new race team. The car was to debut at New Orleans in February 1911, but did not make it. Despite talk of suspending the new team, it was allowed to remain in the sport and debuted that spring at the first Indianapolis 500 race. Now in the role of manager and driver, Strang managed to put the car on the pole. He was the first driver to win the pole position for the first Indianapolis 500 in 1911, driving the red and gray Case automobile. Unfortunately, he had difficulties with the steering after 109 laps.[40]

The presence of drivers such as Strang, who proclaimed the Savannah track to be the best he had ever seen, set the tone for the next three years. He was injured in Kenosha, Wisconsin, in June 1911 when one of his tires burst and he was catapulted through a fence, breaking his arm. A month later, he unwisely drove again with a broken arm and sprained ankle. These injuries may have contributed to his death on July 20, 1911, when he was in Blue River, Wisconsin, scouting a route from La Crosse to Lancaster for a tour. As a farmer came up over a hill he was driving the Case car over, Strang veered off the road and rolled down a ten-foot embankment and was crushed beneath the car. Savannah would lose her first champion in the very year when it finally had won the rights to contest both the Vanderbilt Cup Race and the American Grand Prize in November 1911. Strang would be sadly missed by Savannahians and his fellow drivers. One of America's earliest racing heroes, Barney Oldfield, spoke at length of Strang's career, calling him "a brilliant performer and a genius at nursing a car and picking winning mounts." Oldfield considered Strang's best races to be his wins at Savannah, Briarcliff and the Lowell road races of 1908.[41]

FRED TONE
1908 • Savannah Challenge

Tone was a driver and engineer from 1896 onward. His first foray into the automobile industry was with the Locomobile Company of America. He remained with the company for a number of years before taking a job as an engineer for the Indianapolis-based Marion company. Tone had a dream of building and racing an underslung car. He got the chance to develop one when Harry Stutz left the American Motor Car Company shortly after its start-up and was replaced by Tone as chief engineer in 1906. Tone was instrumental in developing the Underslung chassis.[42] The cars sold at prices ranging from $1,200 to $4,000 at that time.

Tone began racing in 1905 and was a contemporary of Herbert Lytle and Barney Oldfield. Early in August, he raced at Detroit, where Oldfield was badly injured. The sport was at a dangerous time, with automobile technology getting ahead of the Good Roads Movement to keep drivers safe. In the first races in August, Tone entered the five-mile open for stock touring cars with the 50-horsepower American Underslung. His main competitor was George Soules, who had quite a lead in a bigger, faster car. However, Tone drove very well and cut the lead back considerably, pulling all the performance out of the American that was possible.[43] Many were surprised that the car did so well, as it was thought to be too low and would bottom out a lot. But the spring system kept that from happening, and Tone handled the car extremely well, placing second in the event. In mid–August 1905, Tone entered

Fred Tone, driver and designer of the American Underslung cars, driving car number 36, a 50-horsepower American Underslung, at Brooklands in 1908 (with his mechanic).

races as Kenilworth Park in Buffalo, New York. He placed second in the five-mile open and third in the five-mile open for stripped touring cars, driving the American Underslung.[44]

On March 19, 1908, Tone entered the American in the Savannah Challenge in Georgia. It was a 17-mile race. He raced against Louis Strang and Alfred Poole, both driving Isottas, and Herbert Lytle in the Apperson Jackrabbit. The cars were sent off every minute and a half, with Tone leaving in third place, based on the earlier time trials. Again the car impressed many at the start and during time trials. However, Tone encountered much difficulty and brought it to a sixth-place finish, ahead of F.W. Leland in a Stearns and McCulla, who had a collision in an Apperson.[45]

From 1910 onward, Tone's career changed as he became more involved in acting as a representative for American at car shows, events and exhibitions. He participated in major shows in Indianapolis, Detroit and New York as a spokesman and demonstrator for the manufacturer. The cars he would show included some from his racing class: the roadster and touring cars. By 1911, American was having significant financial difficulties and changed its name to American Motor Company. Tone left to work for the Willys-Overland Company in Toledo. American filed for bankruptcy in 1913.[46]

Known as one of the best engineers in the industry, Tone began to move away from racing and concentrated more and more on his business interests. He was very good with finance and highly trusted by the companies he worked with, such as W.P. Kirk of New York, where he served as treasurer. In 1912, he was appointed as receiver of the Electro Light and Starter Company, which had filed for bankruptcy due to cash flow problems. A receiver would be brought in at the request of the creditors, who wanted someone they could trust to handle the firm's affairs and ensure they gained back their assets to whatever extent was possible. Tone, a natural organizer, took his job seriously and began to consider going into business himself. By 1913, the Fred Tone Car Corporation was formed in Indianapolis, although production was primarily in Detroit.[47] With $200,000 in capital, Tone began the company with the idea to produce a $900 five-passenger car. The new car would be built with a single style of chassis and a choice between several standard body types, including a roadster, touring car, light delivery and coupe.[48]

The American Automobile Company merged in 1954 with the Hudson Motor Company, which coincidentally was owned by Mayor Tiedeman's son-in-law Roy Chapin. Tone became interested in aerospace engineering as time passed. He was eventually hired by the United States government as an airplane inspector and was stationed at Curtiss Airplane Company in Buffalo for several years.[49]

Len Zengle
1908 • Southern Runabout Cup and American Grand Prize

Len Zengle was born March 15, 1887, in Dayton, Ohio. His father was Leonard A. Zengle. Young Len grew up in Philadelphia. He worked for the Pennsylvania Motor Car Company based in Bryn Mawr, Pennsylvania, and with the Acme Automobile made by Reber Manufacturing in Reading, Pennsylvania.

Zengle began his racing career with a number of hill climbs. Indeed, he was a master at the hill climb stock car events. On June 20, 1908, he won two events at Point Breeze in the 50-horsepower Pennsylvania race. In the time trials, he placed first with a time of 6 minutes and 27 seconds; he also won in the fifth event for special match stock cars.[50] Zengle's summer racing was working out very well and he would go on to win the first hill climb held in Norristown, Pennsylvania, entering event number six for gasoline-powered stock cars in a Pennsylvania.[51]

On March 18, 1908, Zengle entered the Southern Runabout Cup race, which was intended to have six participants. However, due to several mechanical failures, only three cars appeared: a Pennsylvania driven by Zengle, Herbert Lytle's Apperson Jack Rabbit, and J.B. Lorimer's Thomas Detroit "Bluebird." Zengle's Pennsylvania was flagged to go first and shot down the track and out of sight of the grandstands. Unfortunately, Zengle's good fortune would not hold out long. Shortly after the start, his gears began to show signs of wear and his transmission gave out, leaving him in last place.[52]

Zengle continued racing at a variety of smaller events. By the fall of that year, he was entered in the Fairmount Park Race of October 1908. He was signed to drive the Pennsylvania again, and was allotted car number 16 in the race. The race began at 7 a.m. and the cars were flagged to start at 30-second intervals. Although he did not finish well, Zengle picked up valuable experience from his first race at Fairmount Park that would serve him well in the future.[53]

In November 1908, Zengle returned to Savannah to race an Acme in the Grand Prize race. He held his own against the great Grand Prix drivers of the world and showed his mechanical talent throughout the race. Early on, in lap 3, Zengle had a spring break. He spent two hours repairing it with a block of wood, some wire and rope. Ultimately, he reentered the race and made several more laps, going approximately 75 miles with the repair that he and riding mechanic Frieberg had tried. Unfortunately, he was out of the race on lap 6, but it was not for lack of ingenuity.[54]

Zengle's racing career continued to heat up in 1909. In July, he raced at a number of events at Wildwood, New Jersey, with a 60-horsepower Chadwick 6. He swept all of the events he entered in front of a crowd of 10,000 people. In the one-mile race, Zengle placed first with a time of 44 seconds. He also broke the track record by 1 second, clocking in at 41 seconds. In the kilometer race, Zengle won with a time of 26 seconds; he also took the prize for the free-for-all with a time of 48 seconds. Zengle's fastest time was 87.8 mph.[55] He continued his success in August 1909 at the Algonquin Cup events held by the Chicago Motor Club. Zengle climbed both the quarter-mile Perry Hill and the half-mile Phillipps Place in first place, breaking the record for the Phillipps climb by 1.5 seconds when he came in at 28 seconds.[56]

One of Zengle's favorite races was the Fairmont Park Race, where he often had excellent results. In October 1909, Zengle entered the race in his six-cylinder, 60-horsepower Chadwick with Firestone tires. He had the fastest lap of 7 minutes and 41 seconds. His speed was 63.3 mph. Throughout the first half of the race, Zengle challenged race leader George Robertson for first place. Unfortunately, he suffered mechanical difficulties from an overheating engine caused by leaking water pipes around lap 14 and a few laps later almost had a collision while driving down Sweet Briar Curve. He had to retire from the race early.[57]

After continuing with spectacular results in his hill climbs and setting a new record for the course at Galveston, Texas, during the Cotton Carnival of 1910, Zengle set his sights again on Fairmount Park. His earlier experience at Fairmont lit a fire in Len Zengle and he returned to the race in October 1910 determined to win the race. Zengle's fastest time was 8 minutes and 3 seconds in the Chadwick. With 32 cars entered, winning would be no easy feat. He drove the Chadwick again with a piston displacement of 707 and had a new riding mechanic, Billie Manker. Zengle's time was getting faster as he approached laps 15 and 16 with a time of 8 minutes and 8 seconds per lap. Erwin Bergdoll, who had been leading the race, suffered a mechanical failure on lap 16 and Zengle, chewing a cigar, went on to battle Ralph Mulford for the lead. Zengle got a flat tire near the end but continued racing and won the race, beating Mulford by a mere 6 seconds.[58]

A new chapter began for Zengle in 1911 when he was signed to drive a National. His results were just as impressive as they were in the Chadwick and Pennsylvania. He won the Galveston Beach Races in August, setting yet another new record for the course in the free-for-all at 42 minutes, 9.5 seconds.[59] He struck it lucky at Elgin, winning the Elgin Trophy as well. Unfortunately, there was a terrible mishap at this race where the grandstand collapsed, injuring as many as 100 spectators. The race was restarted after the injured were treated and the track was inspected and judged safe.[60]

Zengle also participated in the Elgin Race and Indianapolis 500 of 1912, driving for Stutz. At Indianapolis he placed sixth and averaged a speed of 73 mph. However, it was the end of an era for Zengle. With the coming of the oval speedways, he and several other drivers lost their interest in racing. As the *Cincinnati Enquirer* sadly recounted in 1919: "racing apparently holds no more thrills for Don Herr, Charley Merz and Len Zengle."[61] Zengle was married around 1915 and had two children. He owned and operated two car dealerships for Chrysler and Plymouth after retiring from the sport. Zengle died September 24, 1963, in Bryn Mawr, Pennsylvania.

5

From Triumph to Tragedy in Savannah

"The Road Race Meet of the Century"
—*New York Times*, November 12, 1911[1]

The Savannah Automobile Club was founded in 1904 by Arthur Solomon, Harvey Granger, Frank Battey and J.J. Rauers, among others. Along with Savannah mayor George Tiedeman, several of these gentlemen had been attending the Vanderbilt Cup Races since they began. They were aware of the troubles that the AAA was experiencing in Long Island, New York. Several of the Savannah members attended the 1904, 1905 and 1906 races and learned of the difficulties first-hand. At that time, Savannahians had become very enamored with motor racing, none more so than the members of the Automobile Club and Mayor George Tiedeman. The Vanderbilt Cup was the crown jewel of American racing, and they admired and loved this fantastic race, and were excited by the drivers, car owners and car club members whom they met while visiting New York. It was during this 1906 visit that the idea formed in their minds that perhaps Savannah could one day host the Vanderbilt Cup.

News of the terrible tragedy that occurred early in the race spread very quickly around the track on that fateful October morning in 1906. Elliott Shepherd was driving a Hotchkiss—a car manufactured by President Hotchkiss of the AAA—when he struck a spectator watching the race. The man was thrown approximately 50 feet and died of a crushed skull and multiple fractures. The saddest part of the tragedy, however, was the identity of the man. Bert L. Gruner was Shepherd's best friend. Shepherd did not complete the race and left the track, weeping inconsolably when he learned of his friend's fate. He was placed under arrest by Nassau County police.[2]

A few laps later, a 14-year-old boy, Ralph Baldwin, was struck by driver Joe Tracey, who broke a record for American drivers that day. Two other boys, John Books and Robert Eyck, were struck while riding their bicycles by an amateur driver, Dr. Weilschott, who plunged down a 36-foot embankment after hitting them.[3] Only five cars finished the 29.71-mile race, which was won by Louis Wagner in a Darracq. Despite the pall that was cast over the races by the tragedy and injuries, the crowd lifted Wagner onto their shoulders and carried him around jubilantly.

The mayor and Savannah Automobile Club members saw the terrible crowd surges personally. The system that was employed at the Vanderbilt Cup to control the crowds was to sound a bugle loudly and make a loud call of "car coming." However, the crowds ignored this warning and piled onto the track to see the cars approach instead of keeping back.[4] Witnessing the pandemonium that ensued was enough to show the Savannah Automobile Club members what they would have to do differently one year later when the Vanderbilt Cup was cancelled and the idea of a new venue was raised.

When it was announced in 1907 that George Tiedeman and Frank Battey, president of the Savannah Automobile Club, would travel up to New York to meet with the AAA to propose Savannah as a new site for the Vanderbilt Cup race, excitement spread like wildfire through the prosperous little city. Georgia governor Hoke Smith was more than willing to commit troops to guard the course. Mayor Tiedeman also promised to provide a police force to assist with securing the portions of the course that were on city land, as the race course was divided between county and city. Savannah was also very fortunate in having extremely talented road builders such as Harvey Granger and Frank Battey to build a course.

It was Arthur Solomon, treasurer for the Savannah Automobile Club, who made a trip to New York in early January to meet with the AAA and iron out the details. He was named Secretary of the Auto Meet for the Savannah Automobile Club and arrived back in Savannah from New York on January 11, 1908, with details about the upcoming chassis races.[5] He assured city officials and Savannah Automobile Club members that everything was in order with the AAA. As early as the next day, the Savannah Automobile Club received a telegram request from Edgar Apperson asking about the entry fee for his Apperson Jackrabbit and the club got started on their plans to set those prices. They met on January 13 to do so and also discussed the major hurdle of how to raise enough money to pay for the grandstand and oil for the roads, which were two of the greatest costs.[6]

Work began on planning the course and race almost immediately. The dates of March 18 and 19 were selected as the race dates and committees were formed to oversee the details. The Transportation Committee would fall to W. Williamson, Charles Ellis and W.B. Stillwell, who assisted in arranging freight and express rates on the trains and began planning parking and coordination with garages for automobiles. Initially, the Race Course Committee was headed by Albert Wylly and A.B. Moore, although Harvey Granger would play a larger role as the events neared and well into the November 1908 race. Trophies would be looked after by J. Baldwin and J.J. Rauers handled the arrangement, printing and distribution of programs.[7]

Aside from the love of the automobile and auto racing shared by the mayor, City Council members and the Savannah Automobile Club, there were other reasons why Savannah wanted the races. Foremost among these was the desire to bring automobile tourists to Savannah. In fact, Mayor Tiedeman specifically wanted to attract Rockefeller to visit with his touring car and make Savannah his regular destination. He was already known to travel regularly to Augusta and Jekyll Island and brought a great deal of media attention to the places he visited. Savannah was known as "the leading automobile city of the South." City officials also wanted the city to become "the leading winter resort of automobile enthusiasts."[8]

Savannah's reputation for being a great automobile city was due, in part, to the number of paved roads—a number that was expanding rapidly. By 1909, $60,000 was being spent per year to pave and grade streets within the city limits.[9] That did not include the county roads, many of which made up the automobile course south of Estill (now Victory Drive). The main streets, such as Bull Street, where the brand-new City Hall had been built, was paved with Trinidad Lake asphalt in 1907. Daffin Park, also a brand-new recreational center for the city, was beautified and used for baseball. A small lake was built there and styled after l'Enfant Tuileries in Paris, France. The central mall of the park was graded to a width of 215 feet and a length of 1,800 feet at a cost of $4,514.94. Four rows of gorgeous live oak trees were planted, totaling 156 trees. It was a breathtaking location for race spectators, families, athletes and curiosity seekers to gather.

One long-held mystery in the city about the palmetto trees lining Victory Drive has had citizens talking for decades. The question always arises as to whether they were placed there after World War I, when Estill Drive was renamed Victory Drive, or sooner, for the races. The answer lies in the city's Annual Report of 1910, where Mayor Tiedeman authorized the planting of a double row of palmetto trees from Bull to Waters and on Atlantic Avenue—the section of the race track which was originally the start–finish line, grandstands, pits and judges stand. It was paved by Barber Asphalt Paving Company in the same year.[10]

A fairly new grandstand had already been built in Daffin Park prior to 1908 for fairground activities. Landscape architect John Nolen designed much of the beautification of Daffin Park, which was undertaken in 1908 and 1909. He also noted that the grandstand located at the southwest corner of the Park could be moved.[11] The race technical committee was in favor of bringing it over to Estill Avenue near the start–finish line and pits. This would add seating in the premium area and, in keeping with the thriftiness employed in all endeavors to bring the races to Savannah, cut down on the cost of building the grandstands.

Tiedeman worked closely with Chatham County on the great races because he felt they "resulted in an amount of advertising for the City, the value of which is incalculable."[12] The mayor also realized the significance of the military contribution, stating, "without their cooperation the races would not have been possible, and I cannot speak in terms too laudatory of the spirit which actuated the members of the military to make the sacrifices incident to the guarding of the course, and of the thorough and effective way in which they performed their duties."[13]

Savannah was among the earliest innovators in using motor vehicles for city functions. This included having the first automobile hearse in 1908, when Marius de Rosa, a young mechanic, wrecked during practice at the November events. It also included being the first city in the world with a fully auto-vehicle fire department in 1911 and requests for automobiles for the Police Department and Park and Trees Department.[14] The city had truly embraced the automobile in every way possible by the period of the "Great Races" of 1908–1911. It was this love of the automobile that propelled city officials to go to great lengths to compete for the Vanderbilt Cup of 1908. Savannah had already achieved a solid reputation for constructing state-of-the-art racing facilities. Back in 1893, it had built the first concrete bicycle racing track in America and the second one of its kind in the world, at Wheelmen's Park. The only other track of this kind was located in Paris, France. Savannah was ready to repeat the process for automobile racing.

Although St. Louis, Missouri, had also bid for the race, Savannah had decades of experience with putting racing events on. This gave the city and Automobile Club a lot of confidence in their ability to build a cutting-edge course, propose an exhibition and solicit the assistance of the AAA in planning it. The two organizations planned an exhibition of speed and endurance races with stock chassis. It would be held around the St. Patrick's Day holiday, with March 18 and 19 being the two days over which three events would be held. The three events would be the Savannah Challenge Trophy, the Southern High-Powered Cup for six-cylinder cars and the Southern Runabout Cup.

The main event of the races was the Savannah Challenge Trophy, which was first known to the media as the Tomochichi Trophy owing to the fact that the race committee planned for the winner's trophy to be a bust of Tomochichi, chief of the Yamacraw Indians. Interestingly, the winner would not receive the trophy itself. Only if the winner won the event three times could he or she keep the trophy. Instead, the winner was given a silver feather, which fit into the headdress of the Tomichichi statue. Two feathers were permitted for each year. The present location of this trophy is unknown at this time.[15] The prize was valued at $3,000 and the race date was fixed for March 19, 1908. Entrants would be limited to a maximum of a 575-cubic-inch engine. They would race 20 laps on an 18-mile course for a total of 360 miles.

The Southern High-Powered Cup race was open to standard stock chassis automobiles. The engines were limited to 375 cubic inches. The participants would also race the full 18-mile course, but would drive only 10 laps (180 miles). The smallest event was the Southern Six Cylinder Cup. It was the first six-cylinder stock chassis race to be held in America. The engines of the vehicles in this race could exceed 575 cubic inches. As in the High-Powered Cup, they would race only 10 laps on the 18-mile circuit. Practices were held on the track daily from 10 a.m. to 12 p.m.[16]

Since crowd control had been such a problem at other races, the track builders used fencing in some areas to improve safety and crowd control. Georgia's governor, Hoke Smith, had provided 1,200 militia to patrol the event. Most of these troops were housed at the Savannah Volunteer Guard barracks located at 342 Bull Street. It was a large red brick building with turrets, wrought-iron balconies and large cannons flanking the main doors, and can be seen today at the corner of Bull Street and Charlton Street.

Visitors arrived from far beyond the local region of South Carolina, Georgia and Florida. Steamships brought spectators from Baltimore, Boston, Philadelphia and New York City. Special trains were also organized from Atlanta and New York to Savannah. Other visitors arrived by automobile, horse, wagon, bicycle and on foot. The cost for entrants to

Volunteer Guard Armory, Bull Street. This view of the Volunteer Guard Armory is from 1908. The Volunteer Guard was organized in 1805 and headquartered at this iconic building in historic Savannah, which is now home to the main offices of the Savannah College of Art and Design. At the time of the races, soldiers from several military and police units came together to patrol the course. They came to this building for rations, weapons, and orders and used it as a place to stay throughout the events.

ship their vehicles down for the race was 28.5 cents per 100 pounds with a minimum of 1,000 pounds.

The Cars of Savannah's March 1908 Races

Three different classes were assigned for the four- and six-cylinder cars. Various manufacturers signed up to race over the two days.

The Apperson Jackrabbit was a shaft drive with three-speed gearset, double ignition with Bosch magnetos, standard band clutch, 4.75 × 5 inch cylinders in separate casting, opposing valves and battery. Diamond tires were on the winning car in the Southern Runabout Cup race.

The Isotta-Fraschini cars were named for company founders Cesare Isotta and Vincento Fraschini, who first worked together assembling Renaults at the turn of the century, then began manufacturing their own cars together in Italy in 1904. They raced at Coppa Florio in 1905 with the Tipo D model. In 1907, they merged their operation briefly with Lorraine-Dietrich, then parted ways again. The cars that raced in Savannah in March 1908 were chain-driven, 50-horsepower engines with cylinders cast in pairs and a 125-inch wheelbase. One car also raced at Briarcliff in 1908.

The Thomas-Detroit had 4.25 × 5.25-inch paired cylinders, valves on the right side and Bosch magnetos. The Thomas famously raced and won the New York to Paris race in 1908. It was also entered in endurance races in Minneapolis and the Rocky Mountains.

Stearns were manufactured in Cleveland, Ohio, from 1898 to 1929. The car which raced in Savannah had a 536-cubic-inch, four-cylinder, 60-horsepower poppet valve engine. The Stearns cars sold for $4,600.

The Acme was manufactured in Reading, Pennsylvania, from 1903 through 1911. The Sextuplet, which drove in Savannah and finished third, was a double-chain drive, six-cylinder, 45-horsepower engine with double ignition, Eisenmann high-tension magnetos, accumulator and coil. It had a four-speed selective change gear and Hess-Bright ball bearings. The front axle was a Cramps manganese bronze I-beam and the rear axle was made of nickel steel. The wheelbase was 126 inches and the car weighed 4,000 lbs. The touring version could accommodate five or seven passengers and sold for $4,500 or $5,500. Acme also entered the car in the 24-hour Brighton Beach Races.

The American Underslung was built from 1905 to 1913 by the American Motor Car Company in Indianapolis, Indiana. As the name implies, the suspension was unique in that it lowered the center of gravity in the car, yet did so without affecting clearance. This 40-horsepower roadster was capable of high speeds. It had 40-inch wheels. The ignition was also high-tension magneto and the vehicle had a conical clutch, sliding gear and shaft and a floating rear axle. The wheelbase was 106 inches and the total weight was 2,200 lbs.

The Pennsylvania "50" was also known by the name "Type C." It was built in Bryn Mawr, Pennsylvania, and had 4.75 ×5.25 inch cylinders with valves located inside the cylinder head; an overhead valve engine with opposing valves operated independently by double-cam shafts. The small parts such as valve housings and springs were easily removed to allow access to the combustion area, which simplified cleaning as there was no need to remove the entire engine. The car had a conical clutch and the gear set was on the rear axle, which incorporated the transmission.

The Lozier was a luxury car manufactured in Detroit, Michigan, from 1900 to 1915.

The Lozier was a favorite and was very popular at the Savannah races of 1908–1911. The car that raced in Savannah in March 1908 was a shaft-drive, six-cylinder, 50-horsepower model painted a light gray that almost looked white. It had a ball bearing crankshaft and double ignition with a storage battery and high-tension magneto. The wheel base was 131 inches. The Loziers sold for approximately $6,000 at that time. In addition to racing in Savannah, Lozier entered its cars in the Vanderbilt Cup Races and Indianapolis 500.

Before the Big Race

The excitement began with a number of developments that occurred in the weeks before the March races. First, a large bet was made by two car owners, Edgar Apperson and V.A. Longaker. The two gentlemen met at a banquet in Chicago only weeks before the Savannah event. Their cars, the Apperson Jackrabbit and the American Underslung, were both being entered in the first Savannah Challenge race. Each man felt his car was certain to beat the other. After a lively discussion on the merits of each man's automobile, the two decided to settle the argument with a bet. Each would put in $500 and whichever car finished better in the race would take home the entire $1,000. Today, that bet would be worth approximately $25,000.

This bet created added excitement for the Savannah Challenge race, as people watched the "race within a race" closely due to the wager, especially on the straightaways where there

Fred Tone, the subject of a famous bet between the owners of the American Underslung and the Apperson Jackrabbit, captured a great deal of interest from the crowd each time he passed the viewing areas and pits on the 17-mile Savannah course.

Fred Tone driving the number 3 American Underslung (with his mechanic) in the Savannah Challenge race of March 19, 1908.

were ample passing opportunities due to the track being wide enough to accommodate three cars running side by side. It was to be a "do or die" competition and the owners instructed the drivers to win at any cost. The drivers who were originally slated to race each other were both known daredevils in the sport. George Robertson had been driving (and wrecking) at the Vanderbilt Cup races up until 1906, and Fred L. Tone—a speed demon—piloted the popular American Underslung car. Tone's mechanic was Joseph Linn.

Unfortunately for Edgar Apperson, events leading up to the race would become talked about more than the results. George Robertson was considered something of a wildcard when he was behind the wheel. He was a fast-or-crash type of driver. After testing for a week or so on the Savannah course, he spoke very highly of it:

> It is an excellent course and I expect to see very fast time made. The eleven turns have all been well banked. The Savannah authorities are willing to do everything necessary to put the course in the best possible shape. They have strong hopes of getting the Vanderbilt Cup race there next fall and realize that their coming meet will aid their cause materially.[17]

This was one of the first accounts of a famous American driver touting the Savannah course so highly. It would not be the last.

Edgar Apperson was a very determined car owner and manufacturer. He was very emotionally invested in the Apperson winning the race and beating the American Underslung car. At a meeting prior to the races, Apperson made a suggestion that a new rule should be included that would prevent participants from using any spare parts to repair their cars during the race. He wanted cars to start and finish with the exact same equipment, thus proving the strength and durability of each part individually. There were numerous objections to his suggested rule and it was not adopted. As originally planned, drivers and mechanics were allowed to carry spare parts, but only the two of them could make the repair during the race.

Sign boards had been put up all over Savannah as practice began in early March. They warned people of the dangers of cars on the course. These dangers extended to the drivers as well. George Robertson, for example, would make more news headlines in his Apperson before race day arrived. On March 11, 1908, the Apperson driver and a young mechanician named Seaton Fariss who had just teamed up with Robertson had an accident. The Apperson spun out after blowing a rear tire and went into a bad skid which caused both rear tires and the detachable rims to come off the car. The same afternoon, Robertson was accused of crashing into Harding's car while it was being towed to the pits for repair.[18]

Edgar Apperson was furious and most likely began thinking back to Robertson's crash in 1906 at the Vanderbilt Cup race. He decided to replace the famous driver. Robertson, however, was not satisfied with being fired without explaining his side of the story. He called a press conference of his own and told the media his own version of events. Robertson explained that he had arrived in Savannah without a mechanic being appointed and had been instructed to choose one from the garage. He stated, "I did not care to take a mechanic I knew nothing about." The accident, he said, was the fault of the inexperienced mechanic and not due to his driving.

The drivers who were entered in the two Apperson cars were now William McCulla, who replaced George Robertson, and Herbert Lytle. McCulla was renowned for racing, testing and automobile engineering. He had driven the year before in the Morris Park 24-hour race in a Darracq. Herbert Lytle, the first American to finish a race in an American car in Europe at the Gordon Bennett Cup race, was wildly popular. From 1904, Lytle had been wowing the crowds in a big Pope-Toledo, forming something of a dynamic duo for America when he teamed up with Billy Knipper. He was a true American racing hero. Lytle was a fantastic driver and Edgar Apperson was very excited to have him. However, Apperson likely misjudged what the outcome would be for a driver who was put in the car without the benefit of a few weeks' practice with the vehicle and on the new course, which had a surface few of the drivers had experienced. Apperson likely came to regret his decision to release Robertson, as McCulla's luck would not prove to be any better.

As titillating as the Edgar Apperson and George Robertson row was during the month of March practice days, nothing compared to the over-the-top tales of John H. Tyson, nicknamed "the Hoo Doo Driver," and his equally infamous Isotta-Fraschini, which was known as the "Flying Death." The Isotta had a colorful mishap with the Apperson car during the Savannah practice of March 11, 1908. During one practice run over the 18-mile course, the Isotta experienced brake trouble. Rather than continue on the lap when the trouble began, the team sent for a tow from one of the large six-cylinder Apperson cars. Once they were attached with a chain, the Apperson began towing the Isotta back to the pits. As the Apperson went into a turn, it slowed down. The driver of the Isotta, which had faulty brakes, was unable to slow down with the Apperson. The car was whipped around the corner and launched into a telegraph pole. The left front wheel was broken and the axle bent. Another Isotta, which was intended to race at Briarcliffe in early April, was sent for to replace the damaged car.

John Hamilton Tyson, owner of the Isotta-Fraschini, was a millionaire with a very colorful background. In the weeks before traveling to Savannah for the March races, he had been speeding in the race car at 86th Street and North River in New York when he struck the steward of the Columbia Yachting Club, Olaf Gunderson. The steward later succumbed to his injuries. It was not immediately known who was responsible for the hit-and-run accident, and some weeks passed while Tyson was in Savannah attending the races before the story began to leak out. Although his chauffeur was with him, newspapers later reported that it was Tyson himself who was driving with two companions. He had confided details of the occurrence to a lady friend, an actress named Virginia Laurence. He told Laurence how bad he felt about the accident and that he wanted to send $500 to the widow as an apology. For her part, Laurence promised to keep the admission to herself.

However, Laurence changed her mind about keeping quiet. Her recollection of the admission of guilt came shortly after May 23, 1908, when Tyson married another woman, Grace Ethel Starr, and took her on a whirlwind romance in his race car. It seems that soon after news of the happy couple's marriage came out, the scorned Miss Lawrence felt compelled to go to the police and tell them what she knew about the accident, claiming she felt guilty knowing the truth all along. When word reached the newspapers, Tyson and his bride disappeared together for a short while before resurfacing in the Northeast. He was indicted for manslaughter in the second degree and pleaded not guilty.

Tyson had garnered a very wicked reputation at his home in Riverside, Connecticut. He was spotted regularly speeding and had very close calls with other residents, who complained to police that he had come close to killing them. Two prominent residents of Riverside had personally threatened Tyson's life if he harmed any member of their family while driving. Indeed, a group of residents from the town set up a "Vigilance League" to try to run him and his Isotta—which they nicknamed "Flying Death"—out of town.

In addition to killing the yacht club steward, Tyson had raced a man named McCormick while McCormick's wife was in the car with her husband. The couple was killed in the crash that resulted. In Stamford, Connecticut, Tyson had been banned from entering the county with his car. His first wife left him in December 1908, after less than six months of marriage, citing his reckless driving as one of the reasons for the divorce. She was awarded a settlement of $10,000 (roughly $250,000 in today's dollars) and $300 per month alimony. That same year, Tyson's chauffeur sued him for forcing him to drive too fast and causing damage to his nervous system. The chauffeur won a settlement of $50,000 (comparable to $1.3 million today).

Tyson remained a regular on the racing scene, including being a notable presence in Savannah. Even after narrowly escaping the manslaughter charges, which were eventually dropped, he did not slow down. In a hill climb in Easton, Connecticut, he went off into the crowd, injuring several spectators and killing one. He married a third wife, Miss Rose Budd Exiner, in 1916 shortly after the death of his second wife. Tyson was a formidable presence and never could be run out of Connecticut. He and his Isotta were welcomed with open arms to the March 1908 races at Savannah, at what turned out to be the height of Tyson's infamy.[19]

The races were steeped in colorful personalities and heroic moments. Unfortunately, the first races of March 1908 in Savannah had suffered several misfortunes building their entrants list. Several of the big-name cars were damaged during shipping or driving to Savannah. In early March, a number of cars were expected to enter the races by the March 15 deadline. They included a Studebaker and a Pullman that were coming from Philadelphia, a Renault, a Fiat, a Simplex, a Mora and a Gearless. Benz did enter a car, but it was damaged during shipping from Ormond Beach, Florida, to Savannah. The Renault, Fiat and Simplex simply did not materialize. But, as they say in Hollywood, the show must go on—and it did.

The Philadelphia to Savannah Endurance Race

The Studebaker and Pullman had a 1,100-mile race of their own from Philadelphia to Savannah, set up by the Quaker City Motor Club in Philadelphia. Frank and Robert Yerger drove a 30-horsepower Studebaker accompanied by an observer named William J. Boyd. The Studebaker left the Hotel Walton in Philadelphia at 9 p.m. on March 4. It took the team 14 days and 8 hours to reach Savannah. They arrived at the DeSoto Hotel at 4:30 p.m. However, everyone was at the races and the drivers had to get a guest of the hotel to sign a statement to certify their arrival time.[20]

The Pullman was piloted by Bob Morton and P.T. Gillette, with A. Daley riding with them as an observer. The car made the trip in 15 days, 5 hours and 5 minutes. The cars did well from Philadelphia to Washington, but they began to encounter serious issues with the dirt roads in Virginia. The Pullman struggled through thick clayey mud for 67 hours in Virginia for a distance of approximately 77 miles. It guzzled 70 gallons of gasoline during this arduous stretch. Both vehicles ended up being pulled out of the mud by mules and horses. However, both cars finally made it to Savannah. The Studebaker was greeted by President Battey of the Savannah Automobile Club and taken to the track to receive resounding applause and a standing ovation for making the grueling trek. Mayor George Tiedeman welcomed the Pullman team in front of the grandstand, where they were met with equal applause and excitement.[21]

The stage was now set for the Savannah Races of March 1908. More than 30,000 spectators would attend the races held in the days after the St. Patrick's Day Parade, along with several local support events, including concerts, picnics, and sporting events. The city had the honor of being the first place in America where soldiers were employed to guard a race course, thanks to Governor Hoke Smith. The groups of militia included more than 300 men from the Irish Jasper Greens, Republican Blues, German Volunteers, and Savannah Volunteer Guards split into four companies, the Hussars, the Chathams and the Naval Reserves. Over 150 soldiers guarded the course each day from 10 different commands.[22]

Early on March 18, the soldiers met at their headquarters, with most checking in at the Savannah Volunteer Guard Armory on Bull Street. They gathered a day's rations, then went out to their designated location on the course. The city leaders and Savannah Automobile Club all knew that the race's success would hinge on a vigilant militia. These soldiers went out to their posts prepared to do whatever was necessary to keep control of the crowds and, at times, to keep the drivers in line. Spectators venturing too close could expect a warning followed by a jab with a bayonet. Track safety was taken extremely seriously and people seemed to understand the necessity, having heard from afar of the trouble that occurred on Long Island. Spectators were not allowed within 100 feet of the road in most places.[23] Savannah needed a flawless record from the start if people were to accept the city as the next mecca of auto racing.

An ample medical staff was also arranged to be on hand. The chief of the medical corps was Dr. T.P. Waring. He oversaw 12 doctors who were stationed around the 17 mile course, each with medical supplies and an automobile to get to a specific location quickly if needed. The doctors on the medical team were Jabez Jones, J.K. Train, E.R. Corson, J.G. Crowter, Ralston Lattimore, G.R. White, William Dancy, A.B. Cleborne, Marion Thomas, Lawrence Lee, R.V. Harris and G.H. Johnson. Many of these names are still familiar in Savannah today, as several of these men went on to do great work for the city and had streets or other notable structures named for them.[24]

The official starter for the race was none other than Fred Wagner. Wagner was the go-to guy for race starting in America. He was on very friendly terms with some of the greatest men of early racing, such as Willie K. Vanderbilt and Henry Ford. "Wag," as he was known, was friends with celebrities such as silent film star Lew Cody. It is almost impossible to recount one of the stories of the earliest races in America without paying homage to Wagner, who, along with John M. Mitchell, authored *Saga of the Roaring Road: A Story of Early Auto Racing in America*. He was the most famous starter in the early days, part of the family of the AAA's Vanderbilt Cup and even earlier of the ACA, since the 1902 New York to Philadelphia race. Wagner worked in this role for nearly 40 years. He knew Charles Duryea when he first started building a horseless carriage and Barney Oldfield when he was burning up racetracks all over America. Wagner was the one who "started" them all: the most famous races of the golden era such as the Vanderbilt Cup races, the Grand Prize of America, the Glidden Tours, and later races as famous as the Indianapolis 500.[25]

Walter Christie was another of the prominent racing figures who attended the March races in Savannah. His presence lent a great deal of credibility to the events, as he was a famous record holder in the early 1900s. Christie had been badly hurt only a few months earlier in a race, so at the time he was not racing very much himself. He traveled to Savannah from Ormond Beach, Florida, for the races and liked the course very much. "The course for stock cars is ideal," stated Christie to reporters on the evening of March 17, 1908. Spectators were not just watching the events from a distance, but were very involved in many aspects of the events. Wagering was very common, and the second event, the Southern High-Powered Cup, seemed to garner the most betting of the weekend.[26]

People traveling from all over the country were familiar with many of the drivers in the field. Mrs. A.H. Shapiro of New York came down to Savannah for the races with her husband and got a pre-race hot-lap ride in the Apperson Jackrabbit with Herbert Lytle. She knew his racing career very well, stating to the Savannah newspaper, "Lytle is a great driver. He is careful, takes care of his car, but 'gets there' just as soon as anyone else. I would be perfectly satisfied in a racing car with him at the wheel. I love to ride fast. I am used to it. We went at least 70 miles an hour on the straightaways of the course."

The people of Savannah considered the races to be a very "American" event and a time to show off their patriotism to the nation. They prepared for the races as if it were the Fourth of July, decking out businesses, homes, farms and sheds all over the city and around the course. Newspapers reported on this, seeing an unusual vigor for auto racing in the southern city. Reports in the *Savannah Morning News* even claimed, "The displays of red, white and blue eclipses anything the Fourth of July has ever done.... Broughton Street today will be tri-colored between the two Broad Streets."[27]

The expenses for each car were believed to include approximately $1,000 to $2,000 for tires throughout practice and between $5,000 and $6,000 for shipping the cars to Savannah, parts and repairs, a private telephone line at the grandstand, staff to score the events and let the drivers know where they were as they raced, and securing a headquarters for the team. Costs could go much higher for drivers who got into accidents. However, the expense was believed to be worthwhile to the manufacturers who wanted to sell the cars

Fred Wagner, the famous race starter for the Vanderbilt Cup races, the American Grand Prize races, and the early Indianapolis 500 races.

to the public. The thoughts of Mayor Tiedeman and local business owners on the benefits to Savannah was clearly echoed in the local newspaper:

> It is undoubtedly a fact that the holding of the first road race for strictly stock cars ever will bring into the city, through the thousands of people out of town, who will attend these races, a great deal of money that will be spent in the local hotels and business houses.... It is also an indisputable fact that the holding of these races has already resulted in giving to Savannah throughout the entire country a far greater amount of publicity than the city has ever before received, in recent years, at least, from any other source.[28]

Race Reports

THE SOUTHERN RUNABOUT CUP RACE

The first race held was raced for 10 laps. It was 10 miles of the original 17.1-mile course. A mile of the start and final stretch from Thunderbolt was visible from the grandstands on Estill Avenue (now Victory Drive). Originally, the course had been measured to 18 miles, but the correct length was obtained shortly before the races. Thirty telephone stations were built along the track and over 60 flagmen employed to alert drivers of the track conditions with red and yellow flags. A green flag was used to tell drivers they had one more lap to the end and a checkered flag was waved to signal that they had completed the race. The first race was limited to stock chassis cars with racing chassis in the runabout class with a maximum engine of 375-cubic-inch piston displacement. The three contenders were very different from one another in terms of cylinder size, and the Pennsylvania was set apart from the other two cars by its rear-axle transmission.

In addition to the grandstands and the high-level course surfacing, there were refueling stops along the course as well as tire walls to control accidents.[29] The runabouts raced first in the 176-mile Southern Runabout Cup race at 10 a.m. on Wednesday, March 18, 1908. The greatest criticism was the small field. Despite correspondence from manufacturers that indicated there would be six entries, only four cars made it to Savannah for this race. Two of the cars were Thomas-Detroits, including the Bluebird driven by Lorimer. Unfortunately, the second Thomas car, which was supposed to be driven by Oliver Light, had blown a cylinder head the day before the event and was unable to race.

No matter—the day was balmy and 16,000 people showed up for the first event. Fred Wagner sent off the first car, the Pennsylvania, driven by Len Zengle. The car roared to life and headed toward the first left turn onto White Bluff (now Bull Street at that intersection). Zengle made it to the long straightaway and picked up incredible speed, gradually disappearing from the sight of the grandstands, which could see the car approach and head south for approximately one mile. After six minutes, Wag sent off the red Apperson Jackrabbit driven by Herbert Lytle. Lytle had spoken of his strategy to win the race, stating to the *Savannah Evening Press* that he would drive at a steady pace, aiming for completing each lap within 20 minutes. A crowd favorite, the car made its own turn onto White Bluff in hot pursuit of the Pennsylvania. Finally, J.B. Lorimer was sent off in the Thomas-Detroit Bluebird and the race was on.[30]

At the end of the Apperson's sixth lap, the crowd saw the Thomas approaching in front of the grandstands. The cars were only 50 feet apart, causing a cheer to go up from the crowd assembled. The people had a great appreciation for seeing the cars brush past each other coming into the turn onto White Bluff. Word came back to the crowd in the grandstands that the Apperson had passed the Thomas in front of the county farm. However, the Thomas regained the lead on LaRoche.[31] The two continued the battle throughout the first half of the race.

After 18 minutes and 54 seconds, Len Zengle appeared back at the start–finish line, having made the fastest lap of the race. The crowd cheered his mile-a-minute time. Unfortunately, the great Zengle would enjoy the crowd's approval for only that one pass by the grandstand. During the second lap, when Zengle turned onto Montgomery Crossroads, he realized he had stripped a gear and destroyed the Pennsylvania's transmission as a result of constant gear changes during such a fast-paced event. He was forced to retire after making it to the second lap of the race.

That left only two competitors on the course: Herbert Lytle and his mechanic George Davis, driving the Apperson Jackrabbit, and J.B. Lorimer, in the Thomas-Detroit Bluebird. Lytle had to stop twice during the race, losing ten minutes. First, he stopped to check his spark plugs and found that one was missing, so he changed all four. His other stop was to refuel.[32] Despite the Apperson's stops, Lytle held a sizable lead. Lorimer struggled with carburetor issues, trouble with his gas tank and a lost tire on the Thomas-Detroit. The driver was forced to make repairs on the side of the road that took more than four minutes, which effectively took him out of the running. This allowed Lytle to pull out a significant lead in the Jackrabbit and he won the $1,000 silver cup. Lytle's time was 3 hours, 35 minutes and 41 seconds, and his average speed was 49 mph.[33]

THE SOUTHERN HIGH-POWERED CUP

The second race at 2 o'clock in the afternoon of March 18, 1908, was the Southern High-Powered Cup race. It was a 10-lap race of the full 17.1-mile track. This event allowed for larger standard stock chassis cars with a maximum engine size of up to 575 cubic inches piston displacement and six cylinders. The idea was to allow people to compare the features and performance of a four-cylinder versus a six-cylinder car. As with the Runabout Cup, three cars were expected to enter: a Stearns Six, owned by Ross Gueard of Savannah; a Thomas-Detroit Flyer; and a Matheson. The latter two vehicles were owned by Atlantans. However, the Matheson was unable to make it to Savannah for the event. There had initially been an entrance application from Harry Levy, owner of a 120-horsepower Hotchkiss, but the car never materialized.

The six-cylinder Thomas Flyer had a similar style of opposing cylinders, like the four-cylinder Bluebird. The larger Flyer had 5.5 ×5.5 inch cylinders, however, and it had the three-disc clutch common on the Thomas cars. An extra gasoline tank was fastened to the back of the car and filled with water, while the gas tank supplying the engine was under the driver's seat, as was typical in the cars. Likewise, the six-cylinder Stearns had the same castings as its four-cylinder model.[34]

Fred Wagner sent off George Salzman in the Flyer first. Salzman had been the assistant superintendent of the E.R. Thomas Company since 1902 and had raced and tested the car more than any other driver. His experience in the Buffalo Derby and Glidden Tours gave him a great deal of experience in long-distance events and the Southern High-Powered Cup would be a short hop, skip and a jump for him. He headed around to the left into the first turn and onto the White Bluff straightaway. The grandstand erupted into cheers. Just two minutes later, Wag sent Frank Leland in the Stearns onto the course. The Stearns accelerated very quickly, impressing the spectators yet again as it rounded turn one and headed south.

The crowd didn't seem to know which car would win: the big, impressive Flyer, which would be preparing to enter the New York to Paris race in a few months, or the Stearns, which had literally leapt to life and taken off at an astonishing speed.

The drama increased on the first lap when Leland gained 40 seconds on Salzman. The cars roared past the grandstand only seconds apart and the crowd was jubilant. They waited in anticipation for the cars to return to see if the Stearns was able to gain even more time on the Flyer. The announcer told the crowd that Salzman made the lap passing through the southside of the course, then Isle of Hope, and was on his way into the hairpin turn at Thunderbolt. When he came into the homestretch and flew past the grandstand, another cheer went up. However, all eyes were looking for his competitor, who had so quickly gained on Salzman in the first lap. The Stearns was a locally owned car, so the crowd was particularly excited to see it race, and hopefully win, against the Flyer. As the minutes ticked past and Leland did not appear, people began to shout, "Where is the Stearns? Where is Leland?"[35]

Unfortunately, the bearings on the Stearns were too tight, which caused a connecting rod to break; it punctured the crankcase and damaged the engine severely. Leland would be forced to retire very early, leaving only Salzman on the race course. Salzman pushed on and gave the crowd the best show he could manage as the sole competitor. Averaging 59.2 mph in the Flyer, he completed the full race in 3 hours, 2 minutes and 25 seconds, winning the silver trophy.

Although it may have seemed anticlimactic for the spectators to not see more cars racing and to have the local car knocked out so early, there was great admiration among those assembled for the Thomas Flyer. Its performance seemed to brighten their mood considerably. Salzman had not only shown his own excellent driving skills, but also had the fastest average speed of all three races.[36] Salzman had broken a world record in the process, since it was the first ever race of six-cylinder cars. Mr. and Mrs. John F. Kiser of Atlanta, owners of the winning car, were thrilled with his performance. For his part, Salzman gave credit where it was due. He commented that he was assisted in the race by the fact that the tires had never overheated and the car had run perfectly. Salzman's humble attitude won him a lot of new friends in the South and his affable demeanor brought both the driver and the Thomas Flyer considerable attention and future job offers in the South.

THE SAVANNAH CHALLENGE

The spectators at the Savannah races did not just confine themselves to the grandstands, although the view afforded three miles of visibility over the track and countryside surrounding it. Many locals climbed trees to gain a similar view or sat on their rooftops to watch the events, while others dotted the countryside alongside the track. The track was considered one of the most best in the world and boasted of five straightaways shaded by oaks and Spanish moss, an S-turn, a hairpin, and professional banking. The roads had also been oiled shortly before the events, which was not normally possible. However, with the cutting-edge surfacing technique of Macadam, it was quite a boon, and added a level of challenge to the races.

Eight cars participated in the 342-mile Savannah Challenge race: two Appersons, driven by William McCulla and Herbert Lytle; two Isotta Fraschinis, driven by Louis Strang and Al Poole; one Acme Sextuplet, driven by Malcolm Neustetter; an American Underslung, driven by Fred I. Tone; a Lozier, driven by Harry Michener; and a locally owned Stearns, driven by Frank Leland. With a field of well-known drivers and cars that garnered a great

The American Underslung driven by Fred Tone at the starting line of the race in March 1908.

deal of interest and excitement, the event was set to be a success from the start. The Isotta-Fraschinis were highly touted as top contenders from the beginning, with one driver, Louis Strang, prepared to take the aggressive approach, and the other, Al Poole, to play it safe. The white Lozier driven by Michener was also heavily staked to keep up with the big Isottas.[37]

Fred Wagner sent off the cars in intervals of 90 seconds. First to go was Herbert Lytle in the Apperson Jackrabbit, followed by Louis Strang in the Isotta, then Fred Tone in the American Underslung, Harry Michener in the Lozier, William McCulla in the Apperson, Al Poole in the second Isotta, Frank Leland in the Stearns Six, and finally Malcolm Neustetter in the Acme Sextuplet.

Strang led with the fastest time for the first five laps, keeping almost entirely under 18 minutes for each. However, that changed on lap 5 when Strang's time dipped and his teammate Al Poole beat him by 25 seconds, while Harry Michener in the Lozier bested him by 6 seconds. Michener was doing a fantastic job with the Lozier, keeping himself in the top three positions in the early part of the race. However, his luck began to sour on the eighth lap. Michener began having difficulties with the exhaust pipe on the car at that time; it was becoming detached from the muffler as he drove. Additionally, he had to take valuable time to refill oil and fuel on the car over the next few laps and had trouble with his tires, dropping his times by the eleventh lap to 27 minutes and 12 seconds.[38]

In the early laps of the race, Frank Leland had driven off course as he approached Isle of Hope and gone through a barbed wire fence. Meanwhile, only three laps into the race,

Fred Tone taking a curve on the Savannah course in the American Underslung.

William McCulla was pressing in on the Isotta driven by Al Poole. While attempting to pass near the Isle of Hope, however, he oversteered and flipped the Apperson Jackrabbit. He and his mechanic, William Wray, Jr., of New York, rolled down a shallow embankment into the marsh, which may have saved them from injury. Poole was not spared from difficulties in the race, either. He had problems with spark plugs and cylinder heads that required him to stop once at the eastern end of the grandstands for a repair. However, that wasn't the end of Poole's problems. His carburetor went and he had to remove it and clean the fuel hoses, giving him a single lap time of 42 minutes and 40 seconds.

The American Underslung driven by Fred Tone also encountered difficulties near Isle of Hope. The team had nicknamed the car "War Cruiser" after its fast times during practice. It had been hitting 70 to 75 mph during practice runs, yet it would not accelerate above 55 mph during the race. When the driver stopped to refuel and make some adjustments to the car, a bystander asked the driver and mechanic if they needed to work on the engine, which seemed to be making some unusual noises. It was later found that the clutch was slipping throughout the race, which was caused by the crankcase losing two bolts. This allowed oil to get into the flywheel and the clutch became saturated.

The mechanic and the driver expressed their frustration with the car, which had not been performing as hoped from the start. The pit crews did their best to keep the driver and mechanic apprised of timing with a large signal board with two-feet-high letters at Bona Bella. With a side bet going on between the owners of the American and Apperson, the

5. From Triumph to Tragedy in Savannah   77

Fred Tone in the American Underslung finished sixth in the Savannah Challenge on March 19, 1908.

pressure of seeing those numbers weighed heavy on the driver and mechanic and they were feeling the pinch.[39] Eventually the car was withdrawn due to the problems with the clutch, which could not be effectively cleaned up.

One of the most exciting battles in the race was between Lytle, Michener and Newstetter in the second half. Lytle fought hard to bring his car from fifth place to second, trying to make up time lost when a copper pipe came loose from the crankcase earlier and from a broken oil pump which caused his mechanic to have to constantly pump oil into the crankcase. The Acme driven by Malcolm Newstetter had an excellent performance and finished third. Neustetter did not have the long auto racing record that some of the other drivers had, but he showed a natural talent. He was only 21 years old when he entered the race in the Acme Sextuplet and from the start he made excellent time, keeping very close to the Isottas and the Lozier. Considering his lack of racing experience and excellent finish on a course with professionally banked corners and long, fast stretches, one can only imagine that Newstetter might have become a legendary driver, had he not passed away only a year and half later in November 1909. He drove a magnificent race, easily holding his own alongside some of the greatest drivers in early auto racing history.

The Isotta team arrived in Savannah with an excellent system in place for winning. Not only did they have the technology and driving talent, but they also had fantastic professional scoring staff who worked from their private office under the grandstands where they had a telephone to call scorers with directions for the drivers. They knew when the driver would come in for pit stops and could tell him how he was doing compared to the other teams. The Isotta and Apperson also kept bulletin boards with times listed on them for the drivers

Top: Fred Tone taking the American Underslung on a wide, sweeping curve of the race course during the Savannah Challenge. *Bottom:* Fred Tone passing over the rural Isle of Hope section of the Savannah course.

Malcolm Newstetter in the number 8 Acme stock car passing a parking area filled with spectators during the Savannah Challenge. Newstetter came in third place in the race, with an average speed of 50 mph.

to read. Strang won the event in 6 hours, 21 minutes and 30 seconds, with a lead of 23 minutes over the second-place finisher, Herbert Lytle in the Apperson in 6 hours, 44 minutes and 37 seconds. Malcolm Newstetter finished in third in 6 hours, 47 minutes and 5 seconds. All of the cars that finished had times within 35 minutes of the race winner's time.

After winning the event, Louis Strang commented, "This is the best course I have ever raced. The only thing that equals it is the kind treatment I have received on every hand since I have been in Savannah."[40]

At the finale for the events, drivers, owners, and elected officials from the city and state, including Governor Smith, joined a large gathering of guests of the Savannah Automobile Club at the Thunderbolt Casino, presided over by Frank C. Battey, president of the Savannah Automobile Club. The winners showed off their beautiful trophies, made by Tiffany and Gorham for the three events, while enjoying crab stew and biscuits. The drivers of the winning cars would receive bronze medals bearing the seal of Savannah on one side and their name and car make on the other. Talk ranged from the bid for the Vanderbilt Cup to a great highway being built that would join Atlanta and Savannah. It was an event thrown in as lavish style as the races themselves had been, and it gave all the attendees—from the AAA members to Mayor Tiedeman of Savannah—a feeling that Savannah was about to become the auto racing mecca of the United States.[41]

6

Drivers of the International Light Car and American Grand Prize Races of 1908

> "You will never know the feeling of a driver when winning a race. The helmet hides feelings that cannot be understood."
> —Ayrton Senna

What would a race be without the faces and personalities who drive the cars? Or without the drama and competition among car owners, engineers and team staff who are trying to prove their mettle and that of their cars by racing? They would be very bland events. The earliest races were no exception to that rule. To read a race report without knowing anything about any of the players lowers the level of engagement to the historical racing audience. The men and women who raced were amazing individuals, and each of them had something to teach or entertain us with. Some were more colorful and heightened the excitement at the racing events. Others were more methodical and showed the determination and pride that went into every car setup, practice and race. So much can be learned from these great individuals, whether they raced at the highest level of the Grand Prix races of Europe and America or the smaller hill climbs. They epitomize the pioneering days of racing.

LOUIS BERGDOLL

1908 • International Light Car Race

Louis Bergdoll was born in Philadelphia in 1890. Bergdoll was of German descent and was part of the family that owned Bergdoll Brewing. A young millionaire, Bergdoll owned much of the land on which "Automobile Row" in Philadelphia was located. He also started the Louis J. Bergdoll Motor Car Company, which built its first cars in 1905. The company was incorporated March 18, 1912, but would fall into bankruptcy on April 11, 1913, with Louis's brother Erwin being accused of improperly taking funds from the bankruptcy settlement. Louis was a conscientious objector who stated his case before President Theodore Roosevelt during World War I.

The year 1908 was probably Bergdoll's busiest year racing. He would never become a race car driver on a full-time basis, but he did enter the racing events he enjoyed over the years. Bergdoll was best known for his win at Ormond Beach on March 4, 1908. Despite the beach being in poor condition that year, with many soft spots to bog the drivers down, Bergdoll won the event driving a 60-horsepower Benz. Granted, he may have been outshone by off-track events. When Gilbert's Packard caught on fire, a bystander tried to help by throwing a bucket of water on it. Unfortunately, the bucket did not contain water, but rather was full of fuel. Also, a Hotchkiss driven by F.B. Shaft caught fire during the race. But Bergdoll's reputation as a racer was sealed and he was quite well known after the win.[1]

On July 4, 1908, Bergdoll raced in the 25-mile championship race at Pamlico, Baltimore, driving a 60-horsepower Thomas. Later that year, he raced at Briarcliffe and Elgin in the 731-cubic-inch Benz. In 1908, he would race at the Fairmount Park races in a six-cylinder, 60-horsepower American Locomotive.[2] In Savannah, Bergdoll drove a Chalmers-Detroit in the Light Car Race, but did not finish due to mechanical problems. He competed at the Point Breeze Race of June 18, 1910. In 1912, he would race at Elgin again, in the free-for-all race in the 750-horsepower Benz. He returned in 1913, but unfortunately ran out of gas during that race.[3]

WILD BOB BURMAN

1908 • International Light Car Race and American Grand Prize
1910 • American Grand Prize
1911 • Vanderbilt Cup and American Grand Prize

Bob Burman, an iconic American racer of the Savannah races, was the famous driver of one of the Buick cars, which were wildly popular at the time. Burman, featured in the Mecca Tobacco Auto Drivers Series Number 1, was out of the Grand Prize on lap 2 in 1908, and he was out with mechanical problems in 1911. In the 1910 American Grand Prize, he placed third driving Buick number 17 with an average speed of 67.07 mph.

Bob Burman was born April 23, 1884, in Imlay City, Michigan. In 1909, Burman won the race at the Columbus one-mile circular track and went on to place third in the five-mile race at Indianapolis. He raced in the Savannah International Light Car Race in November 1908 and in the 1908 Grand Prize race in the Buick. On his return to Savannah in 1910, he placed third in the Grand Prize race. In 1911, Burman raced a Marmon in both the Vanderbilt Cup race and the American Grand Prize race in Savannah. He was very beloved in Savannah, being one of the few drivers who entered the races in all three years, and doing so in the most popular cars: the Marquette Buick and later the Marmon. Burman is also well known for breaking records in the Daytona Beach races in the Blitzen Benz in 1911. Sadly, Burman did not have a long life. He was killed at age 31 in Corona, California, in 1916 while racing in a Peugeot.

WILLIAM R. BURNS

1908 • International Light Car Race

William Burns was aiming for a career in the Vanderbilt Cup races and the Grand Prize. His first foray into higher-level racing came when he drove in the 1908 in the Jericho Sweepstakes in a Chalmers-Detroit. He placed first with an average speed of 46.2 mph.[4] This prepared him quite nicely for his upcoming race in November 1908 in the International Light Car Races in Savannah. He drove a 30-horsepower Chalmers-Detroit, the same car he had driven in the Jericho. Burns was very generous and exchanged car numbers with another driver who had drawn the unlucky 13 for his car. Burns laughed off the superstition, taking 13 for his own car. Unfortunately, that may have been a mistake. Burns was first out of the race, crashing into a tree on lap 1. He lost his four front upper teeth when his mouth came down on the steering wheel. It was disappointing for the crowd because the car had been entered by a local automobile and bicycle dealer, T.A. Bryson. Both driver and mechanic suffered mild injuries.[5]

ALESSANDRO CAGNO
1908 • American Grand Prize

Alessandro Cagno was born May 2, 1883, in Turin, Italy. He was widely known by the nickname "Sandrin." Cagno was a very cerebral child, which translated into genius by the time he was a young man. The multitalented Cagno raced cars; flew and designed airplanes, including the first bomber; set up the first flying school in Italy at Pordenone; and raced powerboats. He was first hired as an apprentice at Fiat in 1896, at the age of 13. He worked his way up quickly to become a riding mechanic and driver by the time he was 18.[6]

Cagno's first race was in 1901 at Saluzzo, where he placed third in a Fiat. By 1902, he was entering more races and hill climbs. He entered his first international race at the Circuit des Ardennes in Belgium, where he placed second in a Fiat. In 1904, Cagno won the Susa-Mont Cenis hill climb and entered the Padua race. He entered the Gordon Bennett race in

Alessandro Cagno at the wheel of the Itala (with his mechanic) in Savannah in 1908 (courtesy John and Ginger Duncan).

a 75-horsepower Fiat and brought the car to tenth place in 7 hours, 23 minutes and 35 seconds. His victories continued to pile up. In 1905, he won the Mount Ventoux hill climb driving a Gordon Bennett. He also raced at the Gordon Bennett race that year at Auvergne, France, placing third. His time was 7 hours, 21 minutes and 23 seconds over the 137-kilometer course.

In 1906, Cagno won the Targa Florio race, driving a 35/40-horsepower Itala, in 9 hours, 32 minutes and 22 seconds. The distance of the race totaled 281.25 miles and 100,000 spectators lined the roads to watch the event near Palermo, which was part of a week-long festival in the town known as La Feste Palermo. Like the Savannah races, the Targa Florio utilized soldiers—4,000, to be exact—to guard the course and control crowds.[7] Cagno won a purse of $800, a fairly small sum for risking his neck driving to the peaks of the Madonian Mountains, passing through deep gorges, remote towns and dangerous broken stone slopes and turns. The owner of the car went home with $5,000. The total purse for the race would go up to $20,000 the following year. Cagno came in fifth in 1907, in 8 hours, 21 minutes and 38.9 seconds, again driving the Itala.[8]

Cagno came to America to race in the Vanderbilt Cup on Long Island, placing seventh, with an average speed of 52.3 mph. He continued his success in the Itala on September 2, 1907, winning the Coppa della Velocita/GP Formula race at Brescia while averaging 65.3 mph.[9] In 1908, Cagno placed 11th at the French Grand Prix. He raced in the Grand Prize race in Savannah, but retired early due to a broken spring. However, Cagno was becoming more and more involved in aviation, and by 1910 he had lost interest in racing automobiles.

He did return to work for Fiat as chief test engineer for race cars in 1912, but once World War I broke out, he joined the war efforts. Cagno returned for one last fling with auto racing in 1923, when he entered the Leningrad to Tiblisi to Moscow race in a Fiat. He went out in a blaze of glory, winning the race and then promptly retiring to concentrate on aviation and powerboat racing, returning to live out his life in Turin. Alessandro Cagno lived a long life, passing away on December 23, 1971, at his birthplace in Turin, Italy.

FORREST FINLEY CAMERON

1908 • International Light Car Race

Forrest F. Cameron was born July 28, 1875, in Shubenacadie, Nova Scotia, Canada. He was partners with his brother, Everett Cameron, in the Cameron Car Co. The brothers began building bicycles in their early teens and moved up from there into building a steam car in 1899. Forrest became a mechanical engineer and built gasoline automobiles, trucks, tractors, engines for airplanes and boats. Cameron married a young woman named Ethel Hall and opened his Cameron Car company in Rhode Island, then moved to Massachusetts and finally Norwalk, Connecticut. The company stopped producing vehicles from 1915 to 1918.

F.T. Cameron entered races, automobile exhibitions, demonstration events and hill climbs. He raced the Cameron Car in Savannah in the International Light Car Race in November 1908. He had the second fastest time during practice at 10 minutes and 23 seconds and his next best practice time was 10 minutes and 34 seconds.[10] Despite the potential to be a contender for the race, Cameron bent the crank shaft on the vehicle, breaking the clutch on lap 3. This mishap put him out of the race.

In 1909, Cameron entered the Cameron Car in the Fort Lee–Edgewater hill climb. Unfortunately, the event suffered from poor crowd control and spectators kept swarming the track when the "car coming" signal was announced. Cameron's hill climb did occur before the events were shut down. He raced up the 20 percent grade with an S-turn for a distance of 0.7 mile. He was the fastest in Class 2.[11]

HERBERT PATRICK CONNORS
1908 • International Light Car Race

Herbert P. Connors was a backup riding mechanic who raced for the S.P.O. (Société Française de Petite Outillage) team during the 196-mile light car race of November 25, 1908, in Savannah, Georgia. The S.P.O. had been manufacturing cars since 1898 and made a taxicab and a town car by 1908. It had a branch on Broadway in New York City and introduced the 24-horsepower Raceabout sports car at auto events such as the light car races in Savannah. After an accident in the car killed the original riding mechanic, Marius De Rosa, the car was taken to the Savannah garage owned by T.A. Bryson, who owned a local bicycle and automobile shop at Bull and York Street. Connors and Bryson's mechanics spent three days rebuilding the car and had it ready by race day.[12] Connors filled in for the injured Juhasz. Juhasz was injured enough to not be able to race, and his riding mechanic, Marius de Rosa was killed when the car flipped over and crushed him.

THOMAS COSTELLO
1908 • International Light Car Race

Thomas Costello entered the International Light Car Race in Savannah, Georgia, on November 25, 1908. He drove the number 12 Maxwell, which had two cylinders and a 4.25-inch bore and weighed 1,000 lbs. In 1909, Costello raced the Maxwell with number 45 on it for the Merrimack Trophy, placing third in Class 4 of the race with an average speed of 46.5 mph.[13] He raced in Savannah again in 1910, placing third in the Tiedeman Trophy Race in the Maxwell car number 48.

Costello also raced in Massapequa that year in the Maxwell. There were six cars in the race, but unfortunately Costello was forced to retire on lap 1 when his engine failed. He entered the Long Island Stock Car Derby, placing second in the Maxwell.

RALPH DE PALMA
1908, 1910 • American Grand Prize
1911 • Vanderbilt Cup and American Grand Prize

Ralph De Palma was born in Italy in 1883. When he was ten, his family immigrated to America. His mother died shortly after the family's arrival. Ralph would begin working and building his racing career soon after. He is reported to have studied mechanical engineering at Brooklyn Polytechnic and Stevens Technical Institute in Hoboken, New Jersey, which gave him a good understanding of early engines.[14] Around 1898, he met Fred Baker, who was the distributor for Pierce Bicycles in Brooklyn, New York. Baker was involved in early bicycle racing and introduced De Palma to the sport. In his early days in bicycle racing, De Palma won races and entered matches alongside some of the world's champions, such as Marshall Taylor, the controversial black world champion who had once been turned away from Wheelmen's Park in Savannah.[15] Like his nemesis, Barney Oldfield, De Palma took the first steps of his racing career in bicycle and motor-paced racing before making the leap to auto racing after the turn of the century.

As a youth, De Palma worked in the family barbershop for a while, then served as a grocery delivery boy around 1900 to purchase a bicycle. He began racing professionally in 1902. While he worked as a chauffeur for the Vanderbilt family, he drove a Simplex, an Isotta-Fraschini and a Fiat.

One of America's earliest heroes in racing, De Palma thrilled spectators from all over the world whether he was racing bicycles, motorcycles or automobiles. He once said, "The most dangerous drive I ever took, in my opinion, was on a one-sixth-mile board bicycle saucer at Passaic, New Jersey, with a 60-horsepower racer."[16] Before moving on to racing cars, he served as a riding mechanic.

De Palma was a relative newcomer to the international motorsports world in 1908 when he came to race in Savannah. He traditionally wore all white to his auto races. He raced first for Fiat, including in the 1908 race in Savannah, where his teammates included the world-famous drivers Louis Wagner and Felice Nazzaro. They were excellent mentors to the younger driver and the three got along famously, hunkered down in their camp at Doyle's horse race track in Thunderbolt, alongside the beautiful Wilmington River. It was an excellent year for Fiat in America—Louis Wagner took home the gold cup from the first American Grand Prix race. De Palma's riding mechanic for the race was Pietro Bordino, who would become riding mechanic for Felice Nazzaro and eventually a celebrated racing champion in his own right. De Palma was running in ninth place when the race was called. In 1910, he was still racing for the Fiat team with Wagner and Nazzaro and returned to Savannah to race for Fiat in the Grand Prize again, unfortunately retiring with a cracked cylinder.[17] However, 1910 was a breakout year for De Palma, as he won the U.S. Dirt Track Championship.

By 1911, when both the American Grand Prize and Vanderbilt Cup races came together for the first time in Savannah, De Palma was beginning to make a great name for himself. He drove a Mercedes that year in Savannah's Vanderbilt Cup race and placed second to Ralph Mulford. He repeated his fantastic performance with the car in the Grand Prize race, placing third behind David Bruce-Brown and Eddie Hearne. If not for a lengthy tire change around lap 18 when he dropped back to fourth, De Palma may have won the Grand Prize race.[18]

De Palma drove a Simplex at Indianapolis in 1911, placing sixth. However, his success with the Mercedes team seemed to have ended after his 1911 races in Savannah. In 1912, his car quit with only two laps remaining in the Indianapolis race. In 1914, the car would not start for the race after a collision during qualifying. Finally, in 1915, De Palma had the Grand Prix Mercedes dialed in and he went on to win the Indianapolis 500. He raced in 1917 and 1918, and drove a Packard in events such as the 10-mile Sheepshead Bay race, where he set new international records for 10, 30 and 50 miles, averaging 111 mph.[19]

Traditionally, De Palma's racing gear was all white. He was considered to be generous, very sportsman-like and very well liked. The only exception was his ten-year-long feud with Barney Oldfield. One of the highlights of that feud came in 1914, when De Palma noticed Oldfield's tires were looking worn about 30 miles from the end of a race. De Palma gave the signal to his pit that he was coming in for tires and Oldfield followed suit. However, De Palma did not stop, but rather kept going, and won the race. Oldfield was outraged when he could not catch up despite racing ferociously through the last laps.[20]

For all of the shrewdness in De Palma, he was also a very considerate and kind man, and a humble racer who respected the men he raced with. Fred Wagner, the famous starter for the Grand Prize and Vanderbilt Cup races and writer for the *New York Times*, spoke at length of De Palma in his book *Saga of the Roaring Road*. Wagner said, "He [De Palma] had traits that were lovable, a heart as big and fine as a mother's.... I respected him not only for his sportsmanship and tenacity, but for his manliness."[21]

In addition to his Indianapolis races, De Palma raced at Brighton, Elgin, Beverly Hills and the French Grand Prix in 1921, where he placed second. He raced for 27 years, beginning with the early Savannah races, completing a long and storied career at Indianapolis and ultimately moving up to the European Grand Prix circuit. He won 2,000 races in that time and was a hero to both Americans and Italians. De Palma passed away in 1956, having lost much of his wealth during the Great Depression. Ralph De Palma was inducted into the Motorsports Hall of Fame in 1991.[22]

Arthur Duray

1908 • American Grand Prize

Arthur Duray was born February 9, 1882. Duray began his racing career before the turn of the century. He was one of the drivers who began as a bicycle racer in approximately 1893. For five years he participated in the sport and then, as automobile racing took shape, he became involved in motorsports. By 1898, Duray was driving the Torpille in the Spa Criterium. He was still driving for Gobron in 1901 and entered several races, including the Paris-Vienne and the Château-Thierry hill climb, with a second place finish in the voiturette class. In 1902, he continued in the Torpille, driving in the Paris to Madrid and Ardennes races. The year 1903 was Duray's greatest year with the team. He broke two land speed records on July 17, 1903, for Gobron at Ostend, Belgium, with an incredible top speed of 134.46 mph, and on November 5 at Dourdan, France, with a top speed of 84.73 mph.[23]

His excellent driving skills won him the notice of Darracq. In 1903 the company hired Duray to drive for it in the Belgium-Ardennes circuit, where he established a world record for the 100-kilometer race. He placed second at Mt. Ventaux and fourth at Brescia in the car. The year 1904 would bring more land speed record-breaking performances. On March 31, Duray topped out at 88.76 mph in Nice, France, driving the Torpille again.

Described by journalists of the time as fun-loving and joyous, Duray's personality easily won over manufacturers who wanted to hire a reliable and even-tempered driver. In 1905, he drove a 130-horsepower De Dietrich to sixth place in the Gordon Bennett Cup race at Auvergne, despite experiencing radiator problems during the race. He also raced

Pictured left to right, drivers Louis Wagner, Ferenc Szisz and Arthur Duray, from an original cover of *La Vie au Grand Air* titled "The Three Champions of 1906."

at Ardennes, placing eighth, and had a big podium finish in second place at Coppa Florio. Duray participated in the La Consuma hill climb that year in the Darracq, placing third in the event. It was an eventful year for the driver as he was offered a new seat, this time by De Dietrich, and raced in four events with the car. In the 1905 Vanderbilt Cup, Duray was expected to be a top contender in the 17-liter, 1,038-cubic-inch De Dietrich, but he had mechanical problems and was out towards the end of the race.

The year 1906 was a busy one both at home and abroad for Duray. He won at the Circuit des Ardennes and went on to enter the French Grand Prix in the Lorraine-Dietrich, placing eighth. Finally, he returned to America and the city of his birth, New York, to race in the Vanderbilt Cup. The Lorraine-Dietrich performed at its peak and Duray had a fantastic race, landing a third-place podium finish in front of his hometown fans. However, it was a tragedy-filled year for the race and it would be cancelled for the following year, after a brief suggestion to hold the race in New Jersey.

Duray's racing schedule was similar in 1907, with races all over the world. He went to Dieppe but was unable to finish, then achieved a great victory in the Moscow to St. Petersburg race in a 60-horsepower De Dietrich. He raced three heats at the Kaiserpreis in Germany, but could get the car no higher than fourth. The French Grand Prix would prove a disappointment for him that year, as he was unable to complete the race, despite having excellent speeds of up to 75.4 mph—the fastest lap turned at the event. A similar fate awaited him at the Coppa Velocita of Brescia, where he ended in seventh place without finishing. Targa Florio proved to be a bright spot in Duray's calendar of races: with his typical good humor, he put his nose back to the grindstone and finished fourth in the race.

Duray did not let up on his racing schedule and traveled to the farthest reaches of the motorsports world in 1908. He began back in Russia at the Moscow to St. Petersburg race, but the car did not cooperate and he was out early. The same result plagued him at Dieppe and Coppa Florio, but he returned to America and entered the new Grand Prix. After practicing and making excellent times for weeks in Savannah in November 1908, his car seemed to have had enough racing. The chain broke and Duray was unable to get out of its path. He received a severe laceration to his right forearm and finished in tenth place.

Duray did not enter any races in 1909 or 1910, perhaps as a result of his injury at Savannah. But by 1911, he was ready to climb back on his horse and go at it again. First up were the two French Grand Prix races, where he placed eighth at Lyon and fourth at LeMans. He drove an Excelsior in the Coupe des Voiturettes.

The following year would bring a similarly slower schedule for the travel-weary driver, but in a new car, an Alcyon. He began at the French Grand Prix, placing tenth in both the Le Mans and Dieppe events, then went on to the Coupe de la Sarthe, placing 11th in the same car. He raced only once in 1913: at the French Grand Prix at La Sarthe, placing fifth in a Delage. Feeling that perhaps his luck was back, Duray returned to the French Grand Prix in the Delage in 1914, intent on bringing in a better result. He placed eighth in Lyon, but was up to fourth at the Le Mans event. Duray decided to return to America with a different combination. He entered the 1914 Indianapolis 500 with a Peugeot voiturette known as the "Baby Peugeot." His Peugeot teammates expressed a lack of faith in the car's ability to compete, but Duray pushed the car to its limits and showed it could certainly keep up at the front of the pack.[24]

World War I ended Duray's racing for the next few years. He became very involved in the war efforts, although he was turned away because of his fame numerous times when he went to recruiting offices to try to join the military. He was part of the General Automobile

Reserve and drove a Delaunay-Belleville car at the front lines from Paris. However, he was captured by the German army and imprisoned briefly.[25] He would not return to racing professionally until 1924. He did work privately to break land speed records in 1914 in a Fiat, as described in one of the company's earliest house journals. Duray gives an accounting of the events in great detail in this journal.

> We have received from the well-known French driver Arthur Duray this description and his impressions of the speed tests he did with one of our 300 HP cars: Prince Boris Soukhanoff bought a Fiat 300 HP car. He came to France to look for a professional driver and I had the pleasure to be chosen. The car was shipped to Brooklands. After just a few laps I realized it was pointless to insist on this track. I had no wish to kill myself. I telephoned Prince Soukhanoff to tell him I was ready to show him the perils of the English circuit. I drove him at a speed of about 200 km/h, but after two laps he signaled me to stop; at one time the centrifugal force almost made me go over the banking where Percy Lambert was killed. I grazed the edge by just 10 centimeters!
>
> At last I found the Ostend road, though it had the shortcoming of not being long enough to allow a good run. I made 14 test runs at over 200 km/h; on some of the runs I reached a speed of 225 km/h on the timing apparatus. The only good tape we could get shows a speed of 211,661 km/h, attained on the 8th December. During the six weeks spent in Ostend I only had two favourable days: there is not just the car to take care of, there is also the organization, laying the wires along the road, getting the time keepers, etc...., all things which require quite a long time to set up. You also have to be aware of people trying to stop the attempts. The Director of the Ostend Tramways—an earnest "autophobe"—called the police whenever he knew we were out for an attempt.
>
> My feelings? To engage first, second or third gear is relatively easy, but when it comes to engage fourth whilst traveling at 190 km/h, that is a different story. One has to hold the steering wheel firmly, push the gear lever forward and pay attention so as not to jump on the sidewalk, because the moment the air enters the carburetor the bounce causes you to feel the seat hurting your back. In the time it takes to say this, you are through the two-kilometer runway. You see the time-keepers. The moment has come to break the record and the timing starts. When speeds like these are reached, the smallest bump on the road makes the four wheels airborne at once, which the spectators see perfectly. As for me, I feel it and it reminds me of the time when I was an aviator.[26]

Duray returned to racing again once the war was over. This time he was in an entirely different type of car and he raced magnificently in the 1924 races, the Coupe de l'Autodrome and Match des Champions, placing second and third, respectively in a 9.4-liter D'Aoust Hispano-Suiza. However, those would be the last of his higher finishes. Duray did race at Le Mans from 1926 through 1928 in an Aries, but his best finish was 21st. He continued to race sporadically into the 1930s, with a fourth-place finish at the Belgian Grand Prix in 1930 driving an Aries. From there he went on to race two more of the 24-hour races he loved, including Spa in 1931 and 1933, where he was first in his class in a BNC and Amilcar, respectively.

The final professional race of Arthur Duray's career was in the 1934 24 hours of Le Mans in Amilcar. He went into retirement immediately thereafter and passed away February 11, 1954, only two days after his 74th birthday.

CHARLES EWING EASTER
1908 • International Light Car Race

Ewing Easter was born March 1, 1882, in Baltimore, Maryland. He had a short racing career, with the only recorded events being in 1906 and 1908. In 1906, he raced in the Open

Air Show of the New York Automobile Trade Association at the Empire Track near Yonkers. He won the first one-mile match he entered driving a 12-horsepower Franklin, but lost the second one-mile match to a 30-horsepower Marmon.[27]

In the racing world, this driver was known as "Little Ewing Easter, the New York Midget."[28] Easter came to Savannah to race in the International Light Car Race on November 25, 1908. He drove an 18-horsepower Buick in the race and was in second place in the first lap. His driving was particularly enjoyed because he liked to give the crowd a thrill by coming up and passing the grandstands side by side with other drivers as often as possible. Unfortunately, Easter went off the road about halfway through the race and hit a tree. His mechanic, Frank Thomas, was badly injured and initially presumed dead. Fortunately, he was taken to hospital and did live.[29]

Easter did not do much more racing, although he worked as an automobile and tire salesman for years afterward. In 1942, he was the person who discovered the bodies of two men missing from a shipwreck near Long Island.[30] He moved overseas to Berlin in the early 1950s and passed away there on July 13, 1962.[31]

Fritz Erle

1908 • American Grand Prize

Fritz Erle was born in 1875 in Mannheim, Germany. As a young man, he trained to become a locksmith and was hired on by Benz in 1894 in that position. However, his mechanical and design talents quickly became apparent to the company and he began working with automobile design. By 1907, Erle was racing the Benz cars he designed. He won the Herkomer Trophy in 1907. The event was six grueling days long, with a break for one day in Vienna, at the halfway point. There were 150 entries for the event, which started in Frankfort and traveled to Munich, Linz, Vienna, Klagenfort, and Innsbruck and finally back to Munich.[32]

Fritz Erle at the wheel of the number 19 Benz (with his mechanic) in the American Grand Prize of 1908. Erle went out of the race on lap 10 when he crashed. He took several weeks to recover in the Savannah Hospital (courtesy Mercedes-Benz Classic Archives).

Erle went on to race in the 1907 Targa Florio Race in the Benz, placing 15th in a time of 8 hours, 53 minutes and 39.2 seconds. In 1908, Erle drove in the French Grand Prix at Dieppe in a 120-horsepower Benz car number 39. He finished seventh. He brought the same car to the November 1908 Savannah Grand Prize race and had a highly unusual race. After being struck in the head by a chunk of tread from a tire, Erle was momentarily stunned and his nose and jaw were broken. He tried to continue racing, but temporarily lost his grip and ran off the course, crashing. The headline in the *Savannah Morning News* for November 27, 1908, read "Unconscious Man Drives Benz Car."[33] Other sources reported that Erle was never unconscious, but simply suffered momentary shock from the heavy blow. He spent several weeks in the Savannah Hospital recovering from his injuries before returning to Europe.

On August 22, 1909, Erle debuted the Blitzen Benz with the new 21.5-liter, 200-horsepower engine. On June 9, 1910, Erle won the Regent of Brunswick Prize with 18.56 points. He would enjoy another victory at the Gaillon hill climb in the same year in the 21-liter Benz car.[34]

Although Erle was not the regular driver for all racing in the Benz cars, he did occasionally continue to enter events up until World War I. In 1913, he broke the climb record in a 200-horsepower Benz. The hill had 2 to 7.5 percent grades and was 2.32 miles in length. Erle's average speed in the climb was 68.26 mph and he accomplished the best time in 2 minutes and 2.5 seconds.[35]

HENRI FOURNIER

1908 • American Grand Prize

Henri Fournier was born in 1871 in Le Mans. He began his racing career in bicycles and motorcycles and by 1900 had graduated to automobiles. His career with the three-wheeled voiturettes included entering a 400-lb Bolée with a 3-horsepower gasoline engine in the Charles River Race in America in the fall of 1898. The machines were judged based on speed, manageability, simplicity, brake efficiency, cost of operation, appearance, durability, grade-climbing ability and price. The judges of the racing competition included MIT professor, Gaetano Lanza.[36] Fournier's first race in 1900 was racing as the riding mechanic to Fernand Charron in a Panhard entered in the Gordon Bennett Cup race from Paris to Lyon. This race proved to be very eventful, as the car was charged by a dog as it went down a hill. Unable to miss the dog, the car spun off the road and into a field. Fournier moved the dead animal off the road and restarted the engine of the car. He got back in the race and won.[37]

Fournier began driving for Mors in 1901 and entered several races. He had an amazing talent for driving and believed that no race of less than 100 miles was an adequate test of a modern automobile. On May 29, 1901, he raced a 60-horsepower Mors in the Gordon Bennett Cup race, also known as La Coupe Internationale. The course for this year went from Paris to Bordeaux, a distance of 555 kilometers. Fournier won the race in the Mors, averaging 53 mph.

A month later, from June 27 to 29, he raced the same car in the Paris to Berlin race.[38] He won this event as well, averaging 44.1 mph. Fournier was a legend in his first year of auto racing in the driver's seat.

Fournier was one of the first of the big-time European race car drivers to want to cross the pond and get involved in U.S. auto racing, competitions and record breaking at the turn of the century. After his excellent year in Europe in 1901, he decided that fall that he would go to America. He visited several cities for auto events, including Fort Erie. On October 12, the Chicago Automobile Club arranged for a race between Fournier and Alexander Winton at Washington Park.[39] On November 23, he planned to try to break the mile record previously set by William K. Vanderbilt, Jr., at Oakley, Cincinnati.

In this event, Fournier would drive before a crowd of 25,000 people on Ocean Parkway in Coney Island, New York. Three men tried to break the mile record at this venue: Fournier, Foxhall Keene and A.L. Bostwick. Fournier succeeded and established the new record of 51.45 seconds, hitting a top speed of 69.5 mph before the assembled crowd.[40] Some claimed that the road had a downward grade and the record should not stand. It was measured and found to indeed have a grade — but it was upward.

Fournier was lucky to have been alive to make the attempt for the record. On October 30, 1901, during his American visit, Fournier was traveling in an automobile convoy with Willie K. Vanderbilt, Jr., and several other men looking for a good road for trying to break the mile record. While in Westbury, Long Island, Fournier crossed a road with train tracks over it. Due to the positioning of buildings on either side of the road, it was impossible to see if a train was coming. There was a Wildcat engine traveling on the tracks at the same time and Fournier, along with others in the car, was involved in a collision. He gave a detailed accounting of the events, pointing out that he was not speeding:

> I had just reached the crossing, and the front wheels of my machine were touching the first rail, when the locomotive loomed up, and I realized that an accident was inevitable. Not having time to reverse power, I gave the handle a quick turn, which moved the front wheels to the right, and then the crash came. The locomotive struck the machine two or three inches behind the left front wheel, throwing it around so the rear of the motor was brought against the locomotive. The first thing I remember is somebody calling out and asking me if I were dead. I think I was unconscious for about a minute. The machine was demolished. It was not one of my racing machines, but was what was known as a touring automobile.[41]

According to H.J. Everall, who was a passenger in the car, "It was the coolness of Fournier that saved us from instant death." If he had not turned the wheels, everyone in the car might have been killed. Several of the occupants of the car, including Fournier, were flung 50 feet. It was a miracle that anyone survived.[42]

The year 1902 was not nearly as eventful for Fournier. It was more of a "win some, lose some" type of year for the driver. His old friend Willie K. Vanderbilt, Jr., had come to Europe to race with him in a Mors car. The pair entered the Paris to Vienna race, which was being run at the same time as the Gordon Bennett Cup race. Fournier was truly a crowd favorite both in America and in Europe. People would jump onto trains after his car was off and get off at a train stop farther ahead to see him pass by again. They watched him zip by at 80 mph. Unfortunately, Fournier's Mors gear shaft broke near Nangis in northern France. He was out of the race early. However, in November of that year, Fournier broke Willie K.'s record for the kilometer in the Mors. He set the new one-kilometer record at 20.15 seconds.

When the year 1908 dawned, Fournier entered the French Grand Prix in an Itala. He was teamed up with Alessandro Cagno. Unfortunately, his luck was not good and he finished 20th in the race. However, Fournier, the first man to exceed 60 mph in America, returned in 1908 to race in the Grand Prix at Savannah, again driving the Itala number 17. He came in eighth place in the race. Fournier's interest in racing had all but fizzled by 1908. He was quoted during the practice period before the Savannah races as saying he "believed automobile racing had seen its best days, and would soon be superseded by races in the air." Fournier had signed a contract to fly in such an event in February 1909 at the Monte Carlo Casino, where he was supposed to fly to Cape Martin and back, a distance of eight miles. The aircraft was being built by Voissin brothers in France at the time of the Savannah races. However, Fournier had never flown before and would have only about one month to learn before the event.[43]

In August 1909, Fournier was indeed entering air racing events. In Reims, an event was held between monoplanes and biplanes built by the Wright brothers, Blériot, Antoinette, Henry Farman and Voisin. Fournier did fly one of three Voisin monoplanes, but two of the planes crashed before making it to one mile. Never one to give up, Fournier came back out the next day and flew a backup airplane for six miles after being bandaged up from the initial crash.[44]

Henri Fournier never fully recovered the love he had for racing after his brother Maurice was killed at the French Grand Prix in 1911. His brothers Achille and Maurice had raced in the French Grand Prix and Targa Florio races from 1906 onward. During World War I, Fournier went to work for the French military running a munitions factory. As the conflict slowed, he went to Philadelphia to run the Searchmont Automobile Company, which was renamed the Fournier Searchmont Co. However, the company did not prove to be lucrative and he returned to France. Henri Fournier passed away in Paris on December 12, 1919.

RENÉ HANRIOT

1908 • American Grand Prize

René Hanriot was born June 11, 1867. Hanriot was famous for racing automobiles, boats and airplanes, beginning with a monoplane. He was also very good friends with Grand Prix champion Louis Wagner, and the two spent much time together flying and racing. They partnered up and started a flying school near Reims, France, in a town called Bétheny.

In his earliest auto racing years, Hanriot raced for Clément-Bayard, usually teamed up with two or three other cars, one of which would be piloted by Albert Clément—at least until his tragic death a few days before the French Grand Prix of 1907. Hanriot drove in the 1903 Paris to Madrid race and disputed the outcome of the race. He was entered by the Clément-Bayard team in the 1904 French Grand Prix at the Circuit des Ardennes. Although he was out of the race after only four laps, he set a speed record of 45 mph in the 30-horsepower car.[45]

On June 16, 1905, Hanriot entered the Eliminations Française de la Coupe International at Auvergne, France. However, he did not have very good luck in the Clément-Bayard and finished tenth, not high enough to put him through to the Gordon Bennett Cup race. In 1906, he was offered a ride with Darracq at the French Grand Prix. It was an excellent decision for both driver and team, and Hanriot fought hard to a second-place finish. He was not so fortunate with Darracq in 1907. Hanriot was entered in the car for both the French Grand Prix, which was held again at Dieppe, and the Targa Florio race, which had a significantly increased purse to tantalize the owners. At the Grand Prix, he suffered engine problems early on and had to retire from the race. At Targa Florio, he suffered a broken half-shaft, shortly after Louis Wagner suffered from the same mechanical failure in his Darracq. The owner was furious and a spat between Wagner and Darracq ensued, which led to the two friends leaving the team.

When Hanriot left Darracq, he received a tremendous offer to drive for Benz. He accepted and entered several races with the car, including the July 7, 1908, French Grand Prix in Dieppe. He was driving a 150-horsepower car and had a third-place finish with a time of 9 hours, 29 minutes and 2 seconds. The Benz team sent Hanriot to Savannah for the first American Grand Prize race in November 1908. One of the most colorful moments in motorsports history occurred at that race.

Hanriot was sent to drive a 120-horsepower Grand Prix Benz car, number 15, at the Grand Prize race. He had an excellent race and came very close to a podium finish, but unfortunately he ran out of gas within a mile of the finish line. The car was left to coast along the final stretch and made it almost to the grandstands. Approximately one to two yards from the finish line, the car ran out of speed. Hanriot and his riding mechanic tried to push on the rear tires to keep the car moving forward. They rocked back and forth trying to get it across the line, but ultimately crossed the finish line in fourth place. The race was over, and Hanriot, annoyed about running out of gas, had fuel brought up from the pits to get the car back to the Benz camp. After refueling, he decided that rather than drive all the way around the 25-mile course to return to the Benz camp, he would simply back up to get there. However, the soldiers who were guarding the course had been given orders to keep the track clear—and that included the drivers. A group of them ordered Hanriot to stop. Hanriot pretended he was going to comply and slowed, but as he approached, he accelerated past them until he reached a second group. Among them was Captain Davant, who witnessed Hanriot's refusal to stop when ordered to do so by the soldiers. He ordered him to stop and shot his tires out, hitting and puncturing the gas tank in the process.[46] Hanriot later apologized for breaking the rules and gave his racing gloves to Captain Davant as a peace offering.

On June 25, 1911, Hanriot was offered the driver's seat in a Lion Peugeot for the Coupe des Voiturettes in Boulogne, France. However, Hanriot had a difficult time with the smaller car after driving the big Benz vehicles and he experienced tire problems. The best time he could make was 51.9 km/h on the track, and he was able to make it for only 6 laps before the car quit. He returned to race in the French Grand Prix at Dieppe in 1912, driving a Lorraine-Dietrich. In a frightening turn of events, the car caught fire, though Hanriot escaped. Shortly thereafter, Hanriot turned his attention more to his aviation business. He was designing and building new models every year and could be found flying more often than driving. On November 7, 1925, Hanriot passed away.

WILLIAM E. HAUPT
1908, 1910 • American Grand Prize

Willie Haupt was born July 10, 1885, in East Cameron, Pennsylvania. He started racing around 1906 and entered hill climbs, endurance races and oval events with much success. He was the first driver to race in a supercharged race car, in an event that he won. Haupt raced at racks including Chicago, Elgin, Indianapolis, Long Island, Minneapolis, Omaha, Philadelphia, Providence, Sheepshead Bay and, of course, Savannah. Although Haupt was most famous for his record-breaking runs in the Big Chadwick 6, he also drove an American Underslung, a Benz, a Duesenberg, an Emden and a Thomas.[47]

In 1908, Haupt drove in the Wilkes-Barre hill climb on the popular, steeply sloped Giant's Despair Course, his greatest rival being Pete Robinson in a Stevens-Duryea. The course had 20 percent grades and included Devil's Elbow, a severe turn on which a car could plunge into a deep ravine if the driver did not take the turn well, and Mountain House, an area that tested a driver's abilities as much as it did the car. Haupt set a new record of 1 minute and 38.6 seconds as his car went airborne at the crest of the hill. Several moments

Willie Haupt (with his mechanic) drove a Chadwick–6 in the 1908 American Grand Prize but had problems with the bearings and was out of the race on lap 5 (courtesy Robyn Quattlebaum).

of this race are depicted by the great Peter Helck in the paintings *Giant's Despair Hill Climb* and *Giant's Despair: Haupts Winning Chadwick*; the latter is featured in the beautifully illustrated book *Great Auto Races* by Peter Helck.[48]

In July 1902, Haupt entered another hill climb in Norristown, Pennsylvania, at Skippack Hill. This course included grades of 3 to 10 percent and was located five miles north of the town. Haupt was a crowd favorite by this time and his Chadwick was equally a great celebrity that people turned out to see. The media loved him, too, and *The Automobile* reports on the event praised Haupt highly: "The Willie Haupt–Chadwick combination is the fastest thing in the hill climbing world in this country, if not the world."[49] Haupt won the event with a time of 57.6 seconds, traveling 75 mph on the uphill portions and 80 mph on the level stretches of the course.

Haupt came to Savannah with his Chadwick and entered the American Grand Prize race on November 26, 1908. He was the fifth driver sent off by Fred Wagner, behind Bob Burman in a Buick. Unfortunately, he was out of the race early on Lap 5 when his brakes failed. Nevertheless, 1908 would not be his only trip to Savannah to race. He would return in 1910 in a 736-cubic-inch Benz, with teammates David Bruce-Brown, who won the race, and Victor Hemery, who placed second. Haupt had an excellent run for the first half of the race, maintaining a place around fifth position until lap 10, when he got his speed up and got into fourth, before moving into first place for the following two laps. He was running down Montgomery Crossroad at a breakneck pace when he lost control of the car and had an off-course excursion into the ditch. His wheel was broken and his race was over.[50]

In 1909, Haupt entered the Fairmount Park Race in a Thomas owned by Louis Bergdoll. Unfortunately, his misfortune followed him and he was out of the race early on only the fourth lap with engine trouble. In 1910, he drove a Benz in the race and placed fifth in Class 4C.[51]

Haupt passed away April 16, 1966, in Elkins Park, Pennsylvania. He was born and died the same years as fellow driver, Harry Cobe.

Lucien Hautvast

1908 • American Grand Prize

Hautvast was born December 8, 1865, in Merkelbeek, Belgium, and became a legendary bicycle racer and auto racer. His father, Pierre-Joseph Hautvast, was a farmer, and his mother, Elisabeth Toussaint, was a francophone from Belgian society, giving young Lucien an excellent command of two languages. However, shortly after the birth of his younger sister Maria, the couple split. The children moved with their mother to a farm in Bombaye, where Lucien was educated at Saint-Hadelin de Vise College.

Hautvast began his life quite differently from many racers in bicycle and auto racing. He chose to become a photographer early on and had his own studio in Liège. But in 1889, at the age of 24, Hautvast embarked on a new career: bicycle racing. He began with a win at the Spa Mile on June 8, 1890. After a number of races that year, he jumped to international competition on September 7 in Cologne, where he became very ill, purportedly from food poisoning. He was forced out of the sport for nearly two years. By 1896, Hautvast was a bicycle racing sensation in Belgium and had successfully opened his own bicycle shop, which supplied the Belgian army. He did a final tour that year, selling his bicycles along the way and preparing to enter the tire industry.

His auto racing career began shortly thereafter in Brussels, where he was a member of the Automobile Club of Belgium. Although Hautvast raced primarily in Belgian-built cars, he also raced for the French manufacturer Clément-Bayard and drove a De Dion Bouton at an automobile race at Spa in 1899. The event featured touring cars racing from Spa to Bastongne and back. Although Hautvast did not complete the event, he impressed the upper echelon of the Automobile Club of Belgium enough for them to ask him to sit as a board member. He later became secretary of the club. Count De Dion was one of the most prominent originators of early automobile racing in Europe and Hautvast was invited to participate in international races with him for several years.

Hautvast raced at the Circuit de Ardennes in a 24-horsepower Pipe, becoming one of the first serious contenders for Belgian manufacturers in the 8.5-hour race. He was competing against 70-horsepower cars manufactured by Mors and Panhard. It was after these races that Lucien Hautvast truly reached the pinnacle of motor racing at the turn of the century. Hautvast was the first to race for the Gordon Bennett Cup in 1904 for Belgium. This time he drove a 13.5-liter Pipe developed for the event. The Gordon Bennett Cup had moved since its inception in 1900 from Lyon and Bordeaux in France to Innsbruck, Austria, for a year, then to Athy, Ireland, and in 1904 to the Taunas mountains of Germany. A year later, the French Grand Prix emerged from the Gordon Bennett Cup races. Hautvast wrote a letter on behalf of the Pipe factory announcing that it would be withdrawing from the competition. Later, the Automobile Club of Belgium withdrew entirely from the race.

Hautvast returned to racing and had his first major victory at the Criterium International in Belgium. In this endurance race and circuit race combined in one event, the Pipe driven by Hautvast and five others dominated. Hautvast averaged 74.5 mph and won the event, giving Belgium its first win at the professional level of racing. He continued with the manufacturer through the 1907 Kaiserpreis, a race that utilized part of the former Gordon Bennett Cup race course. The French media loved the driver, and by 1907 he had catapulted to international fame. Several racing events were named after him, and Belgians were delighted with the acclaim. However, bad luck was just on the horizon. A fatal accident occurred at the Circuit des Ardennes and two spectators were killed. Hautvast and the Pipe company were charged with (but later acquitted of) the wrongful death of the two spectators after his car plunged off course and down a ravine.

Soon after, Clément-Bayard offered the talented Belgian driver a ride on the Grand Prix circuit beginning in 1907. Hautvast happily accepted the offer. Driving the Clément-Bayard Grand Prix car with a 105-horsepower engine propelled him even further down the road to success and solidified his skill in handling the big European machines. He was sent overseas to Savannah, Georgia, to enter the Grand Prize. The driver wrote home during the trip overseas, talking about the hardships of sea travels to the Grand Prix drivers: "Felice Nazzaro never stops saying he is going to die, Arthur Duray has been seasick five times but Victor Rigal seems not to suffer from sea sickness!"

Hautvast also found friends from the past in Savannah, including a fellow bicycle rider with whom he had raced in 1895 in Antwerp. Strangely, Hautvast's correspondence showed he was not in favor of the race track's banks and preferred natural road terrains that did not tax the upper body of a race car driver as much. However, he spoke very highly of the Savannah road surface, saying it was beyond the quality of the circuit of Dieppe and Bologna.

Another interesting point was Hautvast's car number at the Savannah race. A driver from Georgia drew the number 13, but refused to use it and instead put the letter X on the car. Hautvast was given the number instead. The American media were aghast that he would accept the number, and the bad luck associated with it. Some even noted that the hotel room he was staying at was number 156, or 12×13, and pointed out that the numbers $1 + 5 + 6$ equaled 13. On race day, Hautvast joked to the reporters that it was November 26, with 26 equal to 2×13, and that the team consisted of 13 members. Hautvast was quoted as telling friends later, saying, "Never did the Americans understand the casual manner in which I shouldered all the fatalities piled upon me!"

The Savannah race was one of his last races. Hautvast decided to retire immediately afterward in 1908. He was suffering from back issues from the crash in 1907 at Ardennes. His only other race came in 1912 for Sava, when the Automobile Club of Belgium hosted the Belgian Grand Pix at Ostend. Like several other drivers of the golden era who suffered losses of their fortunes directly or indirectly related to World War I and II, Hautvast lost all of his assets during wartime. Hautvast passed away in 1923 and, like several drivers of the time, was never given the acclaim he deserved for his part in the earliest days of racing in Europe and America.[52]

Eddie Hearne

1908 • International Light Car Race
1911 • American Grand Prize

Edward A. Hearne was born on March 1, 1887, in Kansas City, Kansas. He started his career in 1908 in the Savannah International Light Car Races and would go on to make a total of 106 race starts before he retired in 1927. Hearne was the heir to a goldmining fortune and owned many of the cars he raced. He had attended Notre Dame University and played on the second-string football team as quarterback.

Hearne is known mostly for his successes in the big Benz cars he raced in Savannah and his ten Indianapolis 500 races; however, he also participated in many other auto competitions.

In 1908, Hearne raced in the Wilkes-Barre, Pennsylvania, hill climb at Giant's Despair. He had a great run up the hill in a Benz, but unfortunately the timing machine did not record the run and he was asked to do it again once the equipment was working. The second time, the wear and tear on the car from the first run was showing and he broke a jack shaft.[53] Despite the disappointment, Hearne would have another shot at getting his career started at Savannah in November 1908. He drove a Buick in the International Light Car Race and, after a fantastic run against some of the veteran drivers, placed fourth. It was an excellent start to a successful and very busy racing career.

Hearne found himself very much in demand in 1909 when he raced in the Vanderbilt Cup, the Cobe Cup and the Amateur Cup at Indianapolis. 1910 was equally a busy year for the young driver, with appearances in the Fairmount Park Races in the number 26 Benz. He was out on lap 10 due to difficulties with the ignition, but the year was not at all a loss. Hearne went on to break a record at the Algonquin hill climb at Elgin in a 230-cubic-inch, 3.5-liter stock chassis car.[54]

Hearne returned to Savannah in triumph as part of the three-car Benz team. At only 22 years old, he was teamed up with Grand Prix champion Victor Hemery and another young American driver, David Bruce-Brown.[55]

Hearne's Indianapolis 500 record from 1911 through 1927 was packed full of highs and lows. He drove a Fiat in 1911 and placed 21st, and drove a Case in 1912 and placed 20th. He returned in 1919 to his best finish at Indy, placing second and earning a $10,000 paycheck. The year 1920 brought him back in a Duesenberg, which he drove there two years in a row. In 1920 and 1921, he finished sixth and 13th, respectively. He would switch up the formula again in 1922, seeking out the winning formula with a Ballot; he achieved another podium finish, placing third and earning $5,000. But it was not first place, of course. Hearne wanted to try another car there and entered a Miller in 1923. He placed fourth. He raced the following year in the same car, but fell to the back of the pack when a fuel line malfunctioned. His final race at Indy was in 1927, when he returned in the Miller and placed seventh.[56] Hearne retired shortly thereafter. He lived to age 67 and passed away in Los Angeles on February 9, 1955.

Victor Hemery

1908, 1910, 1911 • American Grand Prize

Victor Hemery was born November 18, 1876, near Le Mans, in La Sarthe, France. The village he was born in was Sillé le Guillaume. Early on, he had a talent for engineering and automobiles. Eventually he became an apprentice to Leon Bollée, whom he worked for until 1900. Hemery then received an offer from Darracq to take over as the head of research for the company's race cars—a job that would include driving in races. Hemery happily accepted the offer. By 1902, he was in the driver's seat, paying his dues at tracks such as the Circuit du Nord near Paris and in the Paris to Vienna race, where he placed as high as eighth. Hemery was beginning to display the type of brilliance that he would soon become renowned for in the sport. In 1903, he raced at the Circuit des Ardennes in Belgium, and went on to attempt to enter the Gordon Bennett Cup. However, the Darracq was stymied at this event and Hemery was unable to qualify. The following year, Hemery returned to the Circuit des

Ardennes and Coppa Florio. He was beginning to make excellent progress with the Darracq and the future seemed brighter.[57]

Hemery's greatest year would be 1905, although it was not until after his death that he was named national champion in the United States for his victories. In that year, Hemery had the fastest time at Arles Salon in France at 109.65 mph. He won at Coppa Florio and came to America to win the Vanderbilt Cup race. The mechanic he brought with him was none other than Louis Chevrolet, who would learn a lot from Hemery during their years together. Chevrolet spoke at length of Hemery after winning the Cobe Cup race in Indiana:

> I lost the use of one cylinder as a result of hard jumping over rocks. I almost wanted to give up. But something told me to stay in. It must have been the training I received while a mechanic for Hemery—the greatest motor racing driver the world has ever known. He never has been known to give up. He taught me to drive that way in all my contests.[58]

Known by the nickname "the Surly One," Hemery could become very irate with the race controllers, something that landed him in trouble and got him disqualified more than once during his career. Hemery was a hard charger, however, and took the job of driving very much to heart. It was very personal to him, a matter of pride and honor. When he went to Florida in 1906, hot off his 1905 year, he got into a disagreement with race officials and they would not allow him to race. Louis Chevrolet replaced him.

The year 1907 brought another busy racing schedule for Hemery. It was during this year that Hemery broke with Darracq and went to drive for Benz. It was a natural fit both for the company and for Hemery. He returned to race in the Coppa Florio, coming in second, and raced and won at the Coupe d'Evreux in France. Things were moving along quickly for Hemery, and he began preparing for another great trek overseas to America in 1908.[59]

In 1908, Hemery won the Tsar Nicholas Rally, the 3,000-kilometer race that began in St. Petersburg, moved to Kiev and Moscow, and returned to St. Petersburg. It was a grueling race. Again driving the Benz, Hemery placed second at the French Grand Prix. It was an excellent result and added to Hemery's excitement for returning to the south to race at the 25-mile Savannah course. He was particularly happy to have the opportunity to race against some of his old friends in the Grand Prize race. Louis Wagner, the Fiat driver, was equally excited about traveling to America with his old rival. Wagner once referred to Hemery as "one of the fearless among the fearless."[60] Hemery drove the fastest lap in practice in 22 minutes and 26 seconds and greatly enjoyed the welcome of the people of Savannah. He would make a great deal of men-

Victor Hemery, a great favorite of the Savannah races, drove all three years in Savannah. In 1910, he came in second place to teammate David Bruce-Brown, losing by only one second. After the race, he poured champagne over Bruce-Brown's head to congratulate him, thereby starting this racing tradition.

tion of this love of Savannah in 1910, when the Grand Prize race returned to the southern city. He had similar results as in the French Grand Prix, placing second in the Grand Prize behind Louis Wagner in the Fiat.

The year 1909 was a slower year in Hemery's career, with fewer races entered. However, he had a very strong showing at Brooklands that year. Hemery drove the Lightning Benz, also known as the Blitzen Benz, a 21.5-liter, 1,310-cubic-inch, four-cylinder engine. In 1910, Savannah would have the opportunity to welcome Hemery back, and in return he would start a new tradition that would become a part of auto racing for eternity. Hemery returned to Savannah driving for Benz with a sharp young American driver, David Bruce-Brown, as his teammate. After one of the closest races of the golden era of racing, Hemery came in second place, just one second behind his teammate. When asked about the finish, Hemery explained, "I wouldn't have minded losing by one minute, but one second is hard luck."[61] He took his champagne bottle and poured its contents over David Bruce-Brown's head as he sat in his car in the winner's circle being congratulated.

The following year, on July 23, 1911, Hemery won the French Grand Prix driving a Fiat. He was featured on the front pages of newspapers and the covers of sporting magazines throughout Europe, such as *La Vie au Grand Air*. However, it was a bittersweet moment for the driver. Hemery was very affected by a death that occurred during the race. Maurice Fournier, brother of the famous driver Henri Fournier, had been killed while trying to pass Hemery. The driver broke an axle on the turn and the car flipped, crushing Fournier underneath.[62] An article on the race in *La Vie au Grand Air* clearly shows the dismay on Hemery's face as he is congratulated for his victory. On the opposing page is a full-page story with two photos of the tragic accident of Fournier. One of the photos shows various bystanders, French guards, and a team of medics working on the riding mechanic. In the center is a bottle of champagne and a pair of boots, and to the right is presumably the corpse of Fournier, hands folded across his chest, feet bare, and head, which had been crushed, covered by a small blanket.[63] The death marred the win for Hemery and perhaps even kept him on the sidelines from racing for the next decade.

It would not be until 1922 and 1923 that Hemery would return to the driver's seat. He entered the French Grand Prix in a Rollands Pillain. Later, he owned an auto repair shop and suffered from terrible financial difficulties. Sadly, on September 9, 1950, Victor Hemery committed suicide just two months shy of his 74th birthday. His wife followed suit several days later. Those who knew Victor from the racing world were heartbroken. In 1951, he was named as the national champion in America for his Vanderbilt Cup win of 1905.

WILLIAM M. HILLIARD

1908 • International Light Car Race

William Hilliard was from Boston, Massachusetts, and was involved in both auto racing and (later) aviation. He won and set a record in the July 18, 1905, Climb to the Clouds event at Mount Washington, New Hampshire, in a Napier, winning in the free-for-all category. However, immediately after his win, Hilliard tried to descend the hill again, which was against the rules. Despite being warned to stop by officials due to the dangers of quickly descending, he ignored them and continued to the start for the next event. The officials of the AAA-sanctioned race were furious and barred him from further events.

In 1908, Hilliard raced in a Shawmut at Briarcliffe, finishing in 12th place. In October he raced in the stock car race preceding the Vanderbilt Cup.[64] He went on to Savannah for the International Light Car Race, entered in a Lancia. On November 25, 1908, Hilliard won the race and was awarded a beautiful silver Tiffany trophy. He was working at that time as the resident manager of a company called Hol-Tan as well as being an agent for the Lancia Company in Boston. Hilliard was also becoming fascinated by aviation. In 1910, he purchased a Herring-Burgess airplane, with the intention to one day enter aviation contests. By 1911, Hilliard had gone fully into aviation. He was attempting to get his pilot's license in February 1911 when he crashed his biplane and was badly injured.

CARL W. KELSEY

1908 • International Light Car Race

Carl Kelsey was born July 4, 1887. He was a race car driver and salesman for Maxwell for many years. In 1905, he entered the White Mountains Tour, which was a 12-day tour from the White Mountains of New Hampshire to New York City. He made the trip in a 16-horsepower Maxwell carrying four passengers. The last leg of the trip was 145 miles from Lenox, Massachusetts, in the Berkshires to the Plaza Hotel in New York.[65]

In 1906, Kelsey was to drive a Maxwell in the Vanderbilt elimination trials. To make things more interesting, he placed a side bet with his friend and fellow driver, Gill, who was also entering the trials. Whoever lost would buy the other driver a $100 trophy cup.[66]

The year 1908 was even busier for the driver/salesman. He represented Maxwell at auto shows around the country and entered several competitions, including the National Circuit Meet in October in Cleveland, Ohio. Then it was on to Savannah to enter the International Light Car Race. Kelsey proved to be a very good salesman and host, and the Maxwell Company threw a huge party at the Thunderbolt Casino for the media, making Frank Battey the guest of honor. Kelsey himself served shrimp soup and fried hominy to the newspaper men; as a souvenir, the company gave out miniature steins.[67] Kelsey's race in Savannah was consistent and uneventful. He was the last of the drivers who finished the race, landing in seventh place out of 15 cars. His fastest lap was 12 minutes and 44 seconds and he averaged 46.14 mph.[68]

One interesting note regarding Kelsey is his support of female drivers. He saw that women would be a critical group to whom to direct car sales in the future. As such, he conceived of the idea to set up an event for female drivers. Kelsey would prepare a route for the first woman to drive across country in a 30-horsepower Maxwell. That woman, Alice Ramsey, was a 22-year-old mother from Hackensack, New Jersey. Kelsey ensured that supplies and assistance were available to her on the route. Ramsey reached the West Coast in 59 days and wrote a book titled *Veil, Duster and Tire Iron* about her trip.[69]

By 1911, Kelsey was no longer racing. He had entered the business side of the industry and started the C.W. Kelsey Manufacturing Company. He also served as secretary of the Society of Automobile Engineers (SAE). Later, he returned to his roots in sales and was a sales manager for a private firm when he passed away on September 2, 1959.

JOSEPH MONWEILER (MUNTWYLER)

1908 • International Light Car Race

Joseph Monweiler was born December 3, 1888, in Switzerland. He drove a two-cylinder, 4.5-inch bore Maxwell which weighed 1,000 lbs in the International Light Car Race in Savannah during November 1908. He finished 15th in car number 15 but did not actually finish the race, as it was called when he was still running. Muntwyler spent his life working as an auto mechanic and died in Chicago in 1937.

RALPH KIRKMAN MULFORD

        1908, 1910 • American Grand Prix
        1911 • Vanderbilt Cup and American Grand Prix

Ralph Mulford was born December 28, 1884, in Brooklyn, New York. He was a working-class man who, prior to becoming a race car driver, was a choir master at the Metropolitan Opera House at the turn of the century. His nickname was "Smiling Ralph." Mulford began as an apprentice to Lozier, but had moved on to racing the cars by 1906. Mulford's racing career began to heat up in 1907 when he drove in multiple events for Lozier with great success. On June 19 through 22 of that year, Mulford drove the 40-horsepower Lozier Stock Touring car, number 519, to a perfect score at the 600-mile Sealed Bonnett contest. He continued his great year by winning the Point Breeze race at Philadelphia just a few days later, on June 28 and 29. In this 24-hour race, he was teamed up with Harry Michener in the same touring car. It covered 717 miles in what was known as "the severest track contest ever run."[70] Mulford also had a perfect score in the Boston to Keene (New Hampshire) 206-mile endurance race in 1907.

This put Mulford on a fast track to the bigger racing events that were occurring in America during the golden era. In 1908, Mulford would build on his reputation as a crack driver by winning the 24-hour Brighton Beach race on September 11 and 12. He was teamed up with Harry Cobe for the 1,107-mile race in a 60-horsepower, six-cylinder Lozier. Although they had tire troubles, the pair broke the previous 24-hour record. As Mulford came to the finish of the race, he was surrounded by women applauding and jumping on the car.[71] He would place third at the Fairmount Park Race in the same car in 1908 and finish first in the 5C division in 1910 and second in the same division in 1911.

In November 1908, Mulford traveled to Savannah to enter the first Grand Prix race in America. His mechanic, Beecroft, excelled at putting the car together for big races. Every part was disassembled, polished and inspected, then reassembled in careful preparation. H.A. Lozier himself oversaw the work for the races and attended the Savannah event. Mulford was off second in the race behind Victor Rigal and made the first lap faster than Rigal in the Clément-Bayard. He swept past the grandstands and down toward the first turn, almost losing the engine, which began backfiring until he had completed the turn and roared down the White Bluff straightaway. Unfortunately, Mulford had mechanical difficulties on and off; although he finished the race, he was far out of reach of victory and ended in tenth place.[72]

In 1909, Mulford returned to Brighton Beach to race in the 24-hour event again. The race was held October 16 and would go for 1,196 miles. Mulford teamed up with Cyrus Paschke this time, and the pair won again, averaging 50 mph and establishing a new record for the event.[73]

Mulford kept a busy racing schedule in 1910. In May, he drove a Stearns at Brighton Beach and finished second behind Charlie Basle and Al Poole. He continued on to Elgin in late August and won that race in a Lozier "50," averaging 65 mph and making only one stop for fuel.[74]

The latter part of the racing season was a bittersweet time for Mulford. He entered in his hometown race, the Vanderbilt Cup, on October 2. It was not Mulford's best race, as he was forced to pit at lap 13, losing 11 minutes. However, the worst part of the race for Mulford was the tragedies caused by poor crowd control and rutted roads that sent drivers off course, killing 4 and injuring 20 or more people. The race was not permitted to return and the media were particularly harsh. The *Atlanta Constitution* called it a "Carnival of Death" on October 2, 1910, and *Scientific America* published an expose entitled "The Vanderbilt Cup Race Slaughter" on October 15, 1910. Mulford was not the only driver affected by the result of the race. Along with William Endicott and Herbert Lytle, several drivers announced their retirement immediately after the Vanderbilt Cup race.[75]

Fortunately, a ray of sunshine came back to the sport only days afterward. The American Grand Prize race, which was supposed to be run on the Long Island track six weeks after the Vanderbilt Cup, was moved to Savannah. Mulford knew the track and was reinvigorated at the thought of returning to Savannah. He had an excellent run in the Lozier, placing fourth and not even having to change tires. His driving and the Lozier itself were crowd favorites. Thoughts of retiring were cast aside, and Mulford was anxious to return in 1911 when both the Vanderbilt Cup and American Grand Prize races would come to Savannah.

In May 1911, Mulford entered the first of his most controversial races at the inaugural Indianapolis 500. Mulford was certain he had won and took an extra few laps around the course in the Lozier before returning to the winner's circle—only to find Ray Harroun being congratulated as the winner. Mulford was credited with second place. The judges themselves had a difficult time determining who won, as the drivers were neck-and-neck in the final laps. It was an auspicious start to the great superspeedway.[76]

The following year in 1912, a rule was enacted at Indy stating that the drivers could win the prizes associated with how they placed at the race only if they completed the entire event. Along with riding mechanic Billy Chandler, Mulford had a good race in a Knox and found himself in tenth place, which would earn him $500—if he finished. The rule irritated Mulford, so he slowed to 20 mph, crawling around the track and stopping twice at the pits. During his first stop, he got some fried chicken to eat, the bones of which he discarded as he drove. The second stop to get some ice cream for dessert. He finished the race after 8 hours and 53 minutes and took home his $500 prize.[77]

In 1911, Mulford raced at Elgin in August, but was put out of the race when he encountered problems with connecting rods. However, his luck improved by the end of the year, when he returned to Savannah to enter both the Vanderbilt Cup and American Grand Prize races. He won the Vanderbilt Cup race, averaging 74.06 mph. It was during his fastest lap that Mulford raced an airplane, flown by Beckwith Havens of the Curtiss Flyers, down the home stretch. Although the airplane was faster, Mulford took home the silver Vanderbilt Cup. He had a more

Ralph Mulford, one of America's favorite drivers, was featured in the Mecca Tobacco Auto Drivers Series Number 1. Mulford drove a Lozier in the Savannah races in all three years' events. He won the Vanderbilt Cup race in 1911, averaging 74.06 mph and setting a world record of 74.9 mph while racing Beckwith Havens in a Curtiss airplane down the home stretch.

difficult time in the American Grand Prize race, placing eighth when he went airborne on lap 23 and the car crashed back to the ground, breaking the steering.[78]

The Vanderbilt Cup race next moved to Milwaukee. Although he was thought to be a contender in the race, Mulford was out early with a broken magneto. By 1916, he would be supervising the Hudson team in the Vanderbilt Cup at Santa Monica. He would continue to race at Indianapolis in 1913 and 1914 in the Mercedes "Grey Ghost" owned by E.J. Schroeder, and in 1915 in a Deusenberg. In 1916, he had his best finish at Indianapolis since the race's inaugural year of 1911. Mulford raced a Peugeot and had his second podium finish, placing third in the race. He would return to race there again from 1919 to 1922 in a Frontenac, but retired with mechanical problems in the first and last years in that car.[79]

Ralph Mulford continued with hill climbs into the 1930s and was remembered as one of America's superstar racers. He passed away on October 23, 1973.

Felice Nazzaro

1908, 1910 • American Grand Prize

Felice Nazzaro, nicknamed "the Speed King," was born in Turin, Italy, on December 4, 1881. He was a fan favorite in the early days of Grand Prix racing and was the first race car driver to become an internationally recognized superstar in the sport. One of his youngest fans during his early career was a youth named Enzo Ferrari. Ferrari considered Nazzaro to be the best race car driver in Italy, and perhaps Nazzaro may have been one of his earliest influences. Nazzaro's interest in the automobile began at the age of 14, when he worked on engines for the Ceirano brothers, who founded Fiat.[80] He drove for Fiat along with Vincenzo Lancia, who founded the company making the Lancia automobile. Interestingly, the Lancia Company was acquired by Fiat in 1969, giving the Fiat group a victory in all three years of the Great Savannah Races: the Fiats won the American Grand Prize races in 1908 and 1911, and the Lancia, driven by Billy Knipper, won the Tiedeman Trophy race in 1910.

Nazzaro's first win occurred in 1901 when he raced a four-cylinder, 3.8-liter Fiat at Giro d'Italia, averaging 27.7 mph. The only other race he had entered prior to that time was the 1900 Italian race from Padua to Vicenzo and back to Padua. He entered driving a larger 6-horsepower Fiat, placing second to the Lancia. After the 1901 race, Nazzaro worked part-time as one of the private chauffeurs to Count Vincenzo Florio, who allowed the young driver to enter a number of racing competitions as part of his employment.[81] Chauffeuring was a very common full-time profession for race car drivers and riding mechanics at the turn of the century.

Nazzaro was one of the earliest race car drivers to develop a racing style and strategy that was unique to him. His trademark in the early years of his career was to allow the competition to begin leading the race, scope out their strengths and weaknesses, and then steal the lead and win. Throughout 1903 and 1904, Nazzaro was driving a Panhard in competitions throughout Europe. Ultimately, Nazzaro returned to Fiat in 1905 and produced fantastic results in the car. He placed second in the Gordon Bennett Cup at Circuit d'Auvergne in Clermont-Ferrand, France, despite bookmakers placing 20 to 1 odds against him. He placed sixth at Coppa Florio and second in the French Grand Prix that same year. By 1907, the crowds were cheering him on by name. In 1907, Nazzaro had one of the greatest years of any driver in the period. He won the three major races in the international Grand Prix world: the Kaiserpreis in Germany, Targa Florio and the French Grand Prix, which was in its second

Felice Nazzaro, nicknamed "the Speed King," was an Italian driver who won many Grand Prix races in Europe. He placed third in the number 6 Fiat in Savannah in 1908, with an average speed of 63.96 mph, but did not finish due to mechanical problems in 1910.

year. He raced a variety of cars, ranging from one with an engine size of 7,363 cubic centimeters to another with and engine of 16,286 cubic centimeters.[82]

Nazzaro drove the "Grand Prix" Fiat in 1908, winning at the Brooklands track in Surrey, England, on June 6. The headlines in Britain proclaimed him "The Man Who Could Drive Two Miles a Minute," perhaps in jest over his record-breaking 120 mph "magic lap." The lap was very controversial at the time, with some claiming it did not occur and others certain it did. The race at Brooklands was an unusual one, with a challenge being issued by S.F. Edge, owner of a 90-horsepower Napier driven by Frank Newton. Edge bet D'Arcy Baker 500 pounds that his car could beat Baker's 90-horsepower Fiat Mephistopheles. Baker took up the challenge and hired Nazzaro to drive. Unfortunately for Newton, the Napier did not make it past the third lap due to mechanical difficulties. Nazzaro won the race, coasting through the remaining laps and waving at the crowd, perhaps driving only 2 miles per minute to the finish.[83]

Nazzaro was a very popular contender in the 1908 Grand Prize race in Savannah, along with fellow Fiat drivers Louis Wagner and Ralph De Palma. In that competition, the Grand Prix Fiats were showcased again. The people of Savannah were in awe of Nazzaro's quick pit stops to refuel, check the tires and have a swig from a bottle of champagne. He was baby-faced and very well dressed in his "union suit which displayed his trim lines to advantage."[84] Nazzaro would lead much of the race, outpacing Victor Hemery and Louis Wagner in the early hours. Nazzaro would return with the Fiat team in 1910 driving car number 10, again leading much of the race and schooling the young De Palma and David Bruce-Brown early on. Unfortunately, this would be his final year racing in Savannah; he went out on lap 19 with a broken drive chain.

By 1911, Nazzaro had returned to Turin and joined with Maurizio Fabry, Pilade Massuero and Arnaldo Zoller to start building automobiles under the name Nazzaro & C. Fabbrica di Automobili. The Nazzaro name made his first cars quite popular. The first car came out in 1912 and used a 4.4-liter, 4-cylinder engine with side valves. It was called the Tipo 2. Nazzaro continued manufacturing and driving the Tipo 2 in many races across Europe, including Targa Florio in 1913, which he won by 3 hours. However, the next generation of the car, the Tipo 3, was brought to market at a bad time, after World War I. The manufacturing business ended shortly thereafter in 1923, when Nazzaro returned to work with Fiat.

Nine years after his last race, he reentered the sport with Fiat in the 1922 French Grand Prix and won, beating his old riding mechanic Pietro Bordino, who was the new face of Grand Prix racing. In 1923, Nazzaro placed second in the European Grand Prix, but it would be his last big finish. His wife died the same year in an automobile accident, and perhaps the combination of her demise and a desire to see the younger set have their chance at driving led to Nazzaro's exit from the sport. He retired from racing and became head of Fiat's Competitions Department until the company ceased racing in 1929. He passed away on March 21, 1940, after a prolonged illness.[85]

GIOVANNI PIACENZA

1908 • American Grand Prize

Giovanni Piacenza was born in Torino, Italy, in 1882.[86] Very little is known about this driver due to his short racing career. He was hired as a third driver by Itala in 1908. Itala founders Matteo Ceirano and Guido Bigio named the car driven by Piacenza "Floretta," and it appears in photos to be longer than Alessandro Cagno's and Henri Fournier's Italas. The car had a 12-liter, 100-horsepower engine.[87] Piacenza raced in just two events that year for the company. The first was the French Grand Prix on July 7, 1908. His car was number 45. Unfortunately, he was the second car to drop out of the race due to gearbox problems. The second race he entered in the Itala was the 1908 Grand Prize race in Savannah, along with riding mechanic Cesso, in the number 20 car. Unfortunately, Piacenza made it only five laps. Approximately halfway around the course on the Isle of Hope, Piacenza lost control of the car and went off into the ditch.

VICTOR RIGAL

1908 • American Grand Prize

Victor was born in Paris, France, on September 22, 1879. He was one of the earliest pioneers in auto racing, beginning his career in 1898 when he drove at the Criterium des Entraneurs and the Paris to Bordeaux race in a De Dion. A year later, he drove at the Grand Prix of Verona in a Bernardi-Miari Giusti. This very early car had some similarities in appearance to a Duryea. The company that manufactured it was founded in Padua in 1894 and specialized in three- and four-wheeled vehicles that it entered in races throughout Italy. Rigal drove for the company in 1899 in the Brescia to Mantua to Verona race, with an average speed of approximately 19 km/h.

In 1903, Rigal drove in the Paris to Madrid race in a voiturette. This was one of the races that Willie K. Vanderbilt entered driving a Mors. The race was stopped at Bordeaux because of the fatalities that occurred in what many term as the most dangerous auto race ever held. By 1906, Rigal had secured a ride with Itala in a 35/40-horsepower car at Targa Florio, a circuit to which he would return many times in the years to come. He placed fourth with the car. In 1907, he raced at Targa Florio again, but this time in a Berliet.[88]

The year 1908 brought Rigal to Savannah, Georgia, with the French manufacturer Clément-Bayard, along with teammate Lucien Hautvast. The Clément-Bayards were 13.9-liter, 135-horsepower engines. A heavy southern fog had settled on the morning of the race, delaying the start until the mist had thinned out enough to provide safer visibility for the drivers. Like many of the fogs that roll in during the fall months, it was very wet, making the road slick, saturating the driver in his seat, and covering the steering wheel with a fine sheen. Rigal, with mechanic Gilbert, was unfortunately the first off to try out the course in the inclement conditions. He slid off the course and was unable to gain much of a lead. However, Rigal was a strong, conservative driver and he managed to keep the car going for the entire 16 laps, finishing in seventh place.

In 1911, Rigal drove a Delage at Indianapolis before heading off to Europe for the Grand Prix races. He was first off at the French Grand Prix, driving a Rolland-Pilain in the voiturette class. His career was very busy and he traveled from one race to the other for the next few years. In 1913, Rigal began driving for Sunbeam, entering the spring race at Amiens on March 22, 1913.[89] One of Rigal's best years was 1914, when he entered the French Grand Prix driving the L45 for Peugeot.[90] War World I, however, created tensions that cut deeply into the talented world of motorsports. Rigal, along with Arthur Duray entered the war in 1915 and gave up driving for several years. Rigal became a sub-lieutenant in charge of an automobile convoy.[91] He would not drive again until the war was over. In 1925, he entered Targa Florio on the Peugeot team with his old friends Louis Wagner, Andre Boillot and Christian d'Auvergne.

One of Rigal's final races was in 1929 at the Mille Miglia in an Alfa Romeo. This race was founded by 23-year-old Conte Aymo Maggi, a Brescian nobleman. Maggi was a very humanist, renaissance man; in that fashion, he met with friends Franco Mazzotti, Flaminio Monti and Renzo Castagneta in Milan to argue the merits of bringing racing back to Brescia. All three men felt it was the true birthplace of motorsports in Italy and wanted to resurrect the endurance race to Rome. However, ending in Rome and not back in Brescia seemed as if it would rob Brescia of the victory celebrations and focus, so it was decided among the men that the race would start in Brescia, travel to Rome, and return back to Brescia. Mazzotti is said to have exclaimed, "That is a thousand miles" in Italian, giving birth to the race's name—Mille Miglia.[92] Rigal drove a 1.7-liter 6C Alfa Romeo in the race.

Little is known of Rigal's life afterward. However, there is record of a Victor Rigal with a similar birth date and place, who is recorded to have died in Austria at the Mauthasen Gusen concentration camp on June 22, 1944, after being captured and arrested by the Nazis on April 8, 1944.[93]

JOSEPH MORTON SEYMOUR

1908 • American Grand Prize

Joseph Morton Seymour was also known as J. Seymour, Morton Seymour, J. Morton Seymour and Joe Seymour. Despite the various names the media used to write about him, he seemed to come out of nowhere in 1907, driving like a demon to bring a 50-horsepower Simplex from 21st place to second at Briarcliffe. The crowd was as stunned as the motorsports world. One particular fan whom Seymour gained was none other than Walter Christie, who signed him in 1908 to drive the Christie race car in a number of events. Although the *New York Times* wrote that Seymour had been driving since 1893 when he raced an electric car,[94] Simplex claimed in its advertising that he had "never before driven in any kind of race" prior to Briarcliffe.[95]

In 1908, Seymour partnered with British driver and riding mechanic William Watson to enter the Automobile Topics Tour, which ran from Philadelphia to Savannah. He entered the two-mile event in the Jamaica Speed Trials of New York in early June. Seymour also drove in the Boston Meet on Memorial Day of that year and broke a record in the Exhibition Mile, shaving 2 seconds off the prior record. From there, it was on to Savannah with riding mechanic Pepperday. Seymour had an excellent race. Although the European cars were highly favored, he had the distinct honor of finishing in 11th position, the highest place for the American manufacturers. He entered the race in an 11-liter, 90-horsepower Simplex.

Seymour drove a 50-horsepower, six-cylinder Lozier at the Fairmount Park Motor Races in 1909 and was able to achieve a top time of 8 minutes and 48 seconds. However, he suffered a broken water pump and was the first driver out of the race.[96] He was offered a ride in the 475-cubic-inch Isotta-Fraschini for the Vanderbilt Cup race that year. He was in second place and doing very well holding off Louis Chevrolet in a Buick in that race until lap 6, when his steering broke.

FERENC (FRANCOIS) SZISZ

1908 • American Grand Prize

Ferenc Szisz was born September 20, 1873, in Szeghalam, Hungary. As a young man, he worked as a railway engineer, a locksmith and a coppersmith in Budapest; he later moved to Vienna. However, as the automobile industry grew, Szisz became very interested in automotive technology. He moved to Paris, France, in 1900 and began working for the Renault brothers, Marcel and Louis, as a test engineer. Within two years, he was entering races with Louis and Marcel as their riding mechanic. In 1902, Szisz was riding mechanic to Marcel in the Paris to Vienna race. Tragically, Marcel was killed while racing in the Paris to Madrid race in 1903. Devastated, brother Louis, who had founded the company at the age of 22, stopped driving, turning the driver's seat over to Szisz.[97]

Szisz entered the 1905 Elimination Race at the hilly and wildly curving Circuit d'Auvergne at Clermont-Ferrand for the Gordon Bennett Cup race. He was the third-place driver in a 90-horsepower, 12.9-liter Renault—and only the top three finishers went on. Szisz suffered from cooling problems, as did the other Renaults in the race; they all overheated. However, Szisz was praised for his handling of the car with its mechanical problems, and it amazed many that he was still able to finish in fifth place.

Szisz also went to America that year. Clad in his traditional black leather suit, he entered the Vanderbilt Cup race on Long Island and placed fifth.[98]

In 1906, Szisz entered the French Grand Prix in a red Renault AK90 CV bearing number 3A and won. The race was 769.9 miles. Szisz had an average speed of 64.61 mph with pit stops factored in, but reached speeds of up to 100 mph on the straighter sections of the course. He was timed at the grandstand as the fastest car, hitting a speed of 92.43 mph. Interestingly, the tires he used in practice were detachable wire wheels, but during the race his team used 34-inch fitted artillery wheels with eight nuts holding the rim in place through wedges so that a tire change could be accomplished in just two minutes. Prior to that innovation, tires would be cut off the rim with a knife and new ones forced on in their place.[99] In the end, Szisz held a whopping 32-minute lead on the second-place finisher.

Szisz entered the French Grand Prix in Dieppe in 1907, finishing in second place behind Felice Nazzaro. The primary reason for the second-place finish was a ten-minute pit stop that was required due to the fuel regulations of the race.

In 1908, Szisz came to America to race in the first American Grand Prize race in Savannah as part of his final year in motorsports with Renault. He had an excellent start in the race, working his way through the field to second place. However, he had a broken wheel bearing by lap 6 and had to retire from the race. Renault was souring on being involved in racing and Szisz parted ways with the company, opening a garage at Neuilly-sur-Seine in 1909.

In 1914, Szisz entered the Grand Prix at Lyon in an Alda. He was injured badly while he stopped to make a repair. An Opel hit him, breaking his arm severely. Yet he was back in the driver's seat only a few weeks later in Anjou, driving a Lorraine-Dietrich. However, World War I broke out only a few days later, and Szisz joined the war effort as the head of transport troops in Algeria. He got typhoid and suffered significant illness for the next few years, returning to France. He worked for the Breugeot Aircraft company for the remainder of his life. On February 21, 1944, he died in Auffargis, France.

Louis Wagner
1908, 1910, 1911 • American Grand Prize

Louis Wagner was born near Paris in the town Le Pré-Saint-Gervais, France, on February 5, 1882. In the mid–1890s, Wagner became interested in engines and began looking for a job that would allow him to work on these machines. He found a job as a mechanic's assistant with Leon Bollée, son of Amédée Bollée, the inventor of the three-wheeled car known as a voiturette. In 1899, he received an offer to work for a new French manufacturer, Darracq, located in Suresnes, France.[100] Within four years, Wagner had impressed the team with his mechanical and driving abilities in the voiturettes. He was hired to race for the team from 1903 to 1907 in an 80-horsepower voiturette. Wagner raced at the infamous Paris to Madrid race where at least ten people were killed and the French government stopped the race.[101]

As Wagner built his career, he experienced many highs and lows. In 1904, he entered the French Elimination Race for the Gordon Bennett Cup at Argonne. Unfortunately, the race was a disappointment for Wagner. He was forced to drop out early with engine difficulties. He won in the voiturette class in a two-lap race at Circuit des Ardennes in Belgium in 1905 and began racing in the Vanderbilt Cup races the same year with Victor Hemery. Unfortunately, Wagner went out early in the race when his gearbox cover flew off and the bearings seized on lap 4. His first American race was not encouraging, as he finished third from last among 19 competitors.

However, all that changed in 1906 when Wagner returned to America for the Vanderbilt Cup race. It was a calamitous year for the Vanderbilt Cup, but the dark-haired, debonair foreign driver brought a ray of pure sunshine to the thousands of spectators who lined the course. Wagner wowed the crowds with spectacular driving throughout the race, holding the lead with an average speed of 62.7 mph. Unfortunately, his lasting of impression the Long Island Vanderbilt Cup was marred when he was put in jail for 48 hours. The police had arrested him for speeding on Broadway, ironically the street where Fiat—his future employer—was headquartered. Wagner's 1906 season ended very well, however, and it seemed things could not get better for the driver and his team.

All of the goodwill between the driver and the manufacturer would evaporate at Targa Florio in 1907. Both Wagner and Victor Hemery left the Darracq team after the Targa Florio race. Alexandre Darracq blamed Wagner for leaving the race early and crashing the car carelessly. It was too much for a man of Wagner's reputation and high ethics to take. He told his boss in no uncertain terms how he felt about the false accusations and how he prided himself on work and accomplishment, and stated that he could not continue working for him after receiving such grave insults.

The early years of racing were over for Wagner, but he had proven what he could do. It was only a short time before another team would snap him up. Fiat saw a winning driver in Wagner and hired him immediately. Together, they prepared for an incredible 1908 season which would end with one of the world's greatest races on what was purported by Wagner himself to be the greatest race course in America: the Grand Prize of the Automobile Club of America in Savannah.

Wagner's speeds had increased from the Vanderbilt Cup race and his average speed on the Georgia course was 65.11 mph. He also enjoyed setting a new record at the faster Savannah track, reaching a "flying mile" of 90 mph. Wagner had a special fondness for the Savannah races of 1908, 1910, and 1911. Later in life, as Wagner looked back fondly over his career, he was invited to write a foreword about the Savannah races in Peter Helck's *Checkered Flag* in 1961. Wagner wrote of the charm of the local people and the warm congratulations of George Robertson, winner of the 1908 Vanderbilt Cup, who attended the race as a spectator. "I have recalled those happy days with gripping emotion and relived intensely that great race," Wagner wrote, "certainly the finest in my long career."[102]

The media loved Wagner from the start of his 27-year career to the end. When he came to America to race in the Vanderbilt Cup in Long Island in 1906, newspapers such as the *Atlanta Journal* declared that Wagner "showed dare devil bursts of speed in dangerous places, throwing defiance at death in every revolution of his machine that shot over the earth like a meteor through the sky."[103] After the American Grand Prize in Savannah, the *New York Times* said: "[Wagner] has gained considerable fame as a driver of automobiles ... and made a reputation of nervy, heady driving, coupled with unbounded nerve and courage."[104]

During Savannah's Grand Prize race of 1910, Wagner was less fortunate. His Fiat S61 turned over in the 17th lap of the race. Overall, the 1910 Fiats could not match the performance of the Benz cars, which dominated the race. However, Wagner was happy to be in Savannah and pleased for his long-time friend and past teammate Victor Hemery to place second in such a close race with the young American superstar, David Bruce-Brown. Wagner was

Louis Wagner (with his mechanic) was the winner of America's first Grand Prize race in Savannah in 1908. He raced the number 14 Fiat for Italy, winning the race with an average speed of 65.11 mph.

similarly unlucky in 1911, when he retired with steering problems on lap 15 of the Grand Prize race. This time, however, Bruce-Brown had come over to the Fiat side, and he defended his championship and won the event for Fiat rather than Benz.

The other major highlights of Wagner's career before World War I included a second-place finish at the French Grand Prix of 1912 with Fiat. After this achievement, he left Fiat and signed on with Mercedes, placing second again in the 1914 French Grand Prix with the German manufacturer. This period may have caused some turmoil for the French driver, as tensions between France and Germany were high and war was coming. After the war, Wagner was asked to drive a French Ballot at Indianapolis. The Ballot was designed by Ernest Henry, who had led the design efforts for the Peugeot before the war. Despite being highly regarded, the Ballot did not do well at the race.

Wagner was interested in much more than automobiles throughout his career. He also played a large part as a test pilot for several flying machines, and is strongly associated with the early development of the Hanriot et Cie monoplane and biplane. His interest in flying began shortly after the turn of the century. By 1910, he was on the cover of *La Vie au Grand Air* flying the Hanriot with two passengers in Europe.[105] Several European auto racers shared Wagner's interest in aviation, including Victor Rigal, who drove for Renault in Savannah's 1908 American Grand Prize race.

Wagner appeared to reignite his career with a return to Fiat in 1921. He placed third in the Italian Grand Prix. In 1922, he found himself partnering again with his old friend Hemery to drive for Rolland-Pillain. However, the cars did not do very well. Alfa Romeo offered Wagner a seat to drive for the company in 1924 at the Italian Grand Prix. It was not disappointed with his performance, as he put Alfa Romeo on the podium with a second-place finish.

The year 1925 brought Wagner to yet another new team. The Delage Company took notice of Wagner and signed him to race at the French Grand Prix in 1925, where he placed second. The same year he drove for Peugeot at Targa Florio and brought home another second-place finish. However, Wagner still had one victory left in him, which came in a Delage at the famous Brooklands race in 1926. A year later he went into retirement after racing a Talbot 700.

Wagner was a very good man and remained friends with many drivers and writers, such as Peter Helck, for many years. Sadly, he suffered from bone cancer for several years and lost a leg to the disease. He passed away on March 13, 1960, at the age of 78.[106]

7

International Light Car Race of 1908

After the successful set of events in March 1908, the Automobile Club of America decided to make good use of its right to sanction all international racing events in the country by putting on a weekend of racing on Thanksgiving 1908 in Savannah, Georgia. The sparring that had taken place between the AAA and the ACA had reached a fevered pitch by the summer that year, resulting in a big move by the ACA to contest the International Light Car Race and Grand Prize.

Early Marketing for a Race Destination: Savannah

Marketing of Savannah began in the automotive industry in August 1908. Newspapers talked about the excellent hospitality of the people of Savannah. The media also favorably

City Market, close to Gorrie's Ice House, where the cars were weighed before racing, was home to Del Monico's Restaurant where race organizers met with Mayor Tiedeman of Savannah during prerace celebrations. Team staff and visitors alike could go to the City Market to get supplies of fresh vegetables and meats to take back to their camps.

Broughton Street was the social hub of the races from 1908 to 1911, with its shops, restaurants, music venues, boxing matches and entertainment in its theaters.

described the economy of the city: "Commercially, she is unrivaled on the South Atlantic Coast."[1] The port of Savannah was widely talked about, especially as it pertained to how accessible the city was. Trains came into Savannah from the north, south, and west and the harbors brought in ships from all over the world. This told travelers and potential entrants that it would be easy to travel to Savannah and that it was a thoroughly modern, world-class city used to hosting visitors from around the globe. The media also discussed the types of businesses found in Savannah at the time: it was the third largest port for cotton, the second largest port for lumber, and the largest port for naval stores.[2] "City Beautiful" was the name used to describe Savannah in the media. People were enticed by descriptions of wide boulevards and subtropical parks to stroll through. The river, located high on a 45-foot bluff, was a major topic of conversation, as well as the resort areas around the city, such as Thunderbolt, home of the Thunderbolt Casino, horse racing, yacht clubs, several restaurants, hotels and outdoor musical venues.[3]

Technical Planning for the Automobile

As early discussions took place in August 1908 by the Automobile Club of America and the Savannah Automobile Club, the plans for the Grand Prix and International Light Car Race began to take shape. The Technical Committee of the Automobile Club of America was headed by Henry Souther of Henry Souther Engineering Company of Connecticut, who was in the business of testing metals and materials for automotive and other industries. Initially, the committee recommended that cars in the light car category be a maximum of

850 lbs to match cars on the market stripped to racing form and allowed for a 3.75-inch diameter maximum for four-cylinder motors.[4] The cars expected to fit into these parameters included the Franklin, Ford and Buick for four-cylinder cars. For two-cylinder cars, the possible entrants might include the Maxwell, Reo, Jackson, Moline, Atlas, Rambler, Elmore, Waltham, Autocar and Northern.

The proposal was for cars with four- and two-cycle motors. Four-cycle motors would be allowed:

- 7.50 inches or 190.8 mm of bore for one cylinder
- 5.30 inches of 135.1 mm of bore for two cylinders
- 4.33 inches or 110 mm of bore for three cylinders
- 3.75 inches or 95.4 mm of bore for four cylinders
- 3.66 inches or 77.7 mm of bore for six cylinders
- 2.65 inches or 67.4 mm of bore for eight cylinders

Two-cycle motors would be allowed:

- 6.35 inches or 160 mm of bore for one cylinder
- 4.5 inches or 114 mm of bore for two cylinders
- 3.65 inches or 92 mm of bore for three cylinders
- 3.18 inches or 81 mm of bore for four cylinders
- 2.58 inches or 65 mm of bore for six cylinders
- 2.24 inches or 56 mm of bore for eight cylinders

Souther believed that allowing the two-cycle classes to race alongside the four-cycle classes would provide an excellent opportunity to show automobile industry insiders and potential purchasers the capabilities of the two-cycle cars. He felt that the reports of the media members who would be attending the International Light Car Race in advance of the Grand Prize would open up unprecedented marketing opportunities for these machines.[5]

The proposal for the weight did change slightly in the weeks after the initial parameters were released to the manufacturers. The minimum weight was increased to 950 lbs. The course would be lengthened if the contest received more than 20 entrants. The only changes to the proposed bore sizes dealt with the two-cylinder engines, which were increased to 5.80 inches, and the six-cylinder engines, which were increased to 3.66 inches. For the two-cycle engines, the proposal was altered to include only cars with a three- or four-cylinder engine, with the same bore as originally proposed.[6]

Entrants in the International Light Car Race and the Buick Phenomenon

The entry fees for the International Light Car Race were set at $200 per car, $300 for two cars, $350 for three cars, and half-price ($400) if the company entered four cars. The manufacturer was permitted to change the bore of a stock model car to fit the technical specifications and to strip as much of the stock as it chose to get the car under the maximum weight. The deadline to enter was November 1, 1908.[7] By mid–October, the list of entries included four Maxwells, three Oldsmobiles, two Chalmers-Detroits, one Lancia, one Isotta and one American Aristocrat. There were also three entries made by De Dion and two from Gyroscope that withdrew by mid–October.[8] A Gregoire was added to the list of entrants and was en route to America with the Lancia and S.P.O. on the ship *La Savoie*. But by mid–November, an important entrant had dropped out because it could not get its machines ready in time for the race. This was a blow to the field to some degree, as it was the three Oldsmobiles owned by F.L. Smith that had backed out. These machines were highly anticipated rivals to the Buicks.[9]

The Buicks were a sensation and fans of the car created a very large stir in Savannah. Indeed, a very large number of Buick owners traveled to Savannah for the races. It was the first time the early motorsports media saw how people reacted to the sporting competitions of automobiles that they might own themselves. According to *The Washington Post*, a peculiar phenomenon occurred:

> The enthusiasm for race cars depended largely upon the number of those cars owned by the spectators. The enthusiasm when Buick beat all the American cars—and all but one of the American cars in the small car race—was tremendous, but undoubtedly was caused largely by the fact that there were actually hundreds of these compact little machines present. Where they came from, no one seems to know, but their owners all seemed to be sure that their machine would win, and how they did cheer. The roads were full of Buicks—it seemed to rain Buicks. Some came 3000 miles to see the race, and they didn't waste much time cheering any car but their own.[10]

Many automobile parts companies were offering large sums of money to winners if they used their parts. Continental Tires was one of them. For the International Light Car Race, the company offered a prize of $250 to the first-place finisher, $150 to the second-place finisher and $100 to the third-place finisher, if they raced using Continental tires. Michelin followed suit and offered a first-place prize of $500, a second place-prize of $300 and a third-place prize of $200. The cars themselves would typically cost less than $5,000 to build and expenses, including the drivers' and mechanics' fees, would be less than $20,000 per car.[11]

Practice Report

Practice began Monday, November 16. The track was freshly oiled early each morning. The light cars went out from 11:00 a.m. until 1:30 p.m. while the big cars took to the track once the small cars were through each day. More than 100 guards and flagmen were present to assure the safety of the drivers, race personnel and curious onlookers. The drivers were required to report to the grandstands before starting their practice, so that everyone could be accounted for in the event that someone went off course.[12] Unfortunately, even the best soldiers and an ample number of flagsmen could not completely prevent disaster.

The S.P.O. (Société Française de Petite Outillage) car entered by S. Kjeldsen would, sadly, be the one to feel the tragic wrath of early auto racing. It was something that was accepted as part of the sport—not to be expected, necessarily, but the machinery was still new and being pushed to its limits to win races. It was still an imperfect science when a team of mechanics stripped a stock model car to turn it into a racing machine. The changing weights, use of different tires and varying conditions of a course presented a truly unpredictable environment. The S.P.O. team was not among the wealthiest and had not sent over all of its own mechanics from Europe, being assured that once the team was in New York, many in the industry could fill in. The team traveled from Europe in early November and landed at New York. Almost as soon as they arrived in America, they began looking for a mechanic to assist them.

They found such a mechanic in a local garage. He was a young, recent immigrant who spoke Italian and French. His name was De Rosa. Aside from the facts that he was highly praised for his abilities in the garages the S.P.O. team had visited, and that he was clearly young and very eager to see the world and make a name for himself in the exciting world of racing, not much was known of him. The team hired him anyway and began their journey south with the car. Only a few days before arriving, they learned the lad's first name was Marius. They also learned that he was from a fishing village in southern Italy and had lived in Marseilles.

The S.P.O. team arrived in Savannah on November 19, 1908, and began to practice the next day. Less than 24 hours passed before tragedy occurred. Driver Jean Juhasz was coming up the straightaway on a flat, level section of the course approximately one mile from the grandstands.[13] Suddenly, a large black dog bounded across the road. Juhasz swerved to avoid the dog. Two tires hit the soft sand on the shoulder of the broad course. Juhasz lost control as the car catapulted into the air and struck a tree, which changed its direction. It hit a second tree, then a telephone pole. The driver and mechanic were thrown around like rag dolls and eventually flung from the vehicle as it came to hit a fourth pole which snapped in half. Another car out practicing came across the accident and raced back one mile to the starting point for a doctor.

The two men were rushed to the Savannah Hospital beside Forsyth Park. Jean Juhasz's leg was badly broken at the knee and doctors were not certain whether he would live or die. Unfortunately, De Rosa was in worse shape. He had suffered from a broken arm and leg on his left side, as well as a fractured skull and internal injuries. He was pronounced dead at the hospital, only a few steps from Mayor Tiedeman's home.[14]

Due to the fact that the team did not know the young man very well and they had just arrived in Savannah a day prior, no one seemed to know what to do. The team had never asked about the young man's family, other than learning that he had immigrated to America and was an Italian who had lived in Marseilles, France. However, the realization that the man was so young and had died in a city of strangers tugged at the heartstrings of the organizers from both New York and Savannah. No one seemed to be able to find his family, but they planned to find his mother in Marseilles. There was no mention of his father ever made in the newspapers, suggesting that his mother may have been raising him alone.[15]

De Rosa's funeral was planned and mechanic Herbert Connors went to work on the car in T.A. Bryson's garage. Although it was initially thought to be beyond repair, the vehicle was rebuilt in several days with the help of Bryson's mechanics. A funeral was held for De Rosa, with no family or personal friends knowing he had passed away. Mayor Tiedeman and Frank Battey, president of the Savannah Automobile Club, ensured that no expense was spared. A very lavish ceremony was held at St. John's Cathedral on Abercorn Street and both the mayor and Battey served as pallbearers. De Rosa's body was carried on the automobile in which he had been killed through the city and over part of the course so that people could pay their respects to the young man. It was the first automobile hearse in Georgia. De Rosa was taken to Laurel Grove cemetery and buried in plot number 911, where his grave remains to this day, with the perpetual care cost paid by the sheriff's office.

It was said that word was sent to De Rosa's mother in Marseilles to inform her of her son's death, and that she did not know that he was in Savannah. However, no evidence of these communications exists and a careful study of De Rosa's arrival in America reveals a surprising mystery. In 1907, two different men with similar names arrived in America via Ellis Island. One, Marais De Rosa, arrived from Cherbourg on October 9, 1907. He was a

The S.P.O. car had an infamous reputation during the 1908 Savannah races. The race car served as a hearse for a young riding mechanic, Marius De Rosa, who was killed during practice. It was the first automobile hearse in Georgia (courtesy Robyn Quattlebaum).

25-year-old French chauffeur.[16] The other young man, Marius De Rosa, arrived with his mother Elvira and sister Eva on October 17, 1907, from Le Havre onboard the *Hudson*. The family's residence was listed as Marseilles, France, and they were identified as being of southern Italian nationality.[17] Meanwhile, the records of the Savannah Hospital list the young driver who was killed as being of Belgian descent, deepening the mystery of who De Rosa really was.[18] If the young man who was killed was indeed the son of Elvira De Rosa, she was never contacted in Marseilles as the newspapers state, because she was living in America with her daughter and never returned to Europe after immigrating in 1907.

It would seem that the latter would be the more likely of the two to be the De Rosa who was killed in Savannah. Yet the boy was listed as being only ten upon arrival, or 11 at the time of the races. Sometimes people claimed their children were much younger to get a cheaper passage to America, however, and birth records did not necessarily exist for anyone. It could be that the boy was significantly older, though he would still have to be in his teens to have passed for a ten-year-old at Ellis Island. The ancestors of the boy from Marseilles revealed that their Marius had disappeared from New York late in his teens, but not much else was known about him. The mystery remains unsolved.

Race Report

The International Light Car Race was set to begin Wednesday, November 25, at 11 a.m. George Robertson had arrived to race the Gregoire, but the car had not been prepared to his satisfaction. He refused to race and the car was withdrawn. Another car, the American Aristocrat that was supposed to be driven by Manville, had never made it to Savannah for the race. The first hurdle to starting the event was the thick fog that had settled around the course, which was surrounded by the salt marshes, creeks and rivers of the southeastern side of Savannah. By 10:45 a.m., the sun had burned off most of the fog. The famous race starter Fred Wagner got the race underway. With his watch in hand, he counted off the 30-second intervals between drivers; he would "count loudly the last ten seconds backwards, ending with a 'go,' giving each driver in turn a shove on the back."[19]

The race was on. Wagner sent the drivers off in the following order: Connors in the S.P.O.; Hilliard in the Lancia; Bergdoll in a Chalmers-Detroit; Cameron in the Cameron Car; Poole in the Isotta; Burman in a Buick; See in a Maxwell; Lorimer in a Chalmers-Detroit; Hearne in a Buick; Costello in a Maxwell; Burns in a Chalmers-Detroit; Easter in a Buick; Munweiler (or Muntwyler) in a Maxwell; Jeffers in a Buick; and Kelsey in a Maxwell.

The S.P.O. had been completely rebuilt in three days, to the point that it could be used as an automobile hearse for its original riding mechanic, Marius De Rosa. The car made its appearance with mechanic and driver Herbert Connors at the starting line. The crowd, still very moved by the tragic passing of the young mechanic, erupted in tearful cheers to see the car raced in De Rosa's honor. Connors had done the best he could with the car, but there was no way to replace all of the parts needed for the rebuild with exact replicas on such short notice. He did his best in Bryson's shop, but some parts were not ideal. The rear tires, for example, had a wider tread than the front, affecting the handling significantly. Connors' first lap was uneventful and completed in 19 minutes and 17 seconds. However, Connors knew he was in for a difficult race by lap 2 when engine problems developed. After stopping and making repairs, his lap time was 113 minutes and 48 seconds.[20]

William Hilliard in the Lancia, outfitted with Continental tires, made excellent time on the first lap, crossing the finish line first in 11 minutes and 43 seconds. Hilliard drove a consistently fast, yet conservative race, clocking in around the 11-minute mark on almost every lap. The Chalmers-Detroit driven by William Burns and owned by T.A. Bryson had taken lucky number 13 for the car. Burns had barely started to see what he could do with the car when he reached the second banked turn on White Bluff Road, approximately four miles into his first lap. His front tires, with no tread, could not grip the banked road and the car skidded and crashed into a tree. The riding mechanic was thrown clear and suffered only mild injuries, but Burns stayed in the car as it made the impact. His mouth smashed into the steering wheel, knocking out his top front four teeth, and he suffered other minor injuries. The local man T.A. Bryson's Chalmers-Detroit was first out of the race, much to the crowd's disappointment.[21]

"Wild" Bob Burman, driving the Buick, made a superb first lap, moving through the field from sixth place to third and having the fastest lap at 10 minutes and 58 seconds. The frame of the Buick was underslung and one of the issues that Burman had to contend with throughout the race was that the springs were too light.[22] Hilliard, who had passed Connors in the S.P.O. on lap 1, was closely followed by Bergoll's Chalmers-Detroit. Burman nipped at Bergdoll's heels, intent on challenging the Chalmers-Detroit and Lancia for the lead and taking it by the end of lap 1. Burman would fight to hold this lead for the first ten laps of the race, but the springs began to give him trouble shortly thereafter; by the thirteenth lap, the rear springs had broken. The Buick mechanics had prepared for this problem by attaching two chains and two straps to the rear end prior to the start of the race. This worked for a time, until the connecting rod on the right rear broke and caused the gas tank to come loose. As Burman came into his pit for the repair, a part he needed could not be found and the confusion cost the team eight precious minutes. Even after the gas tank and other repairs were made, the tank came loose again and the riding mechanic had to hold it in place as Burman drove. The required repair slowed Burman down and took him out of contention.[23]

Earl Jeffers, driving a Buick, was out of the race by lap 4 when he suffered a broken steering knuckle. Meanwhile, Forrest Cameron, who had the fastest time during practice and had been the fastest car to pull away at his start, was cruising in fourth position by the fourth lap in the ultra-light Cameron Car. He was making excellent times on his laps, coming in at barely over 11 minutes for three laps. He continued trying to challenge the drivers ahead of him. On the fifth lap when he had just come past the grandstand, it suddenly became apparent that something had gone wrong. Cameron pulled the car into the pits and stopped, remaining in that spot for the rest of the race. He had burned out the clutch and bent the crankshaft, which put him out of the race.[24]

The day became warmer, with skies turning completely blue. Burman had stopped to reattach the gas tank when Hilliard passed and took the lead in the Lancia. Hilliard stopped once for two cans of lubricating oil. His riding mechanic pumped the oil by hand into the motor, while Burman tried his best to get back into the lead. However, he could not overcome the challenge posed by the Lancia. Burman also had his hands full trying to hold off Lorimar in the Chalmers-Detroit, who passed him at lap 14 and held the position for three laps. By lap 17, Burman had wrestled the Buick back ahead of Lorimar, determined to continue his challenge for the lead.[25]

Hearne did an excellent job of keeping his Buick at the front of the field for quite some time, maintaining third position for a while and fighting off Lorimar's Chalmers-Detroit. Despite being an amateur racer, he drove a very consistent race. He drove side by side with Lorimar at one point, thrilling the crowd with their heated battle for position. Costello and Munweiler in their Maxwells ran closer to the back in eighth and ninth positions as the race approached its finale. Munweiler had lost his front left tire on lap 12, but stopped, put it back on, and then continued his race, making up some of the lost time quickly. Costello had also suffered a puncture while running with the Ajax tires. He set a record for the Maxwells, running the fastest lap at 12 minutes and 2 seconds on lap 5.[26]

Poole in the Isotta and See and Kelsey in the Maxwells maintained their positions in the middle of the pack for most of the race. Poole had driven with his usual conservative style, stopping only once at lap 14 for fuel. See made only one stop on lap 15 to take on oil. Bergdoll was out of the race on lap 11 when he snapped a piston ring after a valve fell into one of the cylinders. He had been in Savannah for less than 24 hours and had no time to practice on the course before race day.[27]

Easter in the Buick had what was the most serious accident of the race. The car had a broken axle by lap 14 and crashed close to the grandstand at Waters and Estill while taking the turn. After the right rear tire flew off, the car skidded around the corner and began to flip, rolling several times in full view of the crowd. Easter and his mechanic Frank Thomas were thrown clear, landing very close to two doctors positioned as medics for the race. Both the driver and the mechanic were seriously injured.[28]

The race ended with a comfortable lead of over 6 minutes for Bill Hilliard in the Lancia Lampo, with a final time of 3 hours, 43 minutes and 33 seconds. Bob Burman placed second in the Buick in 3 hours, 49 minutes and 45 seconds. Lorimer landed the third spot on the podium in his Chalmers-Detroit with a time of 3 hours, 53 minutes and 55 seconds. Behind the leaders were newcomer Eddie Hearne, placing fourth in his Buick and finishing in an impressive 3 hours, 58 minutes and 55 seconds. Al Poole placed fifth in the Isotta in 4 hours, 11 minutes and 22 seconds. Two Maxwells filled in sixth and seventh, with See finishing in 4 hours 18 minutes and 38 seconds and Kelsey finishing in 4 hours, 20 minutes and 44 seconds. Costello, Munweiler and Connors in the S.P.O. were still running when the race was called.[29] Italy had won the day with its car, but with a talented American in the driver's seat—and spectators from all over the United States and Europe were thrilled with the results of the first International Light Car Race in America.

8

American Grand Prize of 1908

Cars of 1908 American Grand Prize

THE 1908 GRAND PRIX RENAULTS

The 1908 Renaults entered in the American Grand Prize were 105 horsepower at 1,800 rpm, 737-cubic-inch diameter with 12.07-liter models. The engine was four cast iron cylinders on two blocks. The cars had high-tension Simms-Bosch magnetos. The bore and stroke were 155 × 160 mm and the engine utilized thermo-syphon cooling. Hand-operated drum brakes were attached to the rear wheels with a single band on the transmission which was operated by foot. The wheels used were Michelin wooden artillery tires with detachable rims. The car weighed in at 990 kg and had a top speed of approximately 100 mph. The Renault drivers at Savannah in 1908 were Louis Strang and Ferenc Szisz.[1]

THE 1908 FIATS

Three 1908 Fiat S61 Corsa cars competed in Savannah's American Grand Prize race. The name Fiat stands for Fabbrica Italiana Automobili Torino, which translates to mean "Italian Automobile Manufacturer of Turin." The Corsa was also raced at Targa Florio. The engine was a 12.07-liter, 120-horsepower, 737-cubic-inch diameter model. The top speed for the car was approximately 97 mph. A foot-operated brake worked with the differential gear while a hand brake was located on the rear wheels. It was a four-cylinder engine divided between two blocks. The bore and stroke were 180 × 160 and they were outfitted with Simms-Bosh magnetos. The drivers for 1908 were Louis Wagner, Felice Nazzaro and Ralph De Palma. Louis Wagner was the winner of the race, with third and ninth going to Nazzaro and De Palma, respectively.

THE 1908 BENZ CARS

The 1908 Benz cars driven in Savannah were 150 horsepower, 760-cubic-inch diameter with 12.45-liter displacement. Each car had Siamese cylinder pairs, twin magneto ignition, and overhead V-valves. The water-cooled engine had a bore and stroke of 154.9 × 200 mm. The frame was built out of pressed steel attached in sections. The car also had both hand and foot brakes. The foot brakes were bands that operated on the transmission shaft. The

The Fiat team assembled at a banquet in New York after their 1908 Grand Prize win (courtesy Centro Storico Fiat).

drum brakes, which were controlled by hand, operated in the drive-chain sprockets. The output of the engine was 116 kW. It weighed 1200 kgs and had a top speed of approximately 101 mph. These cars were fielded by Benz of Mannheim for Fritz Erle, Victor Hemery and René Hanriot.[2]

THE 1908 ITALAS

The three Italas entered the Grand Prize with a 737-cubic-inch diameter engine of 12.07-liter displacement. The drive train was fitted onto a steel ladder-style frame. It was a unique car with rear-axle and semi-elliptical leaf springs on the ends of the suspension. The Italas had drum brakes on the rear that were hand operated. The three drivers entered in the Italas were Henri Fournier, Alessandro Cagno and Piacenza.[3]

ENGINE SPECIFICATIONS OF 1908 COMPETITORS

- Clément-Bayard: 852-cubic-inch diameter and 13.96 liter
- Buick: 589-cubic-inch diameter and 9.65 liter

- Chadwick-Six: 707-cubic-inch diameter and 11.58 liter
- Acme–6: 645-cubic-inch diameter and 10.57 liter
- Lozier: 545-cubic-inch diameter and 8.93 liter
- National–6: 589-cubic-inch diameter and 9.65 liter
- Simplex: 672-cubic-inch diameter and 11.01 liter
- De Dietrich: 829-cubic-inch diameter and 13.58 liter

The Million-Dollar Race

The 1908 Savannah event was the very first Grand Prix race in America, so named using the English word "Prize" to substitute for the French term "Prix."[4] Excitement for the first Grand Prix race was apparent all over the United States—newspapers in nearly every state were talking about the event. Many, it seemed, followed the European races very closely. And why not? The society pages were full of news of balls and luncheons attended by the crème de la crème, so why would there be less interest in Willie K. Vanderbilt when he was breaking speed records in France? The people knew the big-name drivers of the French Grand Prix and Coppo Florio such as Felice Nazarro and were aware of his record-breaking 74.25 mph average at the latter event. They knew Henri Fournier, who had broken land speed records in America, and Victor Hemery, renowned for being a demon behind the wheel but a bit testy off the track at times. They knew Wagner, Duray, Mulford and, of course, Louis Strang, who had won in Savannah only nine months earlier. Americans were familiar with the powerful machines of Fiat, Benz, Mercedes and the famous Renaults. They were crazy for the new American cars, the Buicks in particular. Well-informed newspaper coverage was in the stars, from the *Ocala Evening Star* in Florida to the *Hawaiian Star*. Everyone in America was reading about the little city of Savannah, the already legendary 25-mile state-of-the-art course, the heroic deeds of the famous racers, and the intellectual exploits of the driver-inventors, all of whom would risk life and limb to go very, very fast.

Bean counters got in on the act as well, adding up the many costs of putting on an international Grand Prix race of this size and stature. They came up with a total cost of over $1 million to stage the event. This included the cost of manufacturing the race cars, which could be $25,000 or more with a field of 20; the retail value of the vehicles alone was half a million dollars. On top of that, drivers were paid anywhere from $500 to $7,000 each, with three mechanics per driver earning about half the driver's wage each. American drivers made less in large part because they did not have to make the long overseas trip, which could take many weeks. Their salaries could hit a top price of $5,000. In addition, the course expansion from the March races cost $35,000—a big savings due to the use of convict labor. It must be mentioned the convicts were treated so well that they were even escorted to track to watch the races as a reward for their hard work, and their work was much easier than some of the jobs they would normally have undertaken while imprisoned. The Automobile Club of America spent $20,000 to organize the race, including creating the beautiful gold cup ($5,000) and the prize money (a total of $8,000).[5] Outside prizes were offered by manufacturers, with Continental Tires offering $4,500 in prizes, Bosch Magneto offering $2,000 and Michelin offering $2,000 for the first place finisher, $1,000 for second place and $500 for third.[6]

People could drive to the race from cities such as New York on what was a new route

The DeSoto Hotel located on Liberty Street and Bull Street in Savannah served as race headquarters from 1908 to 1911, and in prior years as headquarters to the bicycle racing organizations. Many race car owners stayed at the posh hotel during the races. It was chosen as headquarters due to its prominence as the premier location where many important decisions affecting Savannah were made.

designed by the White Company, which prepared maps for the event. This map gave the distances from all of the major cities that route passed through, including Philadelphia, Gettysburg, Hagerstown, Winchester, Staunton, Roanoke, Winston-Salem, Charlotte, Anderson, Atlanta, and Macon, with a final arrival in Savannah. The route kept drivers away from the coastal areas in locations where the roads were not well updated, opting instead to keep them on the Macadam roads as much as possible. These were more widely available between New York and Charlotte and then picked up again around Atlanta and Savannah.[7]

People began to flood into the city several weeks before the race to catch a glimpse of the practices. Downtown, in what is now the largest and most famous historic district in America, people gathered day and night. The cars would drive in and park on Bull Street, which had been newly paved with Trinidad Lake asphalt. There was a palpable buzz along Bull and Broughton Streets that led all the way up to the automobile garages, which were about half a mile from the heart of the city. Bull Street "is an interesting sight these days," wrote *The New York Times* on November 18, "with the honk-honk and chug-chug of the numerous autos, while the people gaze with admiration upon the little cars and look with awe upon the big speed marvels, capable of doing 120 miles per hour. As each succeeding day passes away the interest gets more intense, if such a thing is possible, and by the time the race starts it is doubtful there will be a man, woman or child in Savannah who will not go out to the races."[8]

Entries: Additions and Withdrawals

The field of automobiles for the 1908 Grand Prize race was up to 24 entrants by early November when the entry deadline closed. The Matheson and the B.L.M. had pulled out by November, unable to prepare in time for the race. That left the following cars: a 90-Simplex driven by Joseph Morton Seymour, and a National, which were late to enter. Italy was well represented in the international competition by three 12-liter Fiats driven by Louis Wagner, Ralph De Palma and Felice Nazzaro, and three Italas driven by Henri Fournier, Alessandro Cagno and Giovanni Piacenza. For Germany, Benz was entering three Benz 760s to be driven by Victor Hemery, Fritz Erle and René Hanriot (who substituted for Poege); however, the third did not race. Mercedes anticipated providing a car to be driven by Salzer, but this car also did not enter the race in the end. France had a solid stable of cars and drivers, including two Clément-Bayards driven by Lucien Hautvast and Victor Rigal, an 829 Lorraine-Dietrich driven by Arthur Duray, and two 737-Renaults driven by Ferenc Szisz and Louis Strang. Last and perhaps most beloved to the spectators were the American cars: a Locomotive driven by Harry Grant was withdrawn before the race, leaving Len Zengle and Cyrus Patscke driving the Acme-Sixes, Ralph Mulford (filling in for the injured Harry Michener) in the 544 Lozier, Bob Burman in an underslung Buick–50, Willie Haupt in a Chadwick–6, Hugh Harding in the National–6 and Seymour in the Simplex.[9] After ten days of practice, the drivers were all ready for the big race.

Felice Nazzaro, the Italian driver who was also known as "the Speed King," was a beloved figure in Savannah. He is seen here with his riding mechanic.

Mercer Camp on LaRoche Avenue in 1908 with the number 12 Itala of Alessandro Cagno and the number 5 Chadwick–6 of Willie Haupt being inspected (courtesy Robyn Quattlebaum).

THE RACE COURSE

The original 17-mile course built for the March 1908 races was lengthened for the Grand Prize race to a distance of 25.13 miles with 30 curves professionally banked, including an S-turn and a hairpin at Thunderbolt that was nicknamed "the Appendix" and would be used only for this race. It was called the fastest course in the world by many in the media and racing industry. The curves would test the driver's skill to the maximum level. On the straightaways a driver could attain speeds of up to 100 mph. The design was methodical and astute, ensuring that there were no parts of the course crossing a railroad track, which was a major problem for automobiles at that time. The main grandstand, on what is now Victory Drive and was known then as Estill, seated up to 16,000 people.[10] However, there were numerous other places to watch the race, from home-made grandstands built in fields, in front of farms, and an orphanage, to watching from automobiles in fields and parks lining the track.

RACE REPORT

As far away as Arizona, Savannah's Grand Prize race was being called "The Greatest Event of the Kind the World Has Ever Seen."[11] Lozier had built a special car to enter the race, which provided a great deal of curiosity to the spectators, drivers and other car manufacturers. The team had Smilin' Ralph Mulford driving for them, fresh off his big win at Brighton Beach. H.A. Lozier attended the races himself and watched his cars from the comfort of a wooden kitchen chair at the judges stand, his hat pulled down over his eyes just

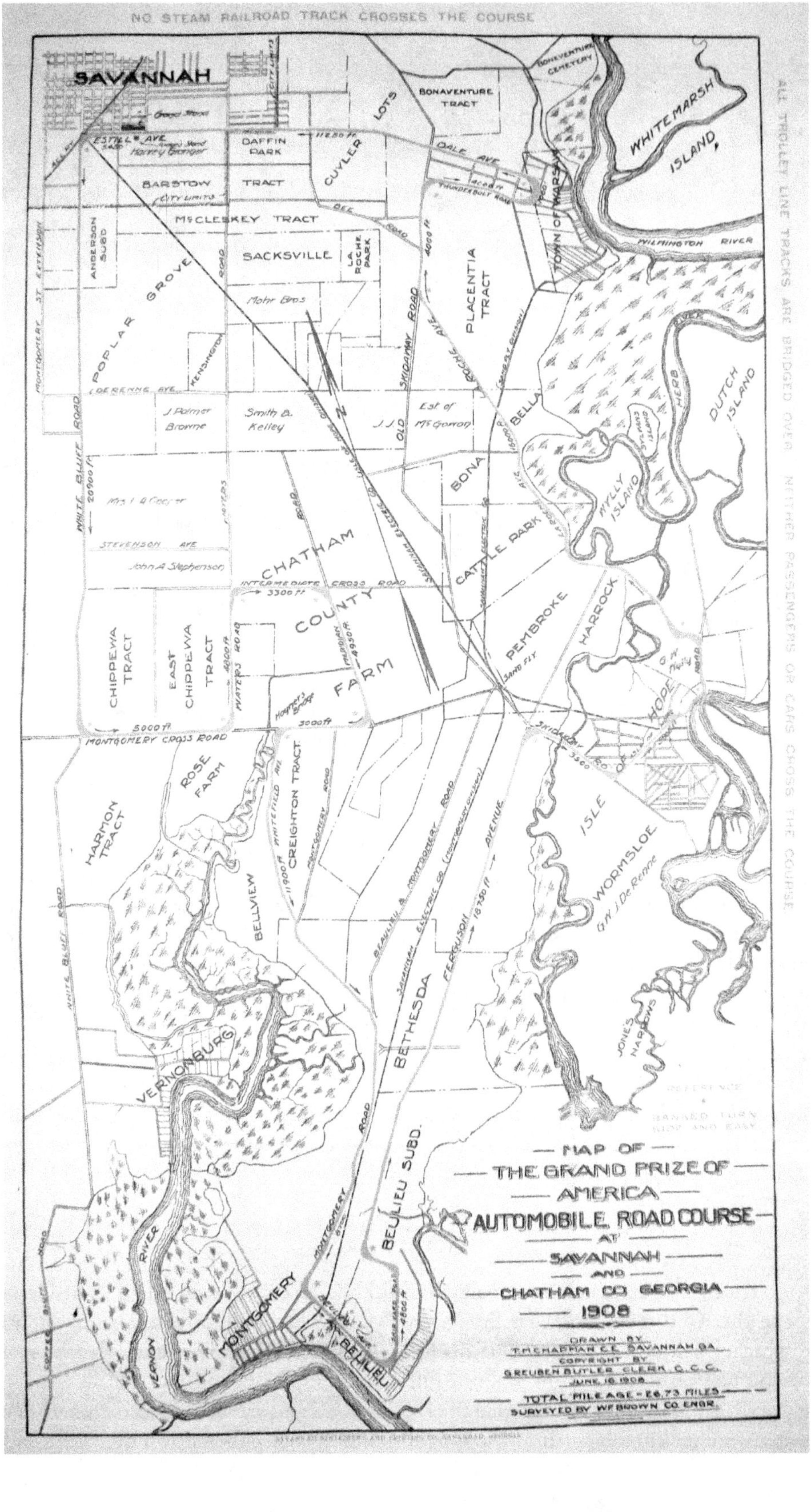
NO STEAM RAILROAD TRACK CROSSES THE COURSE
ALL TROLLEY LINE TRACKS ARE BRIDGED OVER. NEITHER PASSENGERS OR CARS CROSS THE COURSE.
SAVANNAH
BONAVENTURE CEMETERY
BONAVENTURE TRACT
WHITEMARSH ISLAND
CUYLER LOTS
DAFFIN PARK
BARSTOW
TRACT
DALE AVE
THUNDERBOLT ROAD
TOWN OF WARSAW
WILMINGTON RIVER
McCLESKEY TRACT
SACKSVILLE
LA ROCHE PARK
ANDERSON SUBD
POPLAR GROVE
Mohr Bros
PLACENTIA TRACT
SKIDAWAY ROAD
LA ROCHE AVE
HERB RIVER
DUTCH ISLAND
DERENNE AVE
KENSINGTON
J. Palmer Browne
Smith & Kelley
Est of McGorron
BONA BELLA
MONTGOMERY ST EXTENSION
WHITE BLUFF ROAD
Mrs. L. A Cooper
STEVENSON AVE
John A Stephenson
CHATHAM COUNTY FARM
INTERMEDIATE CROSS ROAD
CATTLE PARK
WYLLY ISLAND
PEMBROKE
HARROCK
HOPE
G.W. Wylly
SANDFLY
CHIPPEWA TRACT
EAST CHIPPEWA TRACT
WATERS ROAD
MONTGOMERY CROSS ROAD
SKIDAWAY
ROSE FARM
CREIGHTON TRACT
WHITEFIELD AVE
HARMON TRACT
BELLVIEW
BEULIEU & MONTGOMERY ROAD
FERGUSON AVENUE
ISLE WORMSLOE
G.W. J. De Renne
JONE'S NARROWS
BETHESDA
VERNONBURG
BEULIEU SUBD.
VERNON RIVER
MONTGOMERY
BEULIEU
MAP OF
THE GRAND PRIZE OF
AMERICA
AUTOMOBILE ROAD COURSE
AT
SAVANNAH
AND
CHATHAM CO. GEORGIA
1908
DRAWN BY
T.M. CHAPMAN C.E. SAVANNAH GA.
COPYRIGHT BY
GREUBEN BUTLER CLERK C.C.C.
JUNE 16 1908
TOTAL MILEAGE - 26.73 MILES
SURVEYED BY W.F. BROWN CO. ENGR.

Victor Hemery (on right) in his Benz (courtesy Mercedes-Benz Classic Archives).

enough to keep off the sun and hide his expression as race day dawned. Another heavy fog had settled into the Low Country, delaying the start of the race, which was set to begin at 9 a.m. However, as with the International Light Car Race, the fog lifted once the sun began to burn it off and within 45 minutes it was clear enough to go racing.[12]

As the big cars arrived at the pits, large groups of people who had been admitted to the course before the race started gathered around the cars. The delay due to the foggy mist that had settled around the area gave a little extra time to admire the contestants. The mechanics and staff of all the teams were particularly attracted to the Fiats, Benzes, and Renaults, making close inspections of the cars before heading back to their own pits. Finally, the groups were cleared and the cars prepared for the race start.

Victor Rigal was the first one sent off on the track by Fred Wagner. He drove the big blue number 1 Clément-Bayard car, which took off with a snarl, leaving a trail of smoke behind it as the machine headed for the first turn down White Bluff. Next off was Mulford in the number 2 Lozier. The American car builders were impressed with the machine and the driver was becoming a highly coveted name in motorsports. The crowd loved the white Loziers. Mulford's first trip to the showdown in Savannah would not be his last. He would become one of the most well-known drivers of all time and raced all three years in the city.

Next off was Joe Seymour bearing the number 3 on his Simplex. "Wild" Bob Burman was number 4 in the wildly popular Buick, and Willie Haupt had number 5 in the Chadwick–6 car. Speculation was rampant that the Chadwick would win the race over any of the American cars and Haupt, the first man to race a supercharged car, was assumed to be the

Opposite: **Survey map of the 1908 Grand Prize course (courtesy John and Ginger Duncan).**

Louis Strang in Renault number 16 (with his mechanic) during the 1908 American Grand Prize race in Savannah. Strang finished sixth with an average speed of 59.77 mph (courtesy Robyn Quattlebaum).

Fiat taking a corner during the 1908 American Grand Prize Race (courtesy Centro Storico Fiat).

man who could do it. After the cluster of Americans were sent off behind Rigal, Felice Nazzaro was sent off in the big red number 6 Fiat.[13] The Speed King was another of the drivers who topped the list of potential winners. Nazzaro had been winning races since 1901. On top of that, the odds were placed very high on this driver who had won all three of the major European races only one year before: the Targo Florio, Kaiser Preis and French Grand Prix. Nazzaro had been on the cover of newspapers and magazines around the world throughout 1907 and 1908, becoming known as the Speed King due to his successes.

Behind Nazzaro came Len Zengle in the number 7 Acme, followed by Victor Hemery, the Surly One, in his number 8 Benz. The skies continued to clear as the morning wore on. Arthur Duray was next in his De Dietrich bearing number 9, with Ferenc Szisz in the number 10 Renault and Hugh Harding driving the number 11 National behind him. Alessandro Cagno shot down the track in an Itala with number 12 emblazoned on it, followed by Lucien Hautvast in the other Clément-Bayard bearing the lucky number 13. Louis Wagner was in the number 14 Fiat and René Hanriot in Benz number 15. Little did Hanriot know that he would have what may be the most infamous moment in motorsports, and one that has never been repeated. Behind Hanriot was Savannah's former champion, Louis Strang, piloting the number 16 Renault car. Henri Fournier was in the number 17 Itala and the young newcomer, Ralph De Palma, soon to be one of the greats of the motorsports world, was in the number 18 Fiat. Fritz Erle followed De Palma in Benz number 19 and Giovanni Piacenza started last in the number 20 Itala.[14]

The 400-mile race was on. Soon after Piacenza began his race, the sound of the bugle reverberated in the grandstands to announce the first car was coming onto the home stretch. Ralph Mulford came into sight and the crowd erupted into wild cheers to see an American driver and car first. H.A. Lozier could not contain his excitement and jumped up from his perch to watch his car pass the stands first. However, people looked anxious as Mulford rounded the first corner onto White Bluff and his engine began backfiring and sputtering as if it might quit. Fortunately, he accelerated quickly and the engine was soon humming again.[15]

As the cars began hurtling past, one after the other, it would be another American who would capture the crowd's interest. Ralph De Palma, one of the youngest drivers in the race, was making the best lap times of all the cars in his Fiat after the first lap. He had an average speed of 69.8 mph and set a new course record of 21 minutes and 36 seconds.[16] He repeated his excellent performance on the second lap, raising some eyebrows in the process. However, like many young drivers, De Palma was not quite at the point yet where he could discern how hard to push the car. He was excellent at passing and put on an amazing show, taking on one conservative driver after another and flying past them with ease. But he was too inexperienced to know that the great speeds he was accomplishing would wear his tires out faster, and cause him lubrication problems. Once he realized he had these troubles, De Palma slowed considerably, which would cost him precious time.[17]

Wagner was in second place behind De Palma and watched his young teammate pushing the Fiat hard. He knew it would be only a matter of time before De Palma was forced to back off if he was to make it to the end. Hanriot was behind the two drivers in the Benz, holding third place easily and getting to know the turns more intimately with each pass. He bided his time, waiting to make his move. Meanwhile, Szisz had the Renault humming along in fourth, while Erle pulled himself up from a position of second from last to fifth in the first lap.

The top five drivers in the field remained in the same position on the second lap, but things were heating up behind them as the drivers scrambled to move up. Cagno drove a magnificent lap, taking the turns at the highest speed the Itala could manage. He brought himself from tenth to sixth place, passing the Speed King himself, Nazzaro, who had to settle for seventh. Hemery was already having problems with the Benz and fell from eighth to 12th place.

By lap 3, Burman was experiencing serious car trouble. He was forced to pull off near the county farm, approximately three miles from the starting line, when the engine gave up. Hanriot, also on lap 3, was about to wrestle the lead from De Palma. Haupt was beginning to have problems with the Chadwick and was in tenth place. Zengle was also struggling in the Acme, which was way back in 19th. Nazzaro and Wagner set a scorching pace early in the race, with both drivers passing Szisz in the Renault on lap 4 and cruising into third and fourth place, respectively. Seymour was running in 12th place in the Simplex. Meanwhile Hanriot pushed the Benz to its limits without causing too much wear on the tires. For the next four laps, his hard driving and strategy paid off and Hanriot remained in the lead until lap 8, when he pitted.

Haupt was out of the race on lap 5 with a burned-out bearing. Piacenza crashed one of the Italas on the Isle of Hope, ending his race on lap 6. The car count began to drop steadily with two more drivers out on lap 7: Zengle, who had been struggling with some unknown engine problem which turned out to be the front spring, and Szisz, whose front axle disintegrated on Ferguson. Things appeared to improve over the next three laps of the race until lap 11, when two cars went out. The Europeans were the Kings of the Grand Prix again for the next five laps when Fiats and Benzs blasted into the first four positions for several laps, jockeying among themselves to be top dog.

Felice Nazzaro driving the Fiat number 6 car in the 1908 Grand Prize race in Savannah. Nazarro finished in third place with an average speed of 63.96 mph.

Wagner took the lead on lap 7. He raced neck-and-neck with Nazzaro but then had what appeared to be a near mechanical disaster in the pits. As soon as the car stopped, Wagner's mechanic, Ferro, was out of the car and looking down through the cranks and wheels as the cylinders exploded in front of the breathless crowd. Smoky fumes surrounded Ferro as he gazed beneath the car and made some adjustments. Wagner was replenishing gasoline while Ferro worked. The supply crews had set out two bottles of champagne as they worked and as the men finished, each grabbed a bottle of champagne and drained it to the bottom. The crowd let out a boisterous cheer.[18]

Erle was going approximately 90 mph and putting serious heat on Nazzaro from behind in lap 10, but on lap 11 something very bizarre happened. The heavy, nonskid, steel-studded tread suddenly detached from Erle's front right tire. It flew into the air with an enormous force, striking Erle in the back of the head as he attempted to duck from the flying rubber. His head was driven down into the steering wheel and he was stunned almost to the point of being unconscious. He held the car while in this state for a good quarter of a mile down White Bluff, but then his grip on the wheel began to loosen and he drove off the course and rolled the car. Both the mechanic Muller and Erle were thrown from the vehicle before it crashed into a stone mile marker. Muller was okay, but Erle suffered a mild concussion, dislocated jaw, broken nose and several fractured face bones.[19] He was still conscious when the medics arrived and he walked to their waiting vehicle for a short distance. He and his mechanic were treated at the Savannah Hospital for their injuries.

Cagno, who had worked his way up to fifth by lap 9, was suddenly out on lap 11 with a broken rear spring. Duray, Seymour and Mulford had all been losing time due to various mechanical problems that had them in and out of the pits for repairs throughout the race. The Fiat and Benz crews were impressing the crowds, who stood to applaud them when the cars pitted and rapidly changed tires and replenished fluids. By lap 10, the three race leaders were seesawing back and forth for position. Hemery was in first at the beginning of the epic battle, Wagner in second and Nazzaro in third.

Hemery and Wagner changed positions on lap 11, with Nazzaro behind the race leaders. By lap 12, Nazzaro had gained first over the other two, who battled to get back to the front. From lap 12 to lap 15, it looked like Nazzaro was going to win it with Hemery in second and Wagner in third place. But suddenly, on the final lap, everything changed. First, Nazzaro lost a tire halfway around the course on Montgomery. The stop to put it back on cost him the race as first Hemery and then Wagner screamed past him. Nazzaro worked quickly enough to keep his lead on the fourth-place car of René Hanriot, but the battle for first was left between Victor Hemery and Louis Wagner: Benz versus Fiat!

Hemery's Benz crossed the finish line first, with the driver's fist in the air. The crowd went wild, thinking he had won. The media began sending international wires proclaiming the win for Benz. But it was premature because of the intervals of time over which the cars had started. As Wagner crossed the line behind Hemery, his time was checked. He was 56 seconds faster overall than the Benz. With Nazzaro finishing in third and Hemery in second, Louis Wagner and the big red Fiat had won the first Grand Prix in America: the Grand Prize of the Automobile Club of America.[20] The driver would take home approximately $12,000, of which $4,000 was paid by the Automobile Club of America as the purse, $2,000 came from Michelin Tires, and $5,000 came from Fiat, along with automobile parts prizes from Bosch Magneto.[21]

However, the race was not quite over. René Hanriot, pulling up fourth behind Nazzaro, ran out of fuel approximately one mile from the finish line. He coasted along the straightaway

Fiat headquarters located at the corner of Broadway and 57th Street, with a giant two-story banner announcing its win at the American Grand Prize race in Savannah (courtesy Centro Storico Fiat).

approaching the grandstand and the crowd could see something was off by his slow speed. His mechanic pushed the tire to keep them going across the finish line and Hanriot rocked back and forth in an attempt to keep enough momentum going. He was successful in doing so, and was allowed to get more fuel for the car to return to the pits. But Hanriot decided he did not want to go the 25 miles around the course back to camp; he wanted to join the celebrations back at the finish line. The soldiers lining the track were ordered to keep the track clear until all the cars came in safely. Hanriot was, however, determined to drive his car in reverse back to the finish line. A group of soldiers ordered him to stop and he slowed, pretending he was going to comply, then darted past them when they lowered their weapons. Hanriot came to Captain Davant of the militia, who also ordered him to stop. The driver tried the same thing, but Davant was having none of it. He emptied his pistol into Hanriot's tires and gas tank. The big race ended with a bang and Hanriot later apologized to the captain and sent him his racing gloves and goggles as a peace offering.[22]

News of the race had been wired to media outlets all over the world, reaching as many as 2 million people. The city of Savannah was now famous for having hosted the first International Light Car Race and the First International Grand Prix in America. Over 100,000 spectators had attended in official seats and there were possibly half that number perched on houses or sitting in fields lining the track to watch. The people of Savannah were ecstatic with how well the race had gone. They were certain that with such a wonderful result, they had earned a permanent place as the top center of automobile racing and the races would forever be a Savannah tradition.

Racing Trouble at the End of 1908

Unbeknownst to the Savannah Automobile Club during the race festivities, the ACA and AAA had signed an agreement to put their differences aside. The two cups would be put under the control of the Motor Cups Holding Company and the ACA had agreed not to hold another Grand Prize race in 1909. They would have an opportunity to review that decision after 18 months. Savannah was disappointed, to say the least. So much money and effort had been put into the races and the inhabitants of the city, as well as the Savannah Automobile Club and City Council, had expected a long profitable relationship to result. Instead, the course sat idle and, with such great roads in the areas south of Savannah, houses began to be built.

To put it delicately, the success of the race in Savannah was something of a concern for the AAA, which was rightfully proud of its race. However, this pride may have been the source of some jealousy directed toward the events held in Savannah after such a successful outcome. The highest-ranking members of the AAA had changed their tune, going from the highest of praises for Savannah after the races held in March 1908 in hopes of winning the Vanderbilt Cup for the city to comments that clearly showed jealousy, ire and disdain. The warning signs of this had begun appearing in July, as soon as talk of the Grand Prix race to be held in Savannah by the ACA surfaced. A.G. Batchelder, on March 26, 1908, stated:

> The members of the Vanderbilt Cup Commission feel decidedly happier than they did a year ago knowing that if Long Island cannot be the scene of the race, there does exist a city called Savannah, in a county called Chatham, containing therein a course which will be well guarded, well prepared and most satisfactory for the great automobile race of the year.[23]

However, as pointed out by several media outlets, including *Automobile Topics*:

> In the endeavor to create a partisan advantage for the American Automobile Association and to pass discredit upon the forthcoming race for the Grand Prize of the Automobile Club of America, which is to be run at Savannah on Thanksgiving Day, certain adherants of the former body are going to great lengths, quite regardless of either the truth or their own expressions in the past.[24]

Batchelder was the person to whom the article refers, quite clearly. The article names a letter that Batchelder wrote to the *Paris Herald* where he praised the Vanderbilt Cup race highly and then disparaged Savannah's Grand Prix, saying it was "a single event near a Southern city, a thousand miles from the metropolis, in a sparsely settled region where foreign automobiles are unknown."[25] Media called out the AAA on the matter and the amount of praise and support for the Savannah race was enormous. The sad part was that the good people of Savannah were blissfully unaware that the eyes of some had turned jealous. Whether or not the city had tried to stage an event as great or better than the Vanderbilt Cup, the races put on in 1908 most certainly caused some AAA members' noses to be out of joint. As remains true today, it is always a little bit dangerous to rouse the ire of the wealthy and the powerful.

Many of the members of the AAA were owners of major industries, such as President Hotchkiss and Willie K. Vanderbilt. Many of them believed strongly in monopolies and lived in an environment that feared and loathed any form of competition. Competition was something to be stamped out and destroyed before it could take hold and grow. Thus the success of Savannah's races in March and November was a very real threat that some felt needed to be removed. In fact, other races were treated similarly, as demonstrated by the choice of the AAA to hold the Vanderbilt Cup race on Long Island on the same day as the Fairmount Park Races, forcing race fans in the region to choose only one event to attend.

The path to oppressing racing in Savannah was to pressure the ACA into cancelling the Grand Prize race. The result that was hoped for would be to allow the Vanderbilt Cup race to flourish uncontested on its own on Long Island. The words of AAA President Hotchkiss expressed this view quite clearly: "Extreme care should be exercised not merely in the granting of sanctions, but also and more in the granting of speed contests. May there be as marked a decrease in sanctioned motor racing next year as there has been this!"(21) The AAA had gone from granting 52 race sanctions in 1907 to 24 in 1908. However, it had increased the number of hill climbs it sanctioned from 5 in 1907 to 20 in 1908. Since hill climbs were no less dangerous than other races, it can certainly be considered that allowing a form of automobile contest that did not compete with the AAA's own events was a motivator of its decisions.[26]

Savannah was not the only city or country facing major threats to the future of motorsports. The Society of Motor Manufacturers and Traders of Great Britain oversaw most automobile clubs and manufacturers, much as the AAA did in America. The group prohibited its members from participating in any organized speed contests, ranging from hill climbs to road races. It also requested that the Royal Automobile Club should prohibit the organizing of such events. Many venues would potentially suffer from this ban, such as tracks like Brooklands. The anti-motorist feeling in England was still strong and this move was rather a political one.[27] However, it would not last—nor would Savannah have seen its last great race.

9

Drivers of the 1910 and 1911 Races

Once the races were established in Savannah, many of the drivers returned again and again, enjoying the track and hospitality they found in the southern city. The races also attracted more drivers and teams who had heard of the huge racing crowds and superior race course. They continued to come to Savannah through 1910 and 1911 to experience it for themselves. The number of American drivers and cars began to increase steadily. The words "racing" and "America" became synonymous in Savannah and the Golden Era of Road Racing hit its peak from 1908 to 1910. The men who raced in Savannah were the fuel of the sport itself.

CHARLES BASLE

1910, 1911 • American Grand Prize

Charles Basle was born January 8, 1885, in Paris, France. He immigrated to the United States when he was 18 years old and worked for Mercedes as a mechanic and driver. One of Basle's earliest achievements came when he broke the mile record in a Mercedes known as the Flying Dutchman II at the Boston meet in 1905.[1] He raced at Ormond Beach the same year and set a new record at that meet as well. In 1908, Basle entered the Motor Parkway Sweepstakes for cars that cost over $4,000. He place fifth in a Knox in the 234.6-mile event. He was teamed up with the colorful Louis Strang for the Brighton Beach 24-hour race in 1908, driving a 45-horsepower Renault. They were forced to retire 17 hours into the race after a connecting rod broke.[2]

In 1909, Basle raced at Brighton Beach again in the Renault. He won the event this year after taking the lead in the eighth hour of the race. Unfortunately, he did not do as well in the ten-mile event in Atlanta in the Renault and was out of the race early.

Basle's good fortune in racing began to wane from 1910 onward. He drove in the American Grand Prize race in Savannah in 1910 in the Pope-Hartford number 6. However, after 19 laps, his piston seized and he was out of the race. He raced at Fairmount Park in a Cole in 1911. He suffered carburetor problems and was out on the seventh lap. He also raced at the first Indianapolis 500 that year, but mechanical issues put him out of that race.

In 1911, Basle returned to Savannah in a Marquette-Buick, number 43. His luck was not much better than in 1910: after only ten laps, the engine failed and he was out of the race.[3] On February 4, 1962, Basle passed away at his home in Los Angeles.

David Loney Bruce-Brown
1910, 1911 • Vanderbilt Cup and American Grand Prize

David Bruce-Brown was born August 13, 1887, in New York to a very wealthy and high-society family. His father, George, died when he was only two years old, leaving his mother, Ruth, alone with Bruce-Brown and his older brother, William. She was very protective of Bruce-Brown, yet very involved in his racing career. Early on, she did not want him to race at all. She preferred for her son to attend college, preferably at an Ivy League school, and she was known to threaten legal action against car owners who hired her son to drive. Bruce-Brown reputedly borrowed money to get to Ormond Beach in Florida to race, where he won and broke several records as well. His mother wired him the money to return after his race. She always displayed great pride in him despite her fear of losing him to the dangerous sport, and could most often be found at the finish line, embracing him over and over, as the crowds smiled in amusement.

Bruce-Brown was a tall, husky, and good-natured man who was well liked by the teams he raced for as well as his fellow drivers. He raced as an amateur from 1907 to 1909, when he is considered to have begun racing professionally. His first amateur race was in 1907 at Empire City in Yonkers, where he captured the attention of Emmanuel Cedrino of Fiat.[4] In 1908, his amateur career continued and he entered several different events. He was in the 1908 single hill climb at New Haven, Connecticut, the Briarcliffe road race, and the Ormond Beach races with Fiat. At Ormond Beach, Bruce-Brown managed to break Willie K. Vanderbilt's record on the one-mile straightaway with a time of 33.6 seconds.

In 1909, Bruce-Brown won in the two-mile straightaway event at Jamaica, Long Island, driving a Benz. The same year, he entered and won in the free-for-all at Giant's Despair in Wilkes-Barre, Pennsylvania, breaking the previous record. Bruce-Brown was very good at the hill climbs and also entered the Shingle hill climb that year, breaking yet another record in 51.8 seconds. He won the Sir Thomas Dewar Cup at Ormond and shortened his own record for one mile, set in 1908 at 33 seconds. He won the ten-mile free-for-all at Daytona Beach in a Benz, ahead of another rising star—Ralph De Palma, who was driving a Fiat.[5]

After placing 13th in the Vanderbilt Cup race of 1909, Bruce-Brown was ready to make the leap to professional racing. He was eager to travel overseas and try to find one of the big European teams to take him on. In late July 1910, Bruce-Brown sailed to Europe to meet with Benz and his future teammate Victor Hemery. He would begin testing the car and return with it for training for the Vanderbilt Cup of Long Island and the American Grand Prize race in Savannah.[6]

Bruce-Brown had scarcely begun his career with Benz when he was entered in the tragedy-laden Vanderbilt Cup race of October 1910. The casualties at this race did not help assure his protective mother that her son was safe, and she was adamant that he should not race again. But Bruce-Brown loved racing and when he found out that his next race, the Grand Prize of the Automobile Club of America, was not canceled after all, but rather moved from Long Island to Savannah, he was overjoyed. Along with the Benz team, he packed up and headed south to begin practice, assuring his mother of the difference in track safety in Savannah, which was written about in all the newspapers. Still nervous, Mrs. Bruce-Brown also headed south to see her son race. She would be in the company of the governor of Georgia when her son won the race, becoming the first American to win a Grand Prix race on U.S. soil. Bruce-Brown was also the first man in racing history to have champagne poured over his head by the second-place winner, his teammate Victor Hemery. The event was

David Bruce-Brown being congratulated after winning the 1910 Grand Prize in Benz number 15, with an average speed of 70.55 mph.

captured by photographers and drawn beautifully by Peter Helck, an early race historian and artist, in a drawing featured in his book *The Checkered Flag*. The piece is called *Over the Head of His Conqueror*.[7]

Bruce-Brown went to great lengths to promote track safety, knowing the difference it made in his racing. He advocated for using the course in Savannah due to its high level of safety and the excellent support organization, writing to the company that did final preparation of oil about the matter: "Gentlemen: After driving my Benz car over the Savannah Automobile Course and winning the International Grand Prize over the course of 17.3 miles in 24 laps accounting to 415 miles covered at an average speed of 70.42 miles per hour, I am free to say without favor or prejudice, that this course is the finest in the world."[8] He firmly believed that Savannah should get future renewals due to conducting the race so well: "If Savannah gets the race next year, I will be in it."[9]

After racing in the inaugural Indianapolis 500 in a Fiat S61, Bruce-Brown set his sights on the Vanderbilt Cup and American Grand Prize. Indeed, he was ready to defend his title and to race in the Vanderbilt Cup, which had been moved to Savannah during the Thanksgiving weekend. Bruce-Brown found himself with a different team in 1911, however. He switched to a 90-horsepower Fiat, teaming up with Victor Hemery, Caleb Bragg, and Louis Wagner. He raced in the Vanderbilt Cup and American Grand Prize in Savannah in a Fiat S74. He failed to finish in the Vanderbilt Cup but had another win in the Grand Prize race.

In January 1912, Bruce-Brown traveled to Europe again, this time to meet with the Fiat people. While in Turin, Italy, he signed to drive for the team at the French Grand Prix.[10] It was his first European professional race and he drove a Fiat S74 at the competition in Dieppe. Leading early on, he won the first day's events, but ultimately finished third and then was disqualified because he refueled at a regular race fueling station.[11] In May 1912, Bruce-Brown drove a Benz at the Santa Monica races, starting in sixth place and finishing on the podium in third. He drove a National at Indy, but was out of the race with a broken valve.

The fall of 1912 brought great tragedy and sadness to the Vanderbilt Cup and Grand Prize families. Bruce-Brown showed up for practice a little late. On October 1, he was ready to try out the Wisconsin course, which he could see was in rough shape from the heavy rains and not a state-of-the-art course like Savannah. Many drivers were disappointed by the change in venue and some perceived a much lower level of organization and management of the events. Initially, the race was planned to be held in Greenfield but squabbles with the locals and greedy speculators who wanted to ensure they could not watch for free ensued. They slowed and then halted the plan, which would have provided a much safer and better prepared venue. The race location was moved to Wauwatosa on rural roads only a month before the events were to take place.

Heavy rains had ruined the already heavily rutted, narrow roads and the race was postponed for one week due to the downpours. Finally things had cleared and on October 1, 1912, Bruce-Brown took two to three practice laps shortly before 1 p.m. His session was to end when starter Fred Wagner signaled him in. Bruce-Brown asked for one more lap but Wagner refused him, after noticing his badly worn tires. "You get back to the garage," Wagner commanded, "and take it easy when you do. If you don't, you'll get an ambulance ride. And don't come on this track tomorrow till you've put on new shoes all around."[12]

Bruce-Brown apparently ignored or did not hear the warning and took off. He was no more than a mile away when one of his tires exploded and the car veered off the course and rolled into a ditch. He was traveling 82.2 mph. Wagner recounted that he received the call for an ambulance. Farmers in the area of the crash were trying to get the two unconscious men to the starting line for help. Bruce-Brown and Anthony Scudelari were rushed to Trinity Hospital, where doctors tried to revive them and operate. Bruce Brown died at 3:15 p.m. His mechanic also did not survive his injuries.

The cause of the accident was blamed on various things, depending on who was reporting. Some claimed the culprit was the narrow course, which was quite rough after days of heavy rain; others said it was Bruce-Brown's worn tires, witnessed not only by starter Fred Wagner, but also by several drivers who saw him practicing and had noted the same. Teammate Caleb Bragg reported that he had a conversation with Bruce-Brown before the event and that his friend had stated that he did not like the course. It was too soft, and narrow at only 12 feet, compared to Savannah's wide course. Because the course had been changed at the last minute, it was not oiled until the day before the Vanderbilt Cup race.

Bragg claimed that before the accident, Bruce-Brown agreed that they would not race on the course. The managers, which Bragg described as "shylocks and punks," ran out of money in the end and did not initially pay the winner his purse. Fred Wagner, the starter, supported these claims of the troubles and stated that he, too, had his paycheck bounce. The management and promoters of the event had also apparently been sued by the course builder for nonpayment. All of these factors came together resulting in a terrible tragedy, with the loss of one of America's first racing heroes, David Bruce-Brown.

Arthur Chevrolet

1910 • American Grand Prize

Arthur Chevrolet was born in La Chaux-de-Fonds, in the Canton of Neuchâtel, Switzerland. He was the brother of Louis and Gaston Chevrolet. Louis, the eldest brother, had spent his youth as a mechanic, and later became a driver for Renault overseas in the European Grand Prix events. He immigrated to Montreal, Quebec, Canada, in 1900. He later moved to New York to work for De Dion-Bouton in America. Once he had established himself, Louis invited brothers Arthur and Gaston to join him. They both agreed and traveled to America, entering the automobile racing and building business with Louis.

Early on, Arthur drove a Buick, like his older brother Louis. In 1910, the brothers had both been entered by Buick to drive in the Vanderbilt Cup and American Grand Prize races. Louis was badly injured when his car left the course on Long Island and struck a car with two women in it. At the American Grand Prize in Savannah a few weeks later, his first lap was brilliant and the Buick crowd went crazy, thinking he would certainly win the race. However, Arthur experienced a great deal of problems with his tires and ended up out of the race after 140 miles with a broken crankshaft.[13] In 1911, he co-founded the Chevrolet Car Company with his brothers Louis and Gaston.

Arthur Chevrolet entered the Indianapolis 500 in 1911, but had similar mechanical problems with the Buick and made it for only 30 laps. He gave Indy another go in 1916 in a Frontenac, which was manufactured by the new company he had formed with brothers Louis and Gaston. However, his luck was no better. He had problems with the magneto this time and completed only 35 laps. This would not be the worst luck he would suffer at Indianapolis, however. In 1920, Arthur would crash so badly he was unable to drive again. Gaston won the race in the brothers' Frontenac, only to be killed racing in California just a few months later. Gaston's death sent Arthur into a terrible depression.

Arthur kept on with his mechanical designs, and started the Chevrolet Brothers Aircraft Company with Louis in 1929. However, this venture was less successful than their past ones. The future would be a very different animal and the brothers would begin designing a new type of race car: sprint cars. However, Arthur's depression continued on and off through his life and became worse during World War II. He retired from the business in 1942 and settled in Slidell, Louisiana, just outside of New Orleans. He did not find happiness there, and his depression continued to worsen until his suicide in 1946.

HARRY H. COBE

1911 • Vanderbilt Cup and American Grand Prize

Harry Cobe was born December 17, 1885. In September 1908, Cobe was teamed up with Ralph Mulford in a 50-horsepower, six-cylinder Lozier for the Brighton Beach 24-hour race. They won the first event and entered a second race in early October, where they placed second.[14]

In 1910, Cobe drove a number 14 Jackson in Division 4C for cars with engines of 301 to 450 cubic inches at the Fairmount Park Motor races. He finished second in 3 hours, 46 minutes and 13.16 seconds. In the spring of 1911, Cobe drove the Jackson number 25 in the International Sweepstakes, where he was praised for his quick mechanical abilities when trouble ensued on the track. Cobe drove the Jackson number 5 in the Vanderbilt Cup race in Savannah in 1911, but the engine blew after just one lap and he was forced to retire. In Savannah's American Grand Prize of 1911, he drove a Marquette-Buick, but suffered the same bad luck, completing only two laps before the steering gear went. He drove the Jackson number 25 and finished tenth at the inaugural Indianapolis 500, and later drove a National at Indy, again finishing 10th. At Old Orchard Beach, Maine, Cobe entered the Jackson Flyer in the 50-mile free-for-all race but came in last place. He died July 24, 1966, in Manchester, New Hampshire.

Joseph Crook Dawson

1910 • American Grand Prize

Joe Dawson was born July 17, 1889, in Odon, Indiana. He raced a yellow Marmon in the Vanderbilt Cup race of 1910 and was in contention for third place for a long period of the race. He then led from lap 10 to lap 13, a distance of 50 miles. A longer than anticipated pit stop and the power of Louis Chevrolet's Buick could not be overcome, however, and Dawson had to settle back until he could make up the time and retake the lead. Lap 18 was something the young driver would never forget. He struck errant spectators who had wandered onto the track. Instead of continuing with his race, he stopped to see if they were hurt. Dawson then proceeded to the pits and stopped again to report the accident to the race officials. Harry Grant took the lead in an Alco due to the time Dawson had lost and Dawson came in at second place.[15]

After the multiple tragedies at Long Island in 1910, the Grand Prize race moved to Savannah. Dawson entered two races in Savannah. First up was the Savannah Challenge, where he raced a Marmon number 16. He won the event in 4 hours and 23 minutes, averaging 62.92 mph in the 276.8-mile race. He then went on to be partnered with Ray Harroun on the 318-cubic-inch Marmon entry in the Grand Prize race.[16] After relieving Harroun, Dawson experienced mechanical difficulties with the car. A broken crankshaft forced their retirement, giving them a sixth-place finish.

Dawson was one of the drivers to race in the first Indy 500 in 1911; he placed fifth in a Marmon. He would race there three times in his career, including in 1912, when he won the event in the Marmon. His last race at Indy was in 1914 when he crashed on lap 45.

Joseph Crook Dawson passed away June 17, 1946, at the age of 56.

Louis Disbrow

1910 • American Grand Prize
1911 • Savannah Challenge, Vanderbilt Cup and American Grand Prize

Louis Disbrow was born September 23, 1876, in New York City. The son of a millionaire, Disbrow was accused, but later acquitted, of strangling and murdering Sarah "Dimpie" Lawrence and a married male acquaintance. The case was sensational and reports of it were carried on the front pages of newspapers all over the country. It was a confusing and odd event, full of admissions and retractions, according to the media of the time. Disbrow's defense claimed there was not even enough evidence to prove the deaths had been by violence and were not a boating accident. For his part, Disbrow openly admitted to arguing with the deceased gentleman, Charles Foster, but claimed there was no wrongdoing in the matter. His defense lawyer, Mr. Miles, called Disbrow "a man so palpably innocent."[17]

Many said that due to the wrongful accusations and damaged reputation he suffered (either rightly or wrongly), Disbrow was affected by the event and set out to make something of himself. He chose motorsports as his way of proving himself to the world and to his wealthy father, who had disowned him.

By 1910, Disbrow was racing in numerous professional races, including the Vanderbilt Cup race on Long Island, where he drove the National number 31. He placed fourth in the race with an average speed of 63.6 mph. A few weeks later, he raced in the American Grand Prize in Savannah. He drove lucky number 13, a Pope-Hartford, but was the second person out of the race with a cracked cylinder. This car number had never had much luck in Savannah, and it was always a source of superstitious gossip. When his engine failed, Disbrow pulled his car off the road to wait among the oaks and palm trees until the race ended.[18]

In 1911, he raced at the first Indianapolis 500 but did not finish the race in a Pope-Hummer. Disbrow was actually more of a road racer, and he entered both of the big cup races the same year, with much better results. Both the Vanderbilt Cup and Grand Prize of the Automobile Club of America races were held in Savannah. In the Vanderbilt Cup race, Disbrow drove Pope-Hummer number 3 and finished sixth. In the Grand Prize, he had an even better race and was near the front of the pack nearly all the way in Pope-Hartford number 42. He was the only driver to drive in three events during the Thanksgiving races in Savannah.

It was a great week for the American drivers, who were finally putting some heavy pressure on the Europeans, with Disbrow being one of those American superstars. Disbrow would not race in the Vanderbilt Cup race again until March 16, 1915, when the competition was held in California on the San Francisco World's Fair course. Disbrow drove Simplex number 12 and finished eighth in the 300-laps, 300-mile race.[19]

After his excellent finishes in Savannah, Disbrow decided to try his luck at the Indianapolis 500 a few more times. He returned in 1912, 1913 and 1914. His best finish at Indy was in 1913, when he started 23rd and finished in eighth place in a Case. Disbrow passed away in Philadelphia on July 9, 1939.

HAROLD FLETCHER GRANT
1910 • American Grand Prize

Harry Grant was born July 10, 1887, in Cambridge, Massachusetts, son of a miner who was killed in Colorado. As a young man he worked for Alco and convinced the company's leadership that they should get into motorsports. Grant began entering races himself in 1907 in Readsville, Massachusetts. Throughout 1908, Grant would enter many hill climbs, winning most of the events. He raced in Lowell at the stock car races. He was very successful, winning most of the local races and keeping the car at the front of the pack in the loner events. Grant was the sole driver of Alco's Bête Noir—the Black Beast.

One of Grant's greatest achievements was driving the Alco-6 in the 1909 and 1910 Vanderbilt Cup races on Long Island. He won both events and set the standard for American drivers. Grant raced in the American Grand Prize in Savannah in 1910 in the Alco number 7. He was less successful in that race; after only 11 laps, he was out with stripped gears. However, he would return to Savannah to take on the fastest automobile course in America in 1911.

Grant raced in the inaugural Indianapolis 500 driving the Alco number 19 but was unable to finish the race. The Vanderbilt Cup was held in the South for the first time in 1911, but Alco had retired from racing in September after the Elgin race. Grant accepted a ride with Lozier, driving car number 1, and was teamed up with Smilin' Ralph Mulford. Lozier won the day, but it was Mulford's victory, not Grant's. Behind the Lozier came two Mercedes cars driven by Ralph DePalma and Spencer Wishart. Grant placed fourth behind them, putting the two Loziers in the top five positions alongside the big Mercedes and championship-winning Fiats.

Grant continued racing through 1915. In 1913, he raced at Elgin in an Isotta and brought the car to fourth place. In 1914 and 1915, he entered the Vanderbilt Cup races, which were held in conjunction with the American Grand Prize races. In 1914, he drove an Isotta, but had a problem with the piston at the start of the race and did not complete a single lap. In 1915, he went to San Francisco for the Vanderbilt Cup race; he drove a Stutz and finished 17th. On February 27, 1915, at the American Grand Prize in San Francisco, his Case number 30 was still running when the race ended. He had completed 102 laps out of the total 104.

Grant's final race entry was a very sad event for the world of American racing. Grant entered the Astor Cup at Sheepshead Bay in 1915. During the September 27 practice, his car caught fire. Although the riding mechanic was able to climb out and get to safety, Grant was not so fortunate. It took time to extricate him from the car and he suffered extensive burns. He was taken to the hospital and died from his injuries ten days later, on October 7, 1915, at the age of 38.[20]

Ray Harroun

1910 • American Grand Prize

Ray Waid Harroun was born January 12, 1879 in Spartansburg, Pennsylvania. As a teenager, Harroun enjoyed the bicycle and was one of few in his town to own a high-wheeler. In 1898, he joined the U.S. Navy when the Spanish–American War broke out. In 1902, Harroun moved to Chicago and was taken on as a chauffeur by William Thorne. In 1906, the infamous William Pickens, who would be mixed up in the Louis Strang–Walter Christie feud, offered Harroun a position as riding mechanic in a Buick. The riding mechanic was responsible for the car, the needs of the driver, and taking the wheel or shifting gears on occasion.[21]

In 1908, Harroun became a mechanic for Marmon and was able to deepen his natural mechanical talents. Harroun, who was known as "the King of the Speedway Drivers," won the first Indy 500 and its $14,000 purse. It was a controversial win, where Ralph Mulford believed he had won the race, only to come to the winner's circle and find Harroun being congratulated.

The year 1910 was busier for Harroun. He raced at Fairmount Park in the Marmon number 11. He placed fourth in the Division C cars. Harroun later drove in his only Grand Prix race that year. He would be teamed up with Joe Dawson to drive the 381-Marmon in the Grand Prix race at Savannah—driving 14 laps before Dawson took over. They finished in sixth place after a cylinder cracked. Harroun passed away on January 19, 1968.

Joe Horan

1910 • American Grand Prize

Joseph Horan was born in 1881 in Chicago. He had a short career in racing, lasting just three years. Most of his career was spent as the riding mechanic for Ralph Mulford, but he did get a few rides as the primary driver himself. In 1910, Horan broke the 250-mile speedway record at Atlanta on November 7. His time was 3 hours, 26 minutes and 15.11 seconds.[22] Just a few days later, he came to Savannah to drive a six-cylinder Lozier, number 12, in the American Grand Prize race in Savannah. He was noted for having a conservative style meant to keep the car in the race for the entire event, rather than having a first priority of pressing race leaders or position. His strategy paid off and he placed fifth.[23]

The year 1911 was an unusual one for Horan. He was slated to drive at Indy, but an accident occurred in practice and Horan suffered a broken leg. The story of his accident was also inaccurately reported. Several media outlets claimed that his crash had involved Gaston Morris, who was driving an Amplex—a car manufactured by Simplex—and that the collision put Horan out of the race. However, according to official race reports, Horan crashed alone and the incident had nothing to do with the Amplex.[24]

Horan raced at the Indy 500 again in 1912, placing eighth in the race. He was ready for another go in the Grand Prize at Milwaukee where he drove a Benz number 42, along with Bergdoll and Burman. He would finish seventh in the race. Horan passed away on September 16, 1932.[25]

WILLIAM "BILLY" PETER KNIPPER

        1910 • Tiedeman Trophy
        1911 • Savannah Challenge

Billy Knipper was born August 9, 1882, in Rochester, New York. His racing debut came on October 13, 1906, when he drove at Rochester in the Dugdale hill climb. He piloted a 60-horsepower Thomas and won the event in 51.8 seconds. Knipper subsequently began entering more hill climbs and races.

In 1909, Knipper entered the Lowell races at Merrimac Valley on September 6, 1909. He raced a month later that year at the Vanderbilt Cup race on Long Island, filling in for an injured Bert Dingley in the number 7 Chalmers-Detroit. Knipper led the pack for much of the race and was averaging a speed of approximately 65 mph. Unfortunately, while he was in first place, his oil line was cut and the Chalmers-Detroit went out of the race on lap 20. It was still a podium finish for the driver, however—he placed third.

In 1910, Knipper entered the Massapequa Sweepstakes. Soon after, on November 12, 1910, Knipper had the best race of his entire career. He raced in the Tiedeman Trophy race, driving the number 44 Lancia. He won the event, averaging a speed of 58.48 mph. Knipper was thrilled to find a place that fed his need for speed and appreciation of the finest course he had ever driven in. He was very eager to return to Savannah in 1911, where he would drive Mercer number 27 in the Savannah Challenge. He entered the Indianapolis 500 in 1911, 1912 and 1913, with his best finish being 11th place in 1913. Billy Knipper passed away on September 7, 1968, in Rochester, New York.

CARL LIMBERG

        1911 • Vanderbilt Cup

Limberg was born July 6, 1883, in Mt. Auburn, Iowa. He began his racing career as a bicycle racer. One of his early teammates was Hardy Downing, with whom he raced at Madison Square Gardens in 1904.[26] Limberg placed third in 994 miles at the Brighton Beach race in 1910, driving a Houpt-Rockwell. His teammates were Stanley Martin and Harry Hartman. He drove the car again in the Vanderbilt Cup race on October 1, only a few weeks later, finishing 18th when the race was flagged.

Limberg drove the number 50 Abbott-Detroit in both the Vanderbilt Cup and American Grand Prix races in Savannah in November 1911. Despite starting well in the Vanderbilt Cup, mechanical troubles slowed Limberg until the 14th race, when the event ended.[27] Driving the same car in the Grand Prize, he was in seventh place when the race was called while he was completing lap 22.

In the inaugural 500-mile Elgin race at the new track near Chicago on June 19, 1915,

Limberg entered a Sunbeam.[28] He raced at Indianapolis, teamed with Harry Grant. At the Astor Cup of 1915, he placed sixth. After the event, his employer, Harry S. Harkness, sent him overseas to France to bring back three Delage cars, which had been driven in the French Grand Prix by Duray, Bablot and Guyot. One of those was the Delage that Limberg would drive in the spring of 1916.

Limberg was hired as manager of the team and one of the drivers of the Harkness's cars. He drove the Delage at the Metropolitan Trophy race at Sheepshead Bay Speedway in New York on May 13, 1916. It was a particularly fast and dangerous race, with a minimum qualifying speed of 90 mph required to enter. Limberg and mechanic Roxie Pollotti had a tire blow out and hit the top rail of the course just before the home stretch at a speed of 104 mph. The car came apart and the men were thrown down a 40-foot embankment at the steeply banked curve. Both men were killed almost instantly at the same race where Limberg's former teammate Harry Grant had been killed the year before.

JOE MATSON

1911 • Vanderbilt Cup

Joseph Matson was born March 6, 1881, in Brighton, Massachusetts. One of Matson's earliest races was in the 1909 Massapequa Sweepstakes at Long Island. He beat some of the greatest drivers of the time, including George Robertson at a race in Indianapolis.[29] In 1910, Matson drove at Ascot in Los Angeles. He also raced the number 31 Corbin in Division C at the Fairmount Park motor race. He had problems in that race with the car's magneto and retired very early, after only three laps.

The number 14 seemed to become a fixture in Matson's life in the next few years. In the 1910 Vanderbilt Cup race on Long Island, he drove a Corbin number 14. In the 1911 Vanderbilt Cup, he drove Fiat number 14. In 1912 at the Indianapolis 500, he finished 14th.

Matson drove a Chalmers-Detroit in many races throughout the country. He had raced for only a few years when he decided to retire from the sport. He went to work as an automobile salesman and real estate agent. Later, Matson became a business owner and opened a Studebaker garage. He fought in World War I as a first lieutenant and remained in the service, becoming a captain in the U.S. Armed Forces. Matson died January 4, 1947, in Winthrop, Massachusetts.[30]

EDWARD H. PARKER

1911 • Vanderbilt Cup

Edward H. Parker raced from 1909 through 1911. The year 1909 was his busiest year in racing. He started in June of that year by racing in two events in Portland in a Studebaker bearing number 7. He placed fourth in the first race and tenth in the second. In September 1909, Parker raced at the Lowell meet in Fiat number 7. He finished third in the event and went on to the Vanderbilt Cup race on Long Island on October 30. Driving Fiat number 14, Parker was again very successful and finished the race in second place.

In 1911, Parker raced at the inaugural Indianapolis 500, as a relief driver for Eddie Hearne. He came to Savannah to race in the Vanderbilt Cup on Thanksgiving weekend 1911 and finished fifth in Fiat number 11.[31]

CYRUS PATSCHKE
1911 • Vanderbilt Cup and American Grand Prize

Cyrus Patschke was born July 6, 1888, in Lebanon, Pennsylvania, the town where he lived most of his life. He began his racing career around 1908, and in 1909 drove at Brighton Beach as the teammate of Ralph Mulford. Together, they won the 24-hour event. The following year, in 1909, Patschke was partnered with Al Poole in a Stearns 6 at Brighton. He successfully defended his championship, winning the race again with an average speed of 52 mph.

In 1908, Patschke was also driving for Acme and piloted car number 11 in the Vanderbilt Cup race on Long Island for the factory team. By 1911, Marmom had hired Patschke to drive in several events for the company. One such event was the 1911 Vanderbilt Cup race in Savannah, where he drove the number 1 car. Patschke filled in as a relief driver for Ray Harroun at the Indianapolis 500 in a yellow Marmon Wasp. He also filled in for Joe Dawson in the Marmon number 32.

Patschke was actually more of a road racer than an oval driver. He did not return to Indy to race again, but instead concentrated on road races. At the Santa Monica races held October 14, 1911, one month before the Vanderbilt Cup race and American Grand Prize, he drove the Marmon. In 1914, Patschke traveled to Sioux City, Iowa, where he placed third on July 14 in a 300-mile event. He retired only a year later in 1915 and lived his days out in his hometown of Lebanon as the owner of a Willys automobile dealership and garage.

After participating in only 11 racing events from 1908 to 1914, Patschke was happy with his results and happy to move on in business. Over his career, he had three wins, a second-place finish, two third-place finishes, a fourth and a sixth. Later in his life, Patschke was inducted into the Pennsylvania Sports Hall of Fame for his accomplishments as a pioneer racer. Cyrus Patschke passed away on May 6, 1951, in Lebanon, Pennsylvania.[32]

WASHINGTON AUGUSTUS ROEBLING II
1910 • Savannah Challenge

"Washy" Roebling was named after his uncle, who was one of the designers of the Brooklyn Bridge. He was born on March 25, 1881, the only son of Charles G. Roebling, who was a co-founder of John A. Roebling and Sons. His mother passed away when Roebling was a child. As he grew up, he developed a strong interest in automobiles and racing.

Roebling worked very closely with the Mercer automobile company for a number of years before embarking on founding the Roebling-Planche automobile firm. One of the earliest Roebling-Planche cars was entered in the Grand Prize race of 1910.[33] It arrived for practice in Savannah several weeks after the Vanderbilt Cup race had been held. During practice, the car's engine blew up and it was unable to be raced in the bigger race. However, Roebling had also brought his Mercer race car to Savannah. He drove it in the Savannah Challenge, placing second in the race.[34]

In 1911, Roebling began planning a significant trip to Europe. He left in January 1912 with his Fiat, planning to return to America in several months. On April 10, 1912, he left Southhampton, England, on a brand-new ship called *Titanic*. When the *Titanic* hit an iceberg and began to evacuate passengers, Roebling assisted several parties of ladies and children in getting into the lifeboats. Sadly, Roebling himself perished on April 15, 1912, when the ship sank. His body was never recovered.

Spencer Wishart

1911 • Vanderbilt Cup and American Grand Prize

Spencer Wishart was born December 3, 1888, in Philadelphia. He raced from 1908 through 1914 in a Mercedes, a Mercer and a Simplex. Wishart came from Wall Street money; his father was financier George Wishart. The younger Wishart joined the ranks of young millionaire drivers, who included David Bruce-Brown, Eddie Hearne and Caleb Bragg.[35] A charismatic young man, Wishart bought himself a Mercedes and began racing even while he had little to no experience. Just a few years later, he would be hired by Mercer in 1912, as one of the drivers to replace the equally wealthy Washington Roebling, Jr., who had died on the *Titanic*.

In the 1909 and 1910 Vanderbilt Cup races on Long Island, Wishart raced his own Mercedes, being flagged after 16 laps the first year and after 60 laps on his second go at the track. He went on to Savannah with the Mercedes to race in the Vanderbilt Cup race, where he finished third behind Ralph De Palma and Ralph Mulford. He also raced in the 1911 American Grand Prize but retired early with mechanical problems. Wishart was an early Indianapolis driver as well. He raced there from 1911 to 1914, with a best finish of second in 1913.

In 1911, while driving at Fairmount Park, Wishart finished second. The win caused controversy, however, when Ralph Mulford lodged a formal complaint that Wishart had completed a lap without a riding mechanic on board. Wishart's answer to the complaint was that he was not aware that the mechanic had not climbed back into the car during the pit stop and by the time he realized he was not in the car, he was unable to return for him because the rules prohibited it.[36] However, when Wishart made an appeal to the AAA, its ruling was to disqualify him, based on his failure to comply with Rules 109 and 110, which required a driver to have a riding mechanic onboard at all times. Ralph Mulford and the Lozier team received first place and the $1,000 prize.

In late 1911, after the Savannah races, it was announced that Wishart had invested $25,000 to start a truck manufacturing business in New York, known as the Wishart-Dayton Auto Truck Company. It was his first business venture.[37]

Wishart raced at Brighton Beach, Columbus, Corona, Elgin, Milwaukee, Santa Monica and Sioux City. His only win was in Columbus, where he drove a Mercer. Sadly, Wishart was killed at the Elgin race on August 22, 1914, when his car hit a rough patch and was launched into the air. Strangely, at least one eyewitness of the event claimed that Wishart did not die from the accident, but instead died behind the wheel, having caused the accident. That account was published in several newspapers but was never confirmed. The mechanic, who had been thrown free, did not provide the same account. The eyewitness also claimed that Wishart's hands had to be pried free from the steering wheel, which was his explanation for why Wishart was not thrown from the car as the riding mechanic was.

Eddie Hearne was very moved by Wishart's death and said, "Nothing unnerved me as the death of Spencer Wishart."[38] Hearne was driving behind Wishart and saw the accident occur. He did not think it would prove to be fatal and was shocked to find out his friend had been killed when the race concluded.

10

Cars and Races of 1910

Cars of the 1910 Savannah Challenge

ENGINE SPECIFICATIONS

Marmon: 298.4-cubic-inch displacement, 4.359 bore, 5.00 stroke (driver: Dawson)
Marmon: 286.3-cubic-inch displacement, 4.5 bore, 4.5 stroke (driver: Heineman)
Mercer: 300.7-cubic-inch displacement, 4.375 bore, 5.00 stroke
Falcar: 280.6-cubic-inch displacement, 4.125 bore, 5.250 stroke

Cars of the 1910 Tiedeman Trophy

ENGINE SPECIFICATIONS

Lancia: 211.1-cubic-inch displacement, 3.94 bore, 4.33 stroke
E-M-F: 226.2-cubic-inch displacement, 4.00 bore, 4.5 stroke
Maxwell: 228.4-cubic-inch displacement, 4.1376 bore, 4.25 stroke (drivers: Costello, Wright)
Maxwell: 241.1-cubic-inch displacement, 4.25 bore, 4.25 stroke (driver: Doorley)
Cole: 201-cubic-inch displacement, 4.00 bore, 4.00 stroke

Cars of the 1910 American Grand Prize

ENGINE SPECIFICATIONS

Benz: 920-cubic-inch displacement, 15.07 liter, 6.1 bore, 7.87 stroke (drivers: Bruce-Brown, Hemery)
Benz: 736-cubic-inch displacement, 12.06 liter, 6.1 bore, 6.3 stroke (driver: Haupt)
Marquette-Buick: 593.7-cubic-inch displacement, 9.73 liter, 6.00 bore, 5.25 stroke
Lozier: 544.6-cubic-inch displacement, 8.92 liter, 5.375 bore, 6.00 stroke (driver: Mulford)
Lozier: 369.6-cubic-inch displacement, 6.05 liter, 4.625 bore, 5.50 stroke (driver: Horan)
Marmon: 318.1-cubic-inch displacement, 5.21 liter, 4.5 bore, 5.00 stroke (driver: Harroun)
Marmon: 381-cubic-inch displacement, 6.25 liter, 4.5 bore, 6.5 stroke (driver: Dawson)

Fiat: 615.5-cubic-inch displacement, 10.09 liter, 5.11 bore, 7.48 stroke
Pope-Hartford: 389.9-cubic-inch displacement, 6.39 liter, 4.75 bore, 5.5 stroke
Alco: 565.4-cubic-inch displacement, 9.24 liter, 4.72 bore, 5.51 stroke

The Savannah Challenge Race

Starter Fred Wagner was on hand for the races in Savannah again. As a clear, beautiful day dawned on November 11, 1910, the two small car classes began their races. The Savannah Challenge, a 276.8-mile race, consisted of 16 laps around the shortened 17.3-mile course. The race started at 10:00 a.m. as planned. This race was considered a small car race for automobiles in the range of 231–300 cubic inches piston displacement.

Wagner sent the drivers off at 30-second intervals. First off was Hughie Hughes, with riding mechanic W. Annesberger, in Falcar number 31. Then Lou Heinemann, with mechanic Harry Patton, was on his way in the Marmon. Third off was the man whom Joe Dawson believed to be his greatest rival in the event: Washington Roebling II, nephew of the Brooklyn Bridge designer. Roebling's mechanic was Felix Geschevanter, and the pair drove Mercer number 33. Washington Roebling was slated to drive the Roebling-Planche Car in the big race, but its engine had blown up during practice for the Grand Prize and Roebling decided to drive in the Savannah Challenge instead. Next, came another Falcar, number 35 driven by Frank Gelnaw and his mechanic, L. Johnson. Then Joe E. Dawson, with Bruce Keene serving as his mechanic, was sent off in Marmon number 36. The final car to be flagged onto the course was W.H. Pierce with his mechanic F. O'Brien in a third Falcar, number 37.[1] An entry by Pullman did not make it to Savannah.

View of the automobile course in 1910.

The crowd waited in breathless anticipation for the first car to make it back around and pass in front of the grandstands, located on Waters Avenue. After passing Hughie Hughes in Falcar number 31, Heinemann, in Marmon number 32, was the first to make it back. The crowd went wild with applause to see the first car of the 1910 races passing in front of them. However, the biggest story of the race had already begun during that first lap, when Dawson was able to bring the Marmon into the lead with the fastest time. He did not expect the power of Frank Gelnaw, who was just behind him in the Falcar number 35. Gelnaw presented a formidable force on the track, pushing the race leader very hard. Roebling fell in behind Gelnaw, dueling for the second-place position.

On lap 8, Roebling pitted for fuel and Gelnaw was able to secure second place. However, his luck did not last very long. On lap 9, Gelnaw broke a tie rod on his car on a turn near the back stretch and the car hit the soft, sandy shoulder of the road. This propelled the car up and over the top of first one bank and then another, before veering back onto the course at Bona Bella, where it stopped in front of the American Locomotive Camp.

The Falcar driven by Pierce also had problems, with a broken axle ending that driver's race on the same lap. However, Pierce was a crowd favorite because as he came past the grandstands, he accelerated to the top speed he could get out of the car, skidded toward the ditch and then pulled out of a near crash.[2]

With two Falcar entries out of the race, only one Falcar, driven by Hughie Hughes, the two Marmons and the Mercer driven by Washington Roebling were still running. The leaders were Dawson and Roebling, who stopped for fuel and lost about one minute. Roebling drove the Mercer hard trying to catch Dawson and was gaining on him lap by lap, making up the

W.H. Pierce driving Falcar number 37 (with his mechanic) during the Savannah Challenge race of 1910 (courtesy Robyn Quattlebaum).

Pres. Battey of the Savannah Auto Club, Chief of Police Austin, Governor Brown of Georgia, Mayor Tiedeman of Savannah, and Joe Dawson and his mechanic Bruce Keane after winning the Savannah Trophy

Joe Dawson, driving Marmon number 36, being congratulated after winning the Savannah Challenge trophy in 1910. His speed averaged 62.92 mph and he finished the 276.8-mile race in 4 hours and 23 minutes.

lost 60 seconds. He was counting on Dawson to have to stop at least once for gas and planned to take the lead from him then. But Dawson did not stop for fuel and had a four-minute lead on Roebling. He continued on until the final lap, with Roebling nipping at his heels all the way. Roebling drove the Mercer hard. On lap 16, only one lap from the end of the race, he lost control and the car skidded for a short distance before smashing into a palm tree near Norwood and LaRoche. With his brakes shot and a damaged gearbox that allowed Roebling to drive with only one speed, he pulled back onto the course and continued toward the finish line, with parts dangling behind the car as he drove.[3]

Dawson, now with a spectacular 12-minute lead, won the race in 4 hours, 23 minutes and 39 seconds. His average speed was 62.92 mph. Roebling rolled into second place, while Hughie Hughes finished third in the Falcar number 31, the only one of the three Falcars remaining in the race. Finishing out the top four cars was Heinemann's Marmon, which was on lap 15 when the race was called.

Dawson was magnanimous, as was usual for him. He praised Savannah's course and the safety provided by the soldiers guarding it. The crowd cheered, as the most avid of racing fans knew he had famously stopped during the Vanderbilt Cup race on Long Island to ensure a spectator he had struck was not hurt, thus losing the race. Savannah could not have asked for a finer gentleman to win the second Savannah Challenge. After the race, Dawson was interviewed by the enthusiastic members of the press and told them, "I never opened up once. I drove just as fast as I knew was necessary to win."[4] The top three drivers stopped in front of the grandstands, where Governor Brown of Georgia presented them with huge bouquets of roses to congratulate them.

The Tiedeman Trophy Race

The Tiedeman Trophy race was held in conjunction with the Savannah Challenge. The Tiedeman race cars would start at 11 a.m.—an hour later than the Savannah Challenge cars— so that the two races would run concurrently. This ensured that there would be plenty of great on-track action for the spectators. Also, both groups could complete their race at approximately the same time. The Tiedeman Trophy Race was 190.3 miles in total, and the cars raced for 11 laps of the course. They were sent away at 30-second intervals and required to blend in with traffic already on the course for the Savannah Challenge.

Eight cars were flagged off by Fred Wagner in their scheduled order. First was Harry Cohen with mechanic A.H. Ragdale in number 41 E-M-F, then Ellery Wright and mechanic William Wallie in the number 42 Maxwell. Harry Knight was third with his mechanic Charles Johnson in the number 43 Cole. Billy Knipper and riding mechanic James Maxcey were fourth in the number 44 Lancia. Frank Witt with Francis Lundgreen assisting went off next in the number 45 E-M-F The pair were followed by Martin Doorley and his mechanic Walter Stone in the number 46 Maxwell. Behind the Maxwell came Bill Endicott with brother Harry Endicott as mechanic in number 47 Cole. The last car to be sent off was Thomas Costello with Ernest Briggs as mechanic in the number 48 Maxwell.[5]

Bill Endicott in the Cole number 47 was the first car out of the race, after experiencing engine problems on lap 2. One lap later, Cohen was out in the number 41 E-M-F when he

The automobile course straightaway in 1910, where drivers could get up to their best speeds.

Mayor Tiedeman of Savannah congratulates Willie Knipper after winning the Tiedeman Trophy

William "Billy" Knipper won the 190.3-mile Tiedeman Trophy Race in Lancia number 44, with no pit stops and an average speed of 58.48 mph.

experienced similar difficulties with his engine. Lap 3 also saw the elimination of Knight driving the number 43 Cole when a cylinder cracked.[6] The cars had no tire trouble on the first day of racing, but the speeds were 60 mph and slower, which would not cause the same level of wear as in the bigger machines to come in the Grand Prize race.

Billy Knipper, driving the sole Lancia, led from the very first lap, holding off the E-M-F and Maxwell cars. His first lap was completed in 18 minutes and 10 seconds, only 20 seconds faster than Georgian driver Frank Witt. It was Witt, an Atlantan driver whose car owner was also from Atlanta, who finished second in the Tiedeman Trophy event. He was 8 minutes and 48 seconds behind the race leader. The owner of the E-M-F, George W. Hanson, president of Southern E-M-F Company, had hired Witt to drive. The pair had entered races in Atlanta with great success and were definitely a crowd favorite.[7] All three Maxwells held up very well and finished out the top five in the race. Costello placed third, Wright fourth and Doorley fifth.

Upon arriving for the celebrations at the grandstand, Knipper spoke enthusiastically about Savannah:

> I was much pleased with the course. For the first time in my life I felt absolutely safe from road obstructions. The patrol of the course was perfect, and the road was splendid. On such a course, merit of the car was what spoke volumes. It wasn't a matter of which car could stand the most jolting. My car was never let out. At no time was it necessary for me to open up. I fixed my pace and never varied from it, knowing the capabilities of the car. It was pretty soft for me this time.[8]

Hayner's Bridge was built over soft marshy areas and allowed the cars to cross the creek and move down into the beautiful southern areas of Savannah (courtesy Robyn Quattlebaum).

The light car races were over, and they had shown the world that Savannah still had the best course in America for road racing. Excitement began to build all over America for the big race, the second International Grand Prix race. The appendix portion of the track had been removed, despite the pleas of the Automobile Club of America, which really liked how the course headed down to the river resort area and made a deep hairpin turn. After the first day's race, however, it was clear that the drivers and organizers could not be happier with the location and setup and that it would be an excellent race the next day for the Grand Prize.

The Grand Prize of the Automobile Club of America

The second Grand Prize race was even more popular than the first, with crowd numbers swelling and media outlets analyzing and comparing the event to the Vanderbilt Cup race. *The Horseless Age* put the media's take on the race very succinctly:

> The chief feature of the Grand Prize race is that it is the one international automobile contest. In the eyes of the nations of the world it ranks higher in importance than the Vanderbilt, inasmuch as the cars and drivers represent nations, their entries being made through the recognized automobile clubs of their respective countries. Patriotism is a potent element entering into this contest. All the more honor, glory and prestige for the manufacturers whose brains and ingenuity produce a car able to win this event.[9]

At 9 a.m. on November 12, 1910, everything was in readiness for the 415.2-mile Grand Prize race to begin. The militia would cover every foot of the course, patrolling from one hour before the start to 30 minutes after the conclusion. Due to the short period for planning the race after it was canceled on Long Island, the marketing and transportation efforts were

Picturesque Oglethorpe Drive in downtown Savannah in 1910 was becoming a hub for the automobile and looks much the same in the present day. Many of the garages, such as that operated by T.A. Bryson, where teams could take their cars for repairs during the weeks of practice, were located near Oglethorpe Drive.

Curious children in a rural area coming to watch the photographers snap promotional photos of the race course in 1910.

Military guards lined the course to keep spectators off the course and drivers in line in 1908, 1910, and 1911.

not able to reach as many would-be spectators in time for the race. The attendance was only at 60,000 in the grandstands and surrounding the home stretch. However, the media had arrived in full force, with some hoping for a different ending than what had been experienced after the Vanderbilt Cup. They would find their fairytale in the upcoming battle on the track and the emergence of a new American racing hero.

The Grand Prize of 1910 was the longest of all automobile races at that time, outdoing even the 402-mile race held in Savannah in 1908, despite the track being shortened. The Americans, Germans and Italians would compete without the French this year, due to France's boycott of Grand Prix racing after difficulties at the French Grand Prix. Henry Ford, who was well known in Savannah, was acting as a director on the Technical Committee of the ACA, but at the same time Ford and many other early American automobile manufacturers were not entering racing in the same numbers as their European counterparts. Many of these automobile firms were more interested in selling cars and did not necessarily see racing as a way of showcasing their cars to the public, as the cars were increasingly being custom built for racing.[10]

The original entries numbered 23 in total, but several cars did not make it. Louis Chevrolet was unable to race in the Grand Prize in his Marquette-Buick due to the injuries he had sustained at the Vanderbilt Cup race. Georgian racer Joe Matson did not arrive with the Simplex. There was a serious accident with the Sharpe-Arrow during the final practice which killed the riding mechanic. The Roebling-Planche blew its engine during practice. An American and a Stoddard-Dayton were withdrawn and the two Nationals never arrived in Savannah.[11]

This left a field of 15 cars at the starting line, including one Alco, three Benzes, three Fiats, two Marquette-Buicks, two Marmons, and two Pope-Hartfords. Eight of the drivers

The race course for 1910 was shortened from the original 25 miles to 17 miles and no longer went through Thunderbolt.

had raced at Savannah before and knew the course well. The cars were flagged off at 30-second intervals, beginning with Arthur Chevrolet in the Marquette-Buick number 3 with riding mechanic Seraye. Next was Ralph Mulford and mechanic Chandler in the number 4 Lozier. Charles Basle drove with mechanic and brother M. Basle in the Pope-Hartford number 6. Harry Grant was in Alco number 7 with mechanic Lee. Joe Dawson drove Marmon number 8 with mechanic Keene. Victor Hemery was in Benz number 9 with mechanic Heim. Felice Nazzaro and mechanic Fagnano drove Fiat number 10. Joe Horan was in Lozier number 6 with mechanic Ainsley. Louis Disbrow drove the Pope-Hartford number 13 with mechanic Albright. Ray Harroun and mechanic Goetz were in Marmon number 14. David Bruce-Brown was in Benz number 15 with mechanic Kramer. Louis Wagner, defending champion of the Grand Prize, drove Fiat number 16 with riding mechanic Ferro. Bob Burman was in Marquette-Buick number 17 with mechanic Hall. Willie Haupt was in Benz number 18 with mechanic Feyhl. Finally, Ralph De Palma and mechanic Pozzo drove Fiat number 19.[12]

Victor Hemery was one of the Grand Prize favorites in Savannah. His surly, but impish nature suited Americans just fine. When asked about his racing strategy, he said, "If I can keep cool for the first few laps I'm alright. My big fight is with myself."[13] Hemery completed the first lap with the best time of 14 minutes and 18 seconds and held his lead for the next eight laps. Chevrolet had the second best time in the Buick, completing his first lap in 14 minutes and 19 seconds, only one second behind Hemery's Benz. By the second lap, though, reigning champion Louis Wagner had his Fiat slicing through the salty air around the course, and he was able to steal second from Chevrolet in the Buick.

Chevrolet fought to get the position back for the next two laps, but by lap 4 he was beginning to have problems with his tires and had to make a pit stop. Bruce-Brown took over third place. The current American Grand Prix champion driver, Louis Wagner, was

The Benz cars at the starting line of the race in 1910 (courtesy Mercedes-Benz Classic Archives).

Benz at the starting line in 1910 (courtesy Mercedes-Benz Classic Archives).

Willie Haupt (and his mechanic) in Benz number 17 during the 1910 American Grand Prize race (courtesy Robyn Quattlebaum).

ahead of Bruce-Brown in second place, and maintained this position when he stopped briefly for a tire change at the end of the third lap. Dawson had made a good start in the first few laps, battling two of the Fiats. He fought to keep ahead of De Palma's Fiat and at the same time pressed Nazzaro. On lap 3, Haupt in the Benz and Nazzaro in the Fiat were neck-and-neck for fifth place. Mulford had a very rough start and was at the back of the pack for the first few laps, behind the two Pope-Hartfords of Louis Disbrow and Charles Basle. He would continue to push the Lozier to its limits.[14]

Dawson was first out of the race on lap 5 with a broken crankshaft. Harry Grant in the Alco battled with Burman and De Palma for the sixth, seventh and eighth positions. Bruce-Brown and Haupt seesawed back and forth for fourth place throughout the first ten laps of the race. By lap 9, Disbrow's Pope-Hartford had a cracked cylinder block and was out of the race. Chevrolet went out on the same lap with a broken crankshaft. Nazzaro and Bruce-Brown were neck-and-neck, battling Wagner for first place as the cars completed the first ten laps. On lap 11, Grant's transmission failed and he was out of the race. Haupt took the lead in laps 11 and 12 when Nazzaro and Wagner were flagged off for technical inspections at the starting line by race officials.

Haupt was enjoying the lead when he took the turn at Montgomery Crossroads a little too enthusiastically and skidded. He left the road and the car smashed into a giant live oak, then plunged through a thick wall of bushes which seemed to swallow the car, driver and mechanic whole. They disappeared from sight as spectators, race officials and medics nearby

Opposite, bottom: **Victor Hemery in Benz number 9 in 1910 (courtesy Mercedes-Benz Classic Archives).**

Harry Grant passing under the footbridge leading to the grandstand in Alco number 7 during the 1910 American Grand Prize race. Grant experienced gear problems on lap 12 and was soon out of the race.

Willie Haupt in Benz number 18 on Waters Avenue and Louis Wagner in Fiat number 16 on Dale Avenue (now Victory Drive).

started toward the area. Both men emerged from the shrubbery with only scratches and bruises. They had escaped serious injuries, but the team's race was over.[15]

Nazzaro had the fastest lap in 13 minutes and 42 seconds on lap 7. He took the lead of the race on lap 13. De Palma, the Brooklyn-born Italian, pulled into second and Hemery into third. De Palma was giving the crowd quite a show. At one point, he was coming up fast on Bruce-Brown in front of the grandstands and nearly flipped the car coming into the first turn. The spectators were ecstatic at the performance of both the Americans and their foreign counterparts.

Wagner had fallen from third to sixth to ninth place due to pit stops and the unexpected technical inspection. His Fiat had a shackle dangling from the front axle, which had caught the attention of the technical staff earlier when they called him in for an inspection. They continued to be worried about the car and called Wagner in a second time to assure his safety. He was back out after the quick stop, but by lap 17 his Fiat was not handling well. The spring shackle finally broke. The car veered out of control, struck a stone culvert that crushed the wheel, and went somersaulting over La Roche. Both Wagner and his mechanic Ferro were thrown clear. Ferro landed in some shrubs, which cushioned his fall. Wagner was not so lucky. His body flew high in the air and landed hard on the track. Barely conscious, Wagner crawled to the roadside, covered in oil, and waited for medical assistance. His injuries

Opposite, bottom: **LaRoche Avenue near the German Club, where doctors and emergency services were stationed for the race (collection of Tanya A. Bailey).**

Wagner in Fiat No. 16 rounding the curve from Dale Avenue into Waters Road

Louis Wagner and his mechanic turning off Dale Avenue onto Waters in Fiat number 16 (collection of Tanya A. Bailey).

were minor. His mechanic Ferro was able to stand. He walked to the German Club nearby and was taken to the hospital, where he was treated for broken ribs.[16]

From laps 14 to 17, Burman pushed Hemery hard, trying to get the Buick into fourth, but Hemery would not give him an inch. Nazzaro, who had been leading from lap 13 to 16, began to lose his grip. By lap 17, he had slipped into second place, with De Palma pushing past into the lead. On the 18th lap, Nazzaro knew he had a problem with the car's alignment. He struggled to keep the big Benz on the road. It seemed to want to go its own way, and Nazzaro kept a tight grip on the wheel, putting his whole body behind it as he took the turns. He was barely able to handle the car after the alignment began to fail, and he fell back to fourth. On the next lap, the chain snapped and he was out of the race.

Of the American cars in the competition, Harry Grant's Alco and Bob Burman's Marquette-Buick had the best showings. Meanwhile, the Americans David Bruce-Brown and Ralph De Palma, driving the European Benz and Fiat, respectively, were dueling for first on lap 22. Hemery moved from third to second when De Palma cracked a cylinder on lap 23 and went out of the race. Hemery squeezed everything he could out of the big Benz, chased by Burman and Mulford. It was his turn to take over De Palma's role in putting pressure on his young teammate from New York, David-Bruce Brown. Bruce-Brown, however, held his slim lead in the final two laps.[17]

The crowd was breathless as the cars passed the grandstands and no one could be sure by watching whether Bruce-Brown or Hemery had won. The others behind them were Burman, Mulford, Horan, and Harroun. The top six finishers were closer in time than in any other motorsports event in America. Michelin was very pleased with the results because the top three finishers all had Michelin tires on their cars.

Smilin' Ralph Mulford could not have been happier with his race. He had worked only as a riding mechanic up until his first race, the American Grand Prize in Savannah in 1908. The city and course worked well for him and would always be close to his heart. As the race

Ralph De Palma (with his mechanic) driving Fiat number 19 along Dale Avenue before going out of the race on lap 22.

Bob Burman (and his mechanic) in Buick number 17 on Waters Avenue.

Bob Burman and his riding mechanic changing the tires of the number 17 Buick during a pit stop in the 1910 American Grand Prize race (courtesy Robyn Quattlebaum).

Ralph Mulford in Lozier number 4 on Ferguson Avenue and Joe Horan in Lozier number 12 on Dale Avenue during the 1910 American Grand Prize race.

David Bruce-Brown (with his mechanic) in Benz number 15 coming down Waters Road.

David Bruce-Brown and his mechanic crossing the finish line in Benz number 15 and winning the 1910 race only one second ahead of teammate Victor Hemery.

ended, Hemery began to celebrate for a few moments, waving his hands in victory, believing he had won. However, when the timers displayed the numbers from the timing machine at the finish line, they showed that Bruce-Brown had beat Hemery by a mere 1.42 seconds. Chagrined, but feeling generous toward his likable young teammate, Hemery hoisted a bottle of champagne in the air and poured it on Bruce-Brown's head—the first to start this winner's circle tradition in racing.[18]

David Bruce-Brown took home the gold cup and $6,000 in cash from the race. The media were thrilled with the new young star, as were fans all across America and the world. The racing publication *Automobile Topics* praised him highly, reporting that Bruce-Brown was "driving with splendid dash, daring and skill, and handling his big Benz racer in a manner that compelled the admiration of even the foreign cracks."[19] The young, handsome American hero had not just won the second American Grand Prix, he had saved road racing.

Benz could not have been more thrilled to have its cars place one and two on the podium. It was the culmination of 30 years of hard work for the company to reach this pinnacle as well as a moment that turned the eyes of the world toward the excellent design, workmanship and reliability found in the Benz cars. Hemery, like the majority of drivers, was very impressed by his young American teammate and he did not seem to mind coming in second, but it hurt to lose by just 1.42 seconds. Still, Hemery won the second-place purse of $3,000 and he loved his time in Savannah.

Buick was also very proud to have its car on the podium in third position with Bob Burman at the wheel. The team had started the race with a strategy to go all out right from the start, hoping that by setting a furious pace, the foreign competitors would have their tires burned up as they tried to keep up. The plan almost worked, and it certainly kept Bur-

David Bruce-Brown in Benz number 15 in front of the grandstand as the checkered flag flies for the 1910 American Grand Prize.

man at the front with the leaders. Like Hemery, Burman won a prize of $3,000 cash, although $1,000 of that was awarded for being the first American to finish in an American car.[20]

Burman's feat was the best finish for an American car and driver in a Grand Prix race on American soil. It also lent a great deal of cache to the Marquette-Buick. It was a signal that the company was now an iconic American manufacturer. It was also noted by some in the media that if Burman had not stopped nine times in front of the grandstands to take on fuel and make adjustments, he might very well have taken the gold trophy for Buick.[21]

The international media praised the events. *InterOcean* in Chicago called it the "Blue Ribbon Event of Automobile Contests."[22] *The Horseless Age* said "the Grand Prize was a grand climax for a racing year—motor racing has come into its own again."[23] The *Atlanta Constitution* wrote that the big cars "were doing some of the most thrilling driving in the annals of automobiling history.... Seconds only marked some of the difference in their laps. They seemed more like creatures of flesh and blood than mere racing machines. They shifted position as if in bitter personal rivalry for the vantage of but a few hundred yards. The drivers caught the infection and opened their speed levers wider, and the flying wheels at last refused to stay on the track at the turns."[24]

Considering the tragedy and media firestorm that had erupted only weeks before at the Vanderbilt Cup on Long Island, the tone was set: the public did want road racing. Specifically, they wanted it in Savannah. They wanted the best drivers in the world, on the highest-quality road course, with the race set to the highest standards of safety possible, and no compromise on excitement. Savannah was the only city that would deliver all of these things in the pioneering era of road racing.

11

The November 27, 1911, Races: The Tiedeman Trophy, the Savannah Challenge, and the Vanderbilt Cup

The Tiedeman Trophy Race

Both the Vanderbilt Cup and Grand Prize of the Automobile Club of America were awarded to Savannah in May 1911. Promoting the races began quickly, with the entire state of Georgia joining forces with the local Savannah Automobile Club, the city of Savannah, Chatham County, and the race organizers from AAA and the ACA. The state of Georgia was also promoting the 100-mile endurance run in October 1911 known as the "Round-the-State-Tour," which included 76 participants and stops in over a dozen cities and towns in the state. Savannah was one of the stops in the tour, a role championed by no less than Governor Hoke Smith, Asa Candler, Mayor Tiedeman and the Savannah Automobile Club members.

Supporting events had grown considerably. There would be a football game held between the University of Georgia and Auburn University, a poultry show that allowed people to buy fresh turkey for Thanksgiving, card games for the ladies at several private clubs in downtown Savannah, and dinners and music in Thuderbolt and on Broughton Street. But perhaps the most exciting of the supporting events was the air meet. The Glenn Curtiss Flyers arrived with Beckwith Havens to deliver Savannah's first ever air mail and give an air show to the people in the grandstands. The dirigible *California Arrow* was also present at the events and took off and landed at Athletic Park. The dirigible was more balloonlike than most zeppelins, and the pilot had to move back and forth on the metal frame below the balloon to operate it. The people in Savannah were fascinated and kept busy over the entire week.

It was chilly on the morning of November 27, 1911, when spectators and cars began to arrive at the site of the grandstands and starting line of the race. In the great new athletic park on the east side of the course, an enormous fire had been lit to warm the people. The fire glowed against the sky and could be seen for miles.

The early races were scheduled to begin at 7:45 a.m. and the Vanderbilt Cup race at

The *California Arrow* dirigible flew during the racing week events.

10:30 a.m. An unusual frost settled in, covering everything. Spectators pulled on extra layers of clothes, coats and blankets over their shoulders as they made their way to their spots. The larger Vanderbilt cars were set up in the paddocks across from the grandstands before the light car races, which mostly involved modified stock cars. The teams entered in the Vanderbilt Cup would have an excellent view of the races. Louis Disbrow's Pope-Hummer team was excited to see their driver getting a little extra warm-up and perhaps some advantage in terms of the feel of the track on race day before the big event. Disbrow was entered in the Savannah Challenge in a Case car. He would have to wait: the Tiedeman Trophy Race, an event of ten laps totaling 171.4 miles, with the smallest cars, would be the first off that day.

The E-M-F cars had taken a lot of ribbing in the days leading up the events, with some of the team owners and drivers labeling them with outlandish names, such as Every Mechanical Fault. There were three of them in total in the Tiedeman Trophy race, along with a Ford and two Abbott-Detroits. The E-M-F drivers were Frank Witt, Evans and Tower. Kulick would drive the Ford, and the two Abbott-Detroits were driven by Mortimer Roberts and Hartman. The infamous Barney Oldfield was present in a double capacity: as a celebrity race reporter and to informally advise the E-M-F team on several issues, including which tires to choose. He recommended the new Firestone nonskid tires, which were used for the first time in racing at this event in Savannah and gained even greater popularity in the racing industry over the next few decades.[1]

When the cars were sent off, Roberts and Hartman in the Abbotts got off to a very quick start and were the first to finish the first lap. They crossed in front of the grandstands to thundering applause. Evans came third in an E-M-F, followed by his teammates Tower and Witt. Kulick pulled up last in the Tiedeman event. Hartman was the first to suffer bad luck in the race. He blew out two cylinders on the second lap and retired from the race. This allowed Roberts to keep his lead and Witt in the E-M-F to pull into second place, three minutes behind the race leader. Evans was in third, over a minute behind Witt. Towers was another minute behind him in fourth. Kulick was still at the back, over six minutes behind the race leader.

Roberts was able to hold onto his lead as the cars came around the third time and he made excellent time, pulling out to a 4.85-minute lead over Witt, who remained in second place. Evans was in third behind his E-M-F teammate, but Kulick's Ford passed Tower for fourth place. However, Kulick pushed the car too hard and the radiator began steaming and leaking water. Kulick stopped to replenish the loss with massive amounts of water, costing him ten minutes during the repair. His engine bounced up and down over the track, creating an almost comical sight for the crowd.[2]

The fifth and sixth laps had no change in the order of the drivers and they continued at the same pace they had settled into. But on the seventh lap came the big surprise as Roberts's camshaft broke, causing the Abbott-Detroit to veer off the course and roll off the embankment on Ferguson Avenue. Witt took the lead, holding off his teammates Evans and Tower by only 1.39 minutes and 4.09 minutes, respectively. Kulick remained a good 15 minutes behind the race leader. Witt doubled his lead over his teammate Evans, and continued to pick up an increasingly larger lead through to the end of the race. The three E-M-F cars finished first, second and third, with Kulick a good 20 minutes behind the leader by the end of the race. The outcome was a surprise, but also a vindication for the E-M-F team and the company behind them. Words were eaten and, some say, pink slips exchanged at the unexpected turn of events.

The Savannah Challenge

The Savannah Challenge was run concurrently with the Tiedeman Trophy race, but it was a longer event of 13 laps, for a total race length of 222.82 miles. The entrants for the Savannah Challenge race were Hughie Hughes, William "Billy" Knipper and Barnes in the Mercers; Heinemann and Nikrent in Marmons; and Buckley and Disbrow in Case cars. The cars were sent off 15 minutes after the smaller Tiedeman cars were underway in their event at 8 a.m. Heinemann was first off, followed by Hughes, who took off in a burst of speed. Buckley's Case followed, then Barnes, Nikrent, Disbrow and Knipper. Disbrow, having passed Nikrent, made the best time, completing the first lap in 14 minutes and 10 seconds. The two Mercers came next, with Knipper only 0.81 second behind the leader, followed by Barnes. Hughes had charged around the track, passing Heinemann on Norwood Avenue. He was first to cross the starting line in front of the grandstands in the Mercer in 15 minutes and 52 seconds, putting him in fourth. Heinemann was hot on his tail, only five seconds behind in fifth. Nikrent held several minutes' lead on Buckley, who was having engine problems from the start and took last place.[3]

Disbrow held onto the lead for the next four laps. As he approached the main stretch, Heinemann and Barnes were in hot pursuit, and the three cars grappled for position in front of the crowd. The crowd held their breath as Disbrow pulled away from the other two, then burst into wild applause. Unfortunately, Disbrow would not make it through the fifth lap, as he broke the camshaft soon after finishing the fourth lap. The leader was out of the race.

Lap 5 was to be the beginning of the domination of the three Mercers. Hughes, who

Hughie Hughes winning the Savannah Challenge in a Mercer in 1911 (courtesy Robyn Quattlebaum).

was in second, took over the lead of the race in the Mercer, with teammate Barnes behind him, followed by Knipper. The Marmons were next in line, with Heinemann and Nikrent taking fourth and fifth positions. Buckley continued to struggle at the back of the pack.

On lap 6, Knipper pulled up to second place, ahead of teammate Barnes, who had also been passed by Heinemann's Marmon. Hughes continued on with his sensational driving, thrilling the crowds, but the other two Mercers began to weaken after the eighth lap. Knipper was experiencing engine problems and had to stop for repairs. Barnes could not catch up with Heinemann's Marmon, leaving the Mercer driver in third. Buckley was still at the back of the field.

The eighth lap brought the fastest lap of the day by Barnes in the Mercer. He completed the lap in 14 minutes and 11 seconds. On lap 9, Knipper's engine gave up and he dropped out of the race. The other drivers remained in their positions until the 11th lap, which saw Buckley's struggling Case finally give up the ghost. That left the two Mercers up front, led by Hughes and Barnes, followed by the two Marmons of Heinemann and Nikrent in third and fourth. The two teams battled toward the end and an exciting final lap.[4]

Hughes was still holding his lead easily and Barnes had finished lap 12 with six seconds to spare from Heinemann, but he began having trouble with the car and was forced to make a quick stop. Heinemann and Nikrent got past him, leaving the Mercer in fourth place but still heading for the finish line when the race was called. The winners of both the Tiedeman Trophy and Savannah Challenge races stopped in front of the grandstands, receiving a lengthy standing ovation from the crowds assembled.

The Vanderbilt Cup

The newspapers called it "The Road Race Meet of the Century."[5] Finally, after three long years of reaching out to the AAA, Savannah had secured the race of its dreams: the Vanderbilt Cup. The event would be run on Thanksgiving weekend in 1911 along with the

American Grand Prize race, which was returning to Savannah for its third year. The Savannah Challenge and Tiedeman Trophy races had been held earlier on the morning of November 27, prior to the Vanderbilt Cup race.

Southern race fans were thrilled to have the chance to finally see the great race run in their part of the country, attended by the world's most famous citizens, drivers and automobile teams. The majority of spectators attending the races came from the neighboring states of North Carolina, South Carolina, Florida and, of course, from Georgia. However, many of the Vanderbilt regulars, the elite families of the Meadowbrook Hunt Club and the North Shore of Long Island, would also arrive in great numbers, having traveled in stylish Pullman cars and steamships to Savannah. The advance sale of boxes and reserved grandstand seats was twice what it was for either of the prior Grand Prize races, owing mostly to the addition of the Vanderbilt Cup race. There were over 8,000 people seated in the main grandstand alone, with thousands in the bleachers surrounding the start–finish line and hundreds of thousands in private stands, in cars, on rooftops, or picnicking along the course.

The race purse for the Vanderbilt Cup race would be for $2,750. The *Watchman and Southron* enthusiastically exclaimed, "Never before was such a galaxy of world-famous drivers assembled in one place. The greatest rivalry exists and it is known that these men will enter the races to win at all hazards. It is 'do or die' with them, for the race will make the driver and the manufacturer of the machine rich and world famous. No amount of money could purchase the prestige which winning these races will give the cars."[6]

An interesting moment occurred prior to the races. Celebrity driver and one of the all-time greats, former bicycle racer, and colorful personality from the moment he came onto the auto racing scene around 1902, Barney Oldfield showed up in Savannah. Oldfield was known for driving the "999," the "Winton Bullet," and the "Green Dragon." His nickname was "the Old Master" and he was a polarizing figure around the time of the Savannah races. He had friends and enemies in equal numbers. In his most recent banning for flouting the rules of the AAA, he had been barred from any and all participation in races sanctioned by the AAA since October 1910. Oldfield had come to Savannah as a reporter, to cover the races for several publications.

For its part, the Savannah Automobile Club was delighted to have such a famous driver attending, and its officials issued a military pass for Oldfield to watch the races from the press box. The AAA was furious upon learning of the issuance of this pass and called a meeting with Arthur Solomon and Mayor Tiedeman about the matter. While Oldfield was under no such ban from Automobile Club of America events, the two men nonetheless concurred with the AAA's request to revoke Oldfield's press pass. The Savannah Automobile Club agreed and Oldfield was notified by an apologetic Mayor Tiedeman that the pass was nullified and he would have to attend the events from one of the spectator stands.[7] But the races would not go on without him present. Although he was not in a box shared by members of the upper echelon of the AAA, Oldfield did find some very comfortable quarters from which to watch the race after a stack of invitations to join the elite of Savannah and New York in their private boxes arrived. In the end, he would enjoy all the luxuries of food, beverage and superior views of the events that he could wish for.

Soldiers lined the course under orders from the Georgia governor. They were armed with revolvers, rifles or bayonets and wore ponchos over their uniforms to ward off any rain. The cost to oil the track prior to the Vanderbilt Cup race was $15,000. The race would involve medium-sized cars with a 600-cubic-inch piston limit. The cars assembled included two 597-cubic-inch Mercedes, two 589-cubic-inch Fiats, two 544-cubic-inch Loziers, a 389-

cubic-inch Pope-Hummer, two stock cars by Abbott-Detroit and Marmon, one Mercer, and one Jackson. The weather had warmed up as the smaller cars had raced, and by 11:45 a.m. the crowd was feeling more comfortable.

The cars were sent off by Fred Wagner at 30-second intervals. Harry Grant, driving the Lozier number 1, was first to start and finish lap 1, crossing in front of the grandstands to a chorus of cheers. Behind him was the number 2 yellow Marmon of Wild Bob Burman. Louis Disbrow drove the big red Pope-Hartford with number 3. When Spencer Wishart took off in the big gray Mercedes, a cheer went up from the crowd. Harry Cobe was next in the number 5 Jackson. Another crowd favorite was sent off next: Hughie Hughes, who was fresh off his win in the Savannah Challenge only hours earlier. Hughes drove Mercer number 6. Then came the first of the smaller Abbott-Detroits, with Carl Limberg sent off in the number 7 car. Ralph Mulford had high hopes for his year to turn around as he was flagged off in the big white Lozier number 8. Behind him was another of the Abbott-Detroits, number 9, driven by Leland Mitchell. Ralph De Palma in the German Benz car number 10 was next to go, followed by Edward Parker in the number 11 Fiat. Cyrus Patschke was next in the number 12 Marmon. David Bruce-Brown was behind him in Benz number 14. Finally, the last car, the number 15 Fiat driven by Joe Matson, was sent off.

Cyrus Patschke started the race with a fantastic ride in the Marmon and easily got past Louis Disbrow in the Pope-Hummer, then cruised by Burman and Grant, who had to stop to change a tire early on. Cobe, driving the Jackson, had engine failure and was off the course; however, his retirement would not be officially announced until the race leaders were on the sixth lap. Burman, Bruce-Brown and Hughes in the Mercer came behind the race leaders, seesawing back and forth. Grant fell back into tenth position as the tire change delayed him and the two Abbott-Detroits driven by Mitchell and Limberg fell to the back of the pack.[8]

On lap 3, the race leaders continued to battle and hold on to their respective positions through fourth place. Burman moved up from the positions he had lost to take over fifth. Parker, with his tire change finally completed, started pushing his big red Fiat to the limit and gained back one position to cross the grandstands in ninth place. Matson struggled with his Fiat, which had a leaking connector. He was forced to make an unplanned pit stop to take extra water onboard. It put him back to seventh in the race, with Disbrow behind him in the Pope-Hummer. Hughes's Mercer was experiencing similar problems to Matson's Fiat, with a leak springing up in the third lap that would continue to plague him until the sixth lap. Hughes was falling back quickly, allowing Mitchell and Limberg to pass him in their Abbott-Detroits. Mulford was also having trouble from the third lap with his tire. A tread had come loose and affected the handling of the car. However, Mulford would not stop and lose his position. He took a firm grip on the wheel and continued on with fierce determination.

De Palma was excited to remain in the lead by a full minute in his Mercedes during the fourth lap. It was his first Vanderbilt Cup race, although he had previously experienced great success in many races, ranging from short track events to endurance races to records for durability. Hughes could not contain the Mercer's leak any longer and pulled off the track, retiring from the race much too early for the Mercer fans present. Spencer Wishart was in second in the other Mercedes, pursued closely by Smilin' Ralph Mulford. Patschke began struggling with his car and dropped back to sixth.

In lap 5, Mulford's determination only increased as he pressed the Lozier even harder, pulling out a sizable lead for himself. The American car was applauded as it passed the grandstands in the lead. De Palma continued the fight to keep up with Mulford but fell back by

11. November 27, 1911, Races: Tiedeman Trophy, Savannah Challenge, Vanderbilt Cup   173

The Vanderbilt Cup race starting line in 1911 (courtesy Robyn Quattlebaum).

almost two minutes by the time the fifth lap was complete. Burman took up third position in the Marmon with Bruce-Brown hot on his heels in the Fiat. Wishart struggled through a quick unexpected pit stop to change a tire. A gasp rose from the crowd when the jack collapsed under the car and delayed Wishart for longer than he expected to challenge for the lead. Still, he managed to get back out and defend his fifth-place position against Patschke in the Marmon. Matson's water leak in the Fiat continued to worsen and he was forced to retire with the radiator broken. Behind the field were Parker, Disbrow and Grant. Disbrow in the Pope-Hartford kept his eighth-place position but only with great effort, as Parker's Lozier dogged him through almost the entire course. Disbrow was performing extremely well and many in the crowd cheered to see him out racing again after his run that morning in the Savannah Challenge.

The sixth lap brought Savannah's favorite American Grand Prize champion, David Bruce-Brown, into the limelight, but not for good reasons. He was not destined to have his best race in the Vanderbilt Cup this year. He was forced to retire after holding fourth place early in the race. His rear axle had given out and a tire flew off as he reached Montgomery Crossroads. Meanwhile, Mulford was holding off Burman and De Palma, who fought to take his place. He did not budge and kept his race strategy in place as he continued to lead. In fifth position was Wishart, who had a good two minutes on Patschke in the Marmon. He was followed by Parker and Disbrow, who were only 32 seconds apart. Grant, Mitchell and Limberg made up the back of the field.

During lap 7, the top three held their respective positions. Wishart passed Patschke and took fourth when Patschke began to notice minor engine problems. Disbrow was doing a great job of holding his position in the big Pope-Hartford, which was well known to the crowds for its famous wins at the beach races of Florida. Parker and Grant continued to hold

Montgomery Crossroads in black and white in 1911 (courtesy Robyn Quattlebaum).

their sixth and eighth positions. Mitchell and Limberg remained at the back in ninth and tenth, plugging away with the goal of proving their cars' durability above all else.⁹

The eighth lap brought an early surprise ending to Wild Bob Burman's race as a stone flew up from the road and severed a gasoline line. The fuel poured out so quickly that Burman did not even realize it was gone until it was too late. He was forced to retire the Marmon. Mulford continued his iron grip on the lead of the race, and Wishart found himself in second place, six minutes behind the race leader, with De Palma pushing the Mercedes hard to make up the gap of just over three minutes. The Mercedes driver had lost time with tire troubles and would battle through the remainder of the race to make up for the loss. Patschke's engine troubles continued to worsen and he dropped into eighth place. Parker, Disbrow and Grant continued dueling near the back of the pack. Along with Mitchell, they passed by Patschke's ailing Marmon, which had begun to leak from the pump connector. Patschke was forced to make a quick pit stop to refill the lost fluids. Only Limberg in the Abbott-Detroit remained behind Patschke in last place.

It was the halfway point of the race in lap 9 when Patschke's engine finally gave up completely and he was out of the race in Marmon number 12. Mulford held onto the lead in the Lozier with Wishart and De Palma only a few seconds behind in the two big Mercedes. Louis Disbrow was still moving the Pope-Hartford around the track at fantastic speeds and maintained fourth position, just behind the race leaders. The other Lozier, driven by Harry Grant, the winner of the 1909 and 1910 Vanderbilt Cup races on Long Island, was getting frustrated that he had not been able to get up further than fifth by the halfway point. He continued on with determination, hoping to repeat his win in Savannah. Grant was followed by Parker and Mitchell in sixth and seventh places. Limberg had trouble keeping up the pace

Montgomery Crossroads on the Grand Prize course in 1911.

and remained in last position in the lower-powered Abbott-Detroit, yet he drove magnificently and the crowd enjoyed the sight of the two Abbotts every time they passed by.

On the tenth lap, Smilin' Ralph continued blasting around the track in the lead, with Wishart squeezing everything he could get out of the Mercedes. Mulford knew that the trick to winning a road race was not to just let it out the entire way, but rather to figure out what the top speed was for each turn and maintain that speed. He was doing a fabulous job at it, too. De Palma tried vainly to catch up with the two. With great effort, Grant passed Disbrow's Pope-Hartford and managed to gain 11 seconds on the car. Parker, Mitchell and Limberg rounded out the back, with the Marmon still struggling to keep up with the faster cars.

During the 11th lap, Mulford continued making his best time of the race. Just as he was hitting 74.9 mph on the White Bluff straightaway, another exciting event occurred to heighten the thrill for the crowds. Beckwith Havens of the Curtiss Flyers appeared in the air near the stands and front straightaway, making long swoops over the course and racing over top of Mulford's car, giving the spectators a new battle to watch: automobile versus airplane!

Mulford had to pit soon after, and he made one of the best pit stops of the race on this lap, wowing the crowd by doing everything in less than one minute. Wishart did not fare so well. He seemed to have lost the golden horseshoe on lap 11 when his tires began to wear badly. He was forced to pit to put on a fresh set, and the unplanned stop moved him from second to fifth place. This gave De Palma the opportunity to move into second and challenge Mulford for the lead. Grant pulled the Lozier into third, putting two of the American cars among the leaders. The crowd was excited to see the American vehicles doing so well and shouted their names as they passed the grandstands. Disbrow was up to fourth, right behind Grant, when Wishart rejoined the race behind him. Parker was sixth, with Mitchell and Limberg remaining behind him.

The 12th lap saw De Palma and Grant remaining in their second- and third-place positions, but Wishart was putting on the pressure. He passed Parker's Fiat to get himself back to fourth but could not get past Grant's Lozier quite so soon. Disbrow made a pit stop that was nearly as spectacular as Ralph Mulford's while using a wooden block and mechanical jack. By lap 13, the drivers were holding their pace very steadily, with no unexpected mechanical problems or pit stops. However, Mitchell and Limberg began to slow over the last few laps as the Abbott-Detroits fought to make the full race distance. Limberg was having a particularly hard time—he took four minutes longer on lap 13 than on lap 12. Disbrow had a setback on this lap. A tread had come flying off his car and he swerved toward the water on the bend at La Roche Avenue, sending one of the flagsmen diving into the creek to escape injury.[10] Disbrow fell back to sixth place again as Parker wedged himself in front of the Pope.

On lap 14, the race leaders were able to lap Limberg's Abbott-Detroit toward the end of the race; he was unable to complete the 14th lap when the race was called. Mulford held onto his lead, keeping De Palma 2 minutes and 33 seconds behind him. Wishart pushed hard and finally was able to pass Grant's Lozier and slide back into third place. Parker was a good minute behind the Lozier in fifth and found Disbrow nipping at his heels again in the Pope-Hartford, while Mitchell continued to lose two more minutes.

During the 15th lap, Mulford had to make another tire change. He took only 36 seconds for the quick repair and did not lose his lead due to the brilliant work in the pits. This was part of the plan for the Lozier team. Mulford's car was not strictly stock. It had ⅛ inch bored out of the cylinders to bring the stroke to 5⅜ × 6 inches and the intake had two extra air inlets and two exhaust valves. The changes gave Mulford power to match the Europeans, and a frustrated Ralph De Palma kept pushing his Mercedes, trying to catch up with the Lozier. Meanwhile, Wishart took advantage of De Palma's distraction to come up on him fast and challenge his position. Grant's Lozier also made spectacular time during this lap, giving him a few minutes' cushion over Parker, Disbrow and Mitchell.

On lap 16, the excitement ramped up for the drivers and crowd as the race went into its final two laps. Mulford, De Palma and Wishart stormed on, chewing up the road as they fought for position in the lead. But Mulford had carefully studied this track and knew it perhaps better than any other driver, having raced on it during all three years of the Savannah events. Mulford had sketched it out each time before the race, noting anything unusual where he might run into a problem.[11] This helped him avoid any pitfalls that other drivers might not have noticed. Grant was almost within distance of challenging Wishart's Mercedes. Parker and Disbrow continued the battle. Mitchell would not complete the 16th lap, as the race was called before he arrived at the finish.

Mulford was in the lead, pushing as hard as he could on the 17th lap. He wanted to ensure he would go home with the great silver cup and knew he had the car and team to do it. The greatest battle of the race had been the one between De Palma and Mulford from lap 4. The race speed was 4 mph faster than it had been in the 1910 Grand Prize, and 9 mph faster than in any prior Vanderbilt Cup race. Mulford had not driven for speed, however: he had clearly driven according to his strategy of being consistent—and he was consistently fast.

It was at this moment, when the announcer called out his time to the tens of thousands of spectators assembled near the finish line, that Mulford was dubbed "The Automobile Speed King of the World."[12] De Palma drove a fantastic race. Despite being 2 minutes and 11 seconds behind the leader, he was exhilarated to have battled Mulford and Wishart and to have finished with such a strong showing in the city where he had participated in his first major auto racing competition for Fiat. Wishart fought to shave time off of De Palma's lead, but could not quite get his Mercedes to close the eight minutes separating the cars.[13]

The crowd went wild as each of the three drivers crossed the finish line in first, second and third, followed a few minutes later by Grant, Parker and Disbrow in fourth, fifth and sixth. The race was called for the Abbott-Detroits by Mitchell and Limberg. However, there was a great pride in their performance by George G. McFarland, an early automobile manufacturer from Harrisburg, Pennsylvania. McFarland described himself as "wonderfully pleased with the showing the two forty-fours made. Two entered, two finished, averaging about sixty-three miles per hour for the long grind of two hundred and eighty-nine miles. This is in keeping with all other performances of the Abbott-Detroit 'forty-four' for power and endurance and reliability as compared with high price cars."[14]

Ralph Mulford, ever the humble gentleman, attributed his win to his Michelin tires and the fact that he needed to stop to change them only once. Mulford's record-breaking lap speed of 74.9 mph was later challenged by the National Motor Vehicle Company of Indianapolis. Harvey Herrick had broken the world record in Santa Monica by driving 74.6 mph in the National race. The challenge was based on the difference in track lengths. The Savannah course was 17.14 miles compared to the 8.4-mile track in California. The National Motor Vehicle Company stated that the Savannah track gave Mulford an unfair advantage due to his being able to reach higher speeds on the longer straightaways at the Georgia course. Its furious employees sent a telegram to the press:

> National claims road record is theirs. If the A.A.A. Contest Board attempts to lift the laurel wreath from the brow of one Harvey Herrick, international road racing champion, as a result of the feat of the Lozier car in Savannah, there promises to be some fireworks in the very center of the foremost racing body, touched off by two of the biggest powers in the automobile racing game.... The National Co. claims that it still holds the world's road race record of 74.63 miles per hour.[15]

Ralph Mulford winning the Vanderbilt Cup race in 1911 (courtesy Robyn Quattlebaum).

Most media did not comment when they received the missive from the National Company, except to report that they had received the telegram and record its contents for readers. Mulford's record was not overturned by the AAA as the National Company had hoped. Notably, Felice Nazzaro was only slightly behind Herrick's record, driving 74.25 mph at Coppo Florio, which was the world's record for the 400-mile distance prior to Mulford's achievement at Savannah in 1911.

Starter Fred Wagner weighed in on the controversy in his column for *The New York Times*:

> When Ralph Mulford in his big Lozier car zipped past me to-day at the finish of the seventh Savannah Cup race many conflicting emotions stirred me as I dropped the finish flag on the sterling racer and his most excellent car. I realized that this was the fastest race ever run in the world even before the time was announced, and it seems a pity that it must be robbed of a race record on the technicality that a previous event lacking 80 miles of this one should hold the palm by a measley one one-hundredths of a mile in average.[16]

Despite his praise of Savannah's superior course and ability to stage a race, Fred Wagner was likely the biggest fan of the Long Island Vanderbilt Cup races. He expressed a great deal of disappointment that the Vanderbilt Cup was run on the same day as the minor races and before the Grand Prize. However, as the *El Paso Herald* stated, "The race was run and won without the usual heavy toll of life and limb that has become almost synonymous with automobile races."[17] Surely, the racing gods were looking on Savannah favorably. Despite the success, however, it would be the only Vanderbilt Cup race that Savannah would have the honor of hosting.

12

American Grand Prize of 1911

This was a year of triumph and tragedy for Savannah's great races. Although the highly sought-after Vanderbilt Cup race had finally come to the thrilled southern city, it would be Savannah's only chance to host the event or any other major professional auto race. Things did not start off on the best foot due to a change in securing the track for practice prior to the racing events. Since the 1910 race, an ordinance had been passed that made it illegal to close the public roads for practice. Drivers, therefore, were left to practice with the usual public traffic using the roads.

The Savannah Automobile Club, for its part, tried to get word out to everyone in the

The American Grand Prize and Vanderbilt Cup trophies in 1911.

A curve on La Roche could make or break the driver's lap time (courtesy Robyn Quattlebaum).

city to stay off the course from 11:00 a.m. to 1:30 p.m. when race cars would be practicing. But club members could do nothing to have the course closed or patrolled. It was a lapse in what had always been a flawless record of keeping top security on the course, and one that would cost Jay McNay, of the J.I. Case team, his life. McNay went out on the first day of practice and as he drove down LaRoche Avenue, a wagon came out. McNay veered off the road to avoid hitting the wagon. The Case went down into the ditch and hit a tree, killing the driver and badly injuring Maxwell, his riding mechanic.[1] Savannah's reputation for flawless security was slightly tarnished.

The morning of November 30, 1911, was unusually cold, with temperatures dipping to approximately 30 degrees Fahrenheit. It had drizzled for the previous two days, leaving the ground wet and puddles everywhere. This created a thick, icy surface over the oiled race course and in the ditches alongside the roads. This ice made the trek for spectators heading out to the grandstands or their chosen spots around the track almost as treacherous as it was for the cars to get to the course. To the northerners, it was a slight chill; to the southerners, used to temperatures in the sixties and even seventies in November, it was a freezing cold, windy day.

Nonetheless, the giant fires were lit again in the ball field adjacent to the grandstands and many gathered there to enjoy the warmth as they awaited the delayed start. Several concession waiters circulated among the crowd selling glasses of whiskey for 50 cents.[2] Prohibition laws sweeping the country were the furthest thing from the spectators' minds as they thankfully warmed themselves with the drink. As the day warmed up, both the tragedy of McNay and cold temperatures faded. The big Grand Prize cars and drivers from all over the world began revving up their engines.

Ferguson Avenue with the "Hogless Lard" sponsor's sign.

Despite the bumpy days early on, the "Great Savannah Races," as they later became known, brought in an attendance of approximately 500,000 spectators. By comparison, the inaugural Indianapolis 500 had only 77,000 spectators. Road races were still attracting more than five times the audience, higher car counts and a great deal more investment from sponsorships. Such an event was a massive undertaking, requiring the efforts of almost every resident of the city and consuming a massive amount of resources for many months before the race. Every hotel was filled, with ballrooms set up in hostel style. Advertisements went up in the newspaper for rooms for rent in homes all over the downtown area, now known as the "Historic District." Downtown restaurants were set to serve crowds in unrivaled numbers. Trains, cars, airplanes and bicycles could be seen every day of the events, but especially on November 30 when even the cold would not keep a soul from seeing the greatest race in America and possibly the world. The winner would take home a purse of $7,000 when he won the gold cup.

The stage was set for the cars to begin what would be the final race of the weekend and, unbeknownst to all, the final major automobile race in Savannah's history. The European teams were initially feeling very confident in their chances, as Fiat and Benz had each won one of the earlier Grand Prix races held in Savannah. However, the Fiat team in particular felt shaken by their misfortune in the Vanderbilt Cup race three days prior. Only one of their cars had finished the race, driven by Parker, who had finished fifth. The cars driven by Bruce-Brown and Matson were out of the race early on laps 5 and 7, respectively. It was no time to be overconfident for the Fiat team. The morning brought a more stern and determined approach. Bruce-Brown was now driving one of the Fiat S74s, the new 14.1-liter car, instead of driving against the Italian company for the Benz team. Fiat was filled with hope

The Benz camp in Savannah (courtesy Mercedes-Benz Classic Archives).

Military guards were necessary to keep the course safe and for Savannah to win the bid for the Grand Prize and Vanderbilt Cup races.

for a repeat of its first American Grand Prize championship in 1908. Bruce-Brown's teammates were Caleb Bragg and, of course, Savannah's favorite European driver, Louis Wagner. Part of Fiat's hope was to debut the new car, capture the win and help promote the restart of the French Grand Prix in 1912.[3]

The Benz cars could not quite match the new technology of the Fiats. The company entered the same model car that racers had driven in 1910. The only major adjustment made was to increase the engine to 928 cubic inches. The Benz drivers included another beloved European, Victor Hemery, who congratulated his young teammate by being the first to pour champagne over the winner's head at the end of the American Grand Prize race in 1910 after Bruce-Brown had won. The scene is captured both in photographs and more famously in the painting by Peter Helck, *Over the Head of His Conqueror*.[4]

Mercedes brought two 597-cubic-inch cars to the event to be driven by Ralph De Palma and Spencer Wishart. The team was buoyed by their excellent finish in the Vanderbilt Cup race, where the two Mercedes drivers placed second and third behind Ralph Mulford's Lozier. Both of the Mercedes were privately owned. Spencer Wishart was one of the wealthy young drivers who owned his own Mercedes and entered it in many of the big races. The owner of De Palma's car was the equally rich and well-known Ed Schroeder, who owned a myriad of race cars and yachts that always seemed to compete at the top of their class. Schroeder was very pleased by the Vanderbilt Cup results and had high hopes for a win at the Grand Prize.[5]

The Mercedes formula could definitely compete at the front of the pack, but could the team break through the final barrier and get themselves a first-place finish in an American Grand Prize race? The Loziers felt equally buoyed after their victory during the Vanderbilt Cup race. In fact, the combination of the beloved nature of the Vanderbilt Cup to Savannahians who had wanted the race so badly, for so many years, and the prospect of having an American hero win it driving an American car made Mulford one of the most popular drivers to fans of both major races.

One of the greatest drivers of the time, Felice Nazzaro, was not present. He remained in Europe to oversee his new auto manufacturing business. Indeed, "the Speed King" was greatly missed by both the Americans and his fellow European drivers. However, one new face, soon to become a major star in the Grand Prix circuits of Europe, was working with the Fiat team—namely, Pietro Bordino.[6]

The media called the race that was about to begin "the Fastest Race Ever Run." The track had been given its annual makeover, being trimmed back in size from the 17.3 miles in the 1910 race to 17.14 miles in the 1911 races, with a total distance of 411.36 miles to be raced in 24 laps. The banks were lowered in some places and heightened in others to make the course faster than it had ever been. Soldiers were in place once again to guard the course and control crowds. The race was set to begin with 16 cars competing from Europe and America.

Louis Wagner, winner of America's first Grand Prize race in Savannah, would be the first off at 9 a.m. in Fiat number 41. The other drivers were sent at intervals of 30 seconds. Louis Disbrow was behind Wagner in the Pope-Hartford number 42, then Charley Basle in Marquette-Buick number 43, Leland Mitchell in Abbott-Detroit number 44, Ralph Mulford in Lozier number 45, Bob Burman in Marmon number 46, Eddie Hearne in Benz number 47, David Bruce-Brown in Fiat number 48, Harry Cobe in Marquette-Buick number 49, Carl Limberg in Abbott-Detroit number 50, Cyrus Patschke in Marmon number 51, Erwin Bergdoll in Benz number 52, Caleb Bragg in Fiat number 53, Spencer Wishart in Mercedes

Cars lined up at the starting line of the American Grand Prize race of 1911.

The grandstands on Waters and Dale Avenue in 1911.

Erwin Bergdoll in the number 52 Benz (with his mechanic) during the Grand Prize race of 1911 (courtesy Mercedes-Benz Classic Archives).

number 54, Ralph De Palma in Mercedes number 55 and Victory Hemery in Benz number 56.

The crowd had only five minutes to wait for the sound of the first car coming back around. It was Louis Wagner, champion of the first Grand Prize race in America. Behind him came one driver after another, jostling for position as the timekeepers checked each one crossing the line. Caleb Bragg, the new driver from Cincinnati, was the race leader at the end of the first lap with a time of 13 minutes and 1 second in one of the big red Fiats. David Bruce-Brown, defending champion of the Grand Prize, was only six seconds behind. De Palma was in third, eight seconds behind Bruce-Brown's Fiat. The great Victor Hemery was fourth in the Benz, only ten seconds slower than the leader. Wagner's time was only one second less than Hemery and he was in fifth. Sixth place was a tie between the Mercedes driven by Wishart and the Benz of the millionaire driver Erwin Bergdoll. Hearne, Mulford and Patschke rounded out the top ten drivers on the first lap.

By the end of the second lap, the Fiats dominated. Bragg clocked over 80 mph on this lap and kept a three-second lead over Bruce-Brown, while Wagner pulled into third only 22 seconds behind the leader after passing Hemery. It was the battle the crowd had been anticipating for months: the two Grand Prix heroes fighting tooth and nail. Hemery was beginning to struggle with mechanical problems, but he managed to keep fourth place locked down, ahead of De Palma, Hearne, Bergdoll and Wishart in fifth through eighth, respectively. Mulford was back in ninth in the Lozier. Burman's Marmon was in tenth place and had the fastest lap for an American driver in the race, with a speed of 75.7 mph on the second lap.

Lap 3 brought major problems for the Grand Prix stars from Europe and joy to the

The steep embankment on Ferguson Avenue tested drivers' skills in 1911.

young Americans. Bragg continued to hold off Bruce-Brown for the lead, but only by one second; Bruce-Brown was gaining speed with each lap and had a faster lap this time around. Wagner was forced to pit early for tires, costing him his lead. The "surly" Savannah favorite, Hemery, continued having problems with his exhaust which had begun the lap before. After struggling halfway around the course, his exhaust valve went, and took over half an hour to repair. Hemery's time was 62 minutes for the third lap, taking him out of the running for first place, but one never discounted the driver. He would still have a major surprise in store.

The Mercedes of the wealthy Spencer Wishart was also beginning to groan as its drive chains loosened up. Only 34 miles into the race, Cobe's steering went haywire and he crashed his Marquette-Buick on the inside of the bend at Montgomery Crossroads. De Palma completed the lap in third place, with the two Benzes behind him. Hearne was less than 30 seconds behind the Mercedes, while Bergdoll jumped from seventh to fifth place.

On the fourth lap, the two Fiats of Bragg and Bruce-Brown were forced to pit for fresh tires, allowing De Palma, Hearne and Bergdoll to jump into the first, second and third positions, respectively. Wild Bob Burman pulled every ounce of power out of the Marmon to get into fourth ahead of Bragg, who exited his pit after a quick tire change and landed in fifth. People in the grandstands were on their feet, watching the giant Fiats and the new leaders roaring past. They applauded wildly when their defending champion was able to get back out onto the track in eighth position, not as fortunate as his teammate, but still in the running for a possible win. Hemery, meanwhile, spent most of the time repairing his car, determined to get back out as quickly as he could and give the crowd a thrill.

An interesting change-up occurred in the fifth lap. Hearne suddenly began to take

Hayner's Bridge took drivers over the waterway and down to the south end of Savannah.

charge in the Benz. The car was the same Benz driven by David Bruce-Brown to victory one year before.[7] Hearne pushed hard to steal the lead from De Palma, who had a leaking gas line and had dropped back to fifth. Bragg was zipping around the track, trying to regain the first-place position, but could not better Hearne's time and completed the lap in second place. Mulford pushed the Lozier for all it was worth, streaking around the course in a mere 13 minutes and 20 seconds, and knocking Erwin Bergdoll from third to seventh. Patschke was just four seconds slower than Mulford and he took fourth. De Palma and Wagner were back in the fifth and sixth positions, respectively. The big European cars were being lashed by the American cars, bringing high drama on the track and in the grandstands. Bruce-Brown, Disbrow and Basle rounded out the top ten at the completion of the lap. The crowd was sad to see the beloved Marmon of Wild Bob Burman go out on lap 5 with magneto problems and a broken pump shaft drive.

Amidst all of this fifth-lap excitement came one of the biggest moments in the race. Victor Hemery came back out on the course with a fierce determination to prove his mettle. He did so valiantly, flying around the bends at the highest speeds ever and making the fastest lap of the day. Hemery completed lap 5 in just 12 minutes and 36 seconds at a speed of 81.6 mph! The crowd was on their feet, cheering wildly as he came down Dale Avenue, taking the corner near the grandstands at 70 mph, sliding toward the ditch, then regaining his momentum and continuing down the course. The announcer could barely be heard over the frenzied crowd when he told them it was the fastest time ever made on the Savannah course! Hemery was very gratified, especially given the difficulties he had encountered with the car.

Hearne held his lead on lap 6, with Patschke 1 minute and 16 seconds behind. Patschke was followed by Wagner, who had begun to gain again and was only 8 seconds out of the

LaRoche Avenue near Bona Bella on the American Grand Prize course in 1911.

second-place spot. Fourth and fifth fell to Mulford's Lozier and Bragg's Fiat, respectively. Bruce-Brown was gaining steadily and beginning to pull every ounce of speed out of the Fiat. De Palma, Disbrow, Basle and Limberg were in seventh through tenth places, respectively. Mitchell, Wishart, Bergdoll and Hemery had fallen to the back of the 14-car pack which remained in the race.

Lap 7 proved to be an exciting one for the fans of American drivers and cars. Patchke had a brilliant showing, flying at lightning speed around the bend of the course in just 13 minutes and 23 seconds, and stealing first from Hearne, whose car had turned sluggish. He was two minutes slower than on the previous lap. The top four drivers were within one minute of one another as the race heated up. Hearne did manage to keep himself in second place. Mulford and Bragg completed the lap and were tied for third. Bragg had made the better time on the lap, going around the course in 13 minutes, while Mulford's time was 13 minutes and 43 seconds. The two Fiats of Wagner and Bruce-Brown were just behind them in fifth and sixth places. Basle, with less experience than many of the Grand Prix drivers, was struggling to keep the Buick under control.

The eighth lap was both exciting and heartbreaking for the crowd. Although there was a strong contingent who favored the American cars and drivers, they had a great admiration for the colorful driver Victor Hemery. It was too early in the race for many to see him go out, but problems with the ignition forced his retirement. Another favorite, Erwin Bergdoll, suffered a similar fate, going out on this lap with carburetor issues and a gearbox that seized up because the oil used to lubricate it was too thick and had solidified in the cold temperatures.[8]

Overall, a number of the cars were beginning to feel the wear and tear of the race. Patschke was no exception. Although he managed to hold his lead at the end of this lap, it took him about two and a half minutes longer to get around the track. His car was beginning

The Grand Prize course in 1911.

to show signs of stress from his pushing it so hard to gain the lead. Hearne remained in second, poised to take back the lead if the opportunity arose as Patschke slowed. Wagner rose to third with an excellent lap of just 12 minutes and 55 seconds. The crowd cheered him as he crossed in front of the grandstands. Mulford pulled back ahead of Bragg, and the pair took the fourth and fifth positions. Bruce-Brown was still holding onto sixth place, the same position he had held now for three laps, but he was pushing the Fiat a little harder each round, shaving off exactly seven seconds from his prior lap with each circuit. De Palma seemed to shake off his demons and started making some of his better times in the race again with the Mercedes. He was in seventh, behind Bruce-Brown. Disbrow's Pope-Hartford, Basle's Buick and Limberg's Abbott-Detroit squeaked into the eighth, ninth and tenth positions.

Lap 9 reduced the field of cars to just ten, with five American and five foreign cars still competing. Patchke's "Yellow Jacket" began the lap holding the lead, with the car whipping and dancing around the track like a fiend. Suddenly, disaster struck as the Marmon driver took on the wild bends of Montgomery Crossroads. The car veered off the road, with the engine breaking free of the chassis as the car toppled down the embankment and came to its final resting spot. The Marmon's great run was over and the crowd was disappointed to hear the announcer's bad news for Patschke. Wishart's good luck in the Mercedes had also ended, as he suffered a cracked cylinder and was forced to retire. Hearne blasted back into first place, leading Wagner by 23 seconds. Mulford came up in third, making better time on the lap than the leader. Bragg was behind Mulford in fourth. Finally, Bruce-Brown found himself up a spot due to Patschke's retirement, while De Palma took over the sixth place.

As the tenth lap began, Hearne continued leading Wagner, who remained in second place. Basle blew a cylinder head and retired from the race. Mulford began to have problems

White Bluff Road on the Grand Prize course in 1911.

with the Lozier and dropped back from third to sixth. Bragg was thrilled to push his Fiat up to third, and Bruce-Brown followed closely behind in fourth, doing 80 mph on the main straightaway. De Palma was finally able to get the Mercedes moving and passed Mulford to make it into the top five. Disbrow, Mitchell and Limberg trailed behind at the back.

The 11th lap brought the nine remaining drivers and their cars closer to the halfway mark of the race. Hearne was wowing the crowd as he stayed in the lead with the big Benz. Behind him in second, Wagner was still hanging on to his place, but he had to stop for fresh tires and fuel and was losing time as he tried to keep pace and challenge the Benz driver. An interesting change occurred when Bragg had to stop for tires, fuel and a minor repair. He lost ten minutes and gave up three positions. Bruce-Brown wasted no time pouncing into third, followed by De Palma's Mercedes and Mulford's Lozier. The Pope-Hartford driven by Disbrow had moved up to seventh after a pit stop. At the back of the field, the Abbott-Detroits were hanging on, using a strategy of consistency as they turned lap after lap.

There were no changes at the halfway point in the 12th lap. Bragg put his car back into high gear and snatched the second best time for the lap in 12 minutes and 59 seconds, just a few seconds slower than Wagner's Fiat, which remained in second. All of the drivers held the same position as in the prior lap. The 13th lap was a lucky one for Bruce-Brown, who managed to better his teammate Wagner's time and steal second place. He also gained back several minutes off Hearne's lead when the Benz driver stopped for fuel, but Hearne maintained his overall lead. Wagner was beginning to feel the stress on the car and slipped to third. Behind him were De Palma and Mulford.

In the 14th round, Hearne continued to hold his lead with smart and fast driving that kept everyone on the edge of their seats. Wagner decided to push back on Bruce-Brown with everything the Fiat had. He turned a lap of 12 minutes and 48 seconds and regained second place, with his eyes fixed on the ultimate prize: a second championship win in Savannah. Bruce-Brown was forced to pit, allowing De Palma to take third place and Mulford fourth place in the race. Bruce-Brown was back out on the track, but had fallen back to fifth, with teammate Bragg still behind him.

The hearts of the racing enthusiasts would break for another of their European favorites in the 15th lap. Wagner's indomitable spirit was revived when he returned to second place, but it was not good enough for him. Wagner wanted to win the Grand Prize again and pushed Hearne harder. In a flash, the racing gods snatched victory from him. He took a turn extremely fast and made an error that was not typical for the French driver: he over-steered.[9] The car flew off the track; its rear axle was damaged and the steering snapped when it slammed into a tree. The car was badly damaged, but Wagner was able to limp back to the grandstands in it, where the crowd's hearts fell as one of their greatest heroes withdrew from the race.[10] However, Smilin' Ralph was highly favored by the crowd and received a standing ovation every time he passed the grandstands. They also had the returning young champion, David Bruce-Brown, to shower with cheers and encouragement.

In lap 16, Hearne, Bruce-Brown and Mulford were first, second and third, respectively. De Palma had changed places with Bruce-Brown and drifted back to fourth. Bragg and Disbrow made up fifth and sixth behind the race leaders. Mulford pressed hard and, by the end of the 17th lap, he had pulled the Lozier into second place. All around the track, there was applause when he flew past and a feeling that he might be a double champion for the races. The Vanderbilt Cup fans, in particular, loved the idea of their champion taking home the gold trophy. Mulford did a fantastic job with the car, holding off the Fiat and Mercedes cars and working hard to take down Hearne's Benz. The Abbott-Detroits, although at the back,

The Fiat wreck of Louis Wagner in 1911 (courtesy Robyn Quattlebaum).

were still working hard to make good time on each round, and their durability impressed many.

Mulford was the star of the 17th lap, increasing the Lozier's speed to put pressure on Hearne, who still held the lead. He was within 30 seconds of the leader and had managed to slip into second position. Second place had been held briefly by Bruce-Brown, who still struggled with tire problems. In fact, all the Fiats had difficulties with their tires throughout the race, which put a damper on their otherwise excellent performance. De Palma and Bragg remained behind Bruce-Brown in fourth and fifth. De Palma was within one minute of his time and had a very real shot at a win. Limberg was forced to make a pit stop on the 18th round, but all of the other drivers remained in the same positions, at speeds very close to those achieved on the prior lap.

Things started to heat up again in the 19th lap. Hearne was clearly beginning to grow weary and was slowing down. Mulford seemed to be just warming up. He was able to push the Lozier ahead fast, shortening Hearne's lead to 11 seconds. They completed the lap with a buzz in the air as the 20th round started. The crowd was on its feet, knowing the race was close to reaching its conclusion.

Hearne struggled to keep the car in contention on lap 20. Bruce-Brown, who started the lap back in third, took the occasion to breeze past Mulford and challenge Hearne for the lead. He pushed the Fiat hard and took the lead easily. Mulford maintained his second-place spot, while Hearne dropped back to third. De Palma was in fourth, with Bragg in fifth. The battle for the championship continued to heat up between the top five cars.

Despite starting lap 21 in third place, Hearne was reinvigorated and turned in his fastest lap at 13 minutes and 6 seconds. Hearne was determined to win this race. He had promised his wife he would retire after the Grand Prize since they had a newborn son and he had sworn not to undertake the dangerous sport after this day.[11] Perhaps it was this desire to go out on top that helped him wrestle second place back from Mulford. But it was not enough

A sharp turn to challenge drivers on the course in 1911.

A stretch of the course near Norwood Avenue in 1911.

to overtake the fierce young road warrior leading the race: David Bruce-Brown. Not yet, at least.

Things changed again in lap 22. Hearne was determined to take back the lead and win the race. A series of pit stops would be the determining factor. Bruce-Brown was struggling yet again and pulled into the pits before the frenzied crowd. It took him a full 68 seconds to change his left rear tire. Mulford also made a stop to refuel and took only 36 seconds with his pit stop. Hearne went in for a right rear tire, which took 1 minute to change. When the

The Grand Prize course in 1911.

three drivers came out, it was announced that Hearne had the lead again. The crowd went wild!

As they started on the 23rd lap, Mulford was uncharacteristically frantic to gain the lead. Instead of slowing across the Isle of Hope streetcar tracks on Ferguson Avenue, Mulford hit them at full tilt. His car went up, then bottomed out, ripping the prop shaft to shreds and destroying all hopes of an American driver winning the Grand Prize. Mulford was not alone in suffering the sudden end of the race with only one lap to go. Only a few seconds after Mulford's accident, which took the big Lozier out of the race, Hearne heard a loud bang from his car. A tire had been punctured and he would have to stop to replace it only moments after replacing the rear tire in the pits. Bruce-Brown surged ahead in first place, flying around the track in his excitement and completing the lap in 12 minutes and 53 seconds, at an average speed of 80 mph. Hearne was able to make the repair quickly and kept himself in the top two, with De Palma still a couple of minutes behind in third, followed by Bragg in fourth and Disbrow in the Pope-Hartford in fifth.

The green flag was thrown for the last lap at the starting line as American David Bruce-Brown screamed past the grandstands in the big red Fiat: the Italian manufacturer's second Grand Prize championship in America was within reach. Bruce-Brown was the sentimental favorite for many fans, and the crowd cheered, hugged one another, and jumped up in down in their finery. When his team informed him that Hearne was delayed, the driver slowed a little to ensure that he did not have to contend with tire problems or any other unexpected mechanical issues brought about by pushing too hard. There was also the matter that his fuel was a little low: if he went all out, Bruce-Brown might run out of gas—as René Hanriot had done in the Benz car in 1908, at the first American Grand Prix race in Savannah. Having

Whitefield Avenue in 1911 on the American Grand Prize course.

raced with Benz in the prior year, Bruce-Brown knew that story only too well. But time was on the young Fiat driver's side, and all he had to do was make the final lap and conserve as much fuel as possible with a comfortable cushion of time between him and the second-place driver, Eddie Hearne.

Bruce-Brown took the checkered flag and drove out of sight, followed by Hearne, who was still in second place, but two minutes behind Bruce-Brown. De Palma's Mercedes was only three minutes behind the leader. It was almost an hour before the race was called for the other drivers, however. Bragg and Disbrow rounded out the top five finishers. The Abbott-Detroits were still going, but were waved off as the race was called. The crowd cried Mulford's name over and over, waiting in vain for the retiring driver to come around, but he did not make it back to the grandstands. David Bruce-Brown, the young man who was once bound for Yale, was instead a second-time champion in the third Grand Prize race of America. He drove at an average speed of 74.66 mph, bettering his average speed of 1910, which was 70.55 mph in the Benz car.[12]

After driving around the track for his victory lap, Bruce-Brown stopped before the stands where his team, his friends, other drivers, and, of course, his mother surrounded his car. Everyone cried out congratulations to him. Mrs. Bruce-Brown, with tears in her eyes, moved forward to claim her young son in a giant hug and showered him with kisses. She came away covered in the oil and grit of the road, but smiled through it, unconcerned. The men picked the champion up on their shoulders and carried him around in front of the stands while the crowd screamed with excitement. Bruce-Brown was given one enormous bouquet after the other in congratulations and finally set down. He looked around to find his colleagues and ran over to them, congratulating Hearne and De Palma on a great race.[13] Hearne was particularly disappointed since he would not be racing again, but De Palma was hearty in his congratulations.

Bruce-Brown was surrounded by race reporters shortly thereafter and gave a statement on his win:

I won the race by driving like the devil toward the early part of the race. I had to make nine tire changes, had to put in a new bolt in the front axle and stalled my motor altogether. I was up against and wanted to make better my victory than I did last year. I did it by driving furiously in the first of the race and then easing down toward the latter part.[14]

Most notable to race historians, and especially Peter Helck, was the strength in the showing of American cars and drivers in this race, when they were tip to tip with the vastly experienced European Grand Prix favorites. Mulford's Lozier had beaten the Mercedes Grand Prix model cars and had been very close to taking both the Vanderbilt Cup and American Grand Prize trophies for the American manufacturer. The Pope-Hartford was the only American car to finish, with the noteworthy Louis Disbrow at its wheel. The races in Savannah were over and questions of many sorts would soon arise as various parties and interests tried to decide what the future would hold.

13

What Happened to the Great Savannah Races After 1911?

The days of the Great Savannah Races ended with the 1911 events. In 1912, the two major races, the American Grand Prize and the Vanderbilt Cup, moved to Milwaukee. The drivers and teams expressed disappointment over the location, which was first settled and then changed to a more rural location. Many of the people involved with the race were unhappy with this venue and felt it was unsafe and unsuitable for road racing. The change of venue would prove to be even more disastrous than everyone feared. Drivers were worried about the rudimentary roads, and some were claiming they would refuse to drive in the races. And America lost its beloved young superstar, double Grand Prize champion David Bruce-Brown, who was killed practicing for the race.

His friend and teammate Caleb Bragg had a very negative view of the course and told media that Bruce-Brown felt the same and that the two discussed pulling out of the race. Their fears were that the course was too narrow and riddled with potholes after heavy rains in the days prior to the event. Bragg was not one to sugarcoat things and told the newspapers that the management and promoters were lacking in ethics and, even worse, were incompetent. Milwaukee would hold the two great road races only once. The disasters that ensued made many realize how fortunate they had been in Savannah.

There were many reasons why the races did not return to Savannah, but it was definitely not for a lack of trying to bring about their return on the part of the Georgia organizers. There is no single explanation or single person responsible, but rather a complex combination of factors and varying perceptions by the parties involved that affected the outcome. Dr. Julian Quattlebaum's book *The Great Savannah Races* puts forth the local explanation for the races ending: Savannahians had a perception there was nothing to be gained by holding international contests at the time. Moreover, he added, there was a great deal of local opposition to the races.[1]

The continuation of foreign teams at the Indianapolis 500 and the Grand Prize and Vanderbilt Cup races of 1912–1917 would suggest that there was not a lack of interest in international racing overall. Perhaps what Quattlebaum perceived was that local interest in the international races had waned under the strain of the event, which had grown to an almost unmanageable size. Quattlebaum's assertion that there was some disappointment in the events of 1911, which caused disenchantment among Savannahians and the organizers, is true and well reported. However, not all parties felt that way.

Fiat team 1912 at the Grand Prize race in Milwaukee (courtesy Centro Storico Fiat).

Fiat team in Milwaukee in 1912 (courtesy Centro Storico Fiat).

13. What Happened to the Great Savannah Races After 1911?

> It is doubtful Savannah will have any more big races. Mayor Tiedeman who has been very active in the management of these runs says he does not think the city will bid for any more and Harvey Granger, President of the Savannah Automobile Club, says it will be for the first people of Savannah to say whether there will be more racing or not.[2]

However, the true question to ask is: Why did certain parties sour on the races when they had gone so very well? Did the locals realize that some members of the AAA and Vanderbilt Cup race authorities had not really wanted to come to Savannah, where there was little of the New York society atmosphere? Did they realize that despite all of their hard work, some of the AAA members were resentful of the success and safety of the races in Savannah because these were things that had eluded Long Island's events? No accounting tells us how human nature might have affected Savannah's racing after 1911.

We do know something about the perspective of Savannahians. The local opposition was apparently very short-lived. After Milwaukee held the two major races in 1912, Savannah definitely wanted the races back for 1913. On January 6, 1913, a committee was sent to the Waldorf-Astoria Hotel in New York to meet with the Motor Cups Holding Company and begin negotiations for a fall event that year or an early 1914 race. The representatives from Savannah included Harvey Granger, Mayor George W. Tiedeman, Alderman R.M. Hull, Oliver T. Macon, J. Ward Motte (representing Chatham County), and Arthur W. Solomon of the Savannah Automobile Club. In January, newspapers across the country reported, "Negotiations have proceeded to such a state that it seems probable that the races will be held in the fall of 1913 or early 1914."[3]

Yet, by the latter part of 1913, despite being granted the rights to host the Grand Prize and Vanderbilt Cup races, Granger, one of the lead organizers, was unable to get entries for the races. The question is why? It was truly a fantastic event when held in Savannah. There should not have been any fear that the race would turn out as it had in Milwaukee. Savannah's events had widely been referred to as superior to any other major race held previously in America, in terms of reliability, engagement of the local and regional population, safety, quality of the infrastructure needed for the race and sport, and a top-notch course. This opinion was shared by drivers, teams, and even the famous European Grand Prix promoter, Victor Breyer. Breyer had organized races at Bologna, Dieppe and Le Mans.[4] He claimed that the first American Grand Prize compared favorably with the French Grand Prix and the Coppo Florio. He spoke very highly of the quality of the course, putting it even above the Grand Prix course in Dieppe:

> Another point where the A.C.A. and the Savannah promoters got us Europeans badly beaten is in the oiling of the road. Despite numerous inquiries, I am yet at a loss to understand the exact composition of the material used in Savannah, but I noticed that there was not one speck of dust on that homestretch, even when three cars came tearing along it, while on our side, dust has always been a cause of nuisance."[5]

By 1913, Savannah had contracted to have the races return for Thanksgiving weekend. One of the top foreign teams in 1913 to help pull teams on board was Peugeot. It had made a huge splash in Galveston at the Cotton Carnival races. It was the president of Peugeot on whom Granger was most dependent, since Fiat was not racing in America that year. The agent for Peugeot, A.G. Kaufman, was very enthusiastic until suddenly as the deadline to enter cars approached in early October, he broke off talks with Granger and sailed home to France. Granger was said to be "scouring New York" for entries, but then gave up and returned to Savannah before the October 4 deadline for entries.[6]

One possibility is that Peugeot may have been influenced by Carl Fisher of the Indianapolis 500. If Peugeot had demurred to meet the wishes of Fisher and put the Indy 500 first, other teams may also have declined to enter, influencing others in a domino effect. Indy presented very sizable interests and Peugeot had won first place at the race in 1913. Fisher remained in regular contact with Peugeot, which sent two cars to the Indy 500 that year.[7] Just as the city had offered huge sums of money to try to get the Vanderbilt Cup and American Grand Prize races in prior years, so Indianapolis offered very large sums of money to the automobile manufacturers for their participation in the Indy 500. These funds far eclipsed anything that Savannah or the purses of either of the two major races could offer to bring the cars back to Savannah.

From a purely business standpoint, Indianapolis would become the sole major race in the United States with the demise of the Grand Prize and Vanderbilt Cup. The organizers of the Indy 500 could not have wanted the competition, especially at a venue that received higher attendance and larger fields of cars than their own. Savannah garnered audience numbers that could not even fit in the grounds of the speedway. A return to racing in Savannah—which was still very highly acclaimed and referred to as the "Greatest Race in America"—would put quite a serious crimp in Fisher's plans to make Indy the premier race in America. This would be especially harmful if it evolved into the solid, annual event that Indy aspired to become.

The organizers could not have been happy when Galveston's beach races garnered higher attendance numbers than the fledgling Indianapolis 500 in 1913. No doubt, the overall popularity of racing in the South presented a threat at some level to northern and western venues battling to establish themselves. With keen respect for the Indianapolis 500 and what it has given to American racing, it is important to note that it is and was a business, first and foremost. Reducing your competition was a common business strategy at the turn of the century. It may not be the sole reason why the 1913 Savannah races did not work out and why auto racing ended in Savannah, but it is certainly easy to understand that it would not have been normal for a new race like the Indy 500 to encourage its competition rather than discourage it.

Another factor in why the races left may have arisen from the rivalry that had always existed between the AAA and the ACA. Despite these organizations finally coming together in Savannah in 1911, the Vanderbilt Cup's most ardent fans felt like their race had become a supporting event or held lower stature somehow. How ironic, given that to Savannah, the Vanderbilt Cup race was the pinnacle of the sport, a race officials had courted for years and revered so much that they sought to host it again and again. That very desire to have the Vanderbilt Cup and finally gaining it, and putting on the best organized race the Vanderbilt Cup had ever experienced, might even have played a part in undoing Savannah's great achievements in building the finest road race course in America. Resentment against Savannah and the ACA simmered hotly among the major players of the AAA. This jealousy is described in many books, such as Peter Helck's *Great Auto Races*, where he talks about the lament of the Vanderbilt Cup Race supporters: "Our older classic now suffered small-brother status."[8] Even in some modern accounts of the early road races, there is sometimes an expression of resentment against Savannah's races, which some claim was an inferior event. Yet the press, teams, and racing experts of the time claimed just the opposite. This need to put down Savannah's accomplishment is nothing short of puzzling. It is sad to think that some have seemed to want to strip a small, beautiful city and its people of their history and the tremendous contributions and significance they gave to American motorsports and road building.

Overall, a number of factors worked against a revival of the Savannah auto races. Money from other cities tempted away the Motor Cups Holding Company and the AAA and ACA. The automobile manufacturing industry positioned itself in the North and would want to showcase cars closer to home. The Indianapolis 500 was determined to be the biggest and best race in the country and had a great deal of money, power and influence to make that happen. Savannah was growing rapidly, especially in the areas surrounding the course, and the city had been a little bit overwhelmed by the enormous size of the races in 1911.

There were even some who felt certain businesses in Savannah had been greedy with visitors and teams. Examples were given in several newspapers of a few isolated cases of overcharging for garage services and travelers' needs. One such account came from none other than Fred Wagner, starter of the races. In an article he wrote for *The New York Times*, Wagner expressed great sadness that the Vanderbilt Cup race was overshadowed by the American Grand Prize in Savannah and spoke of his anger at local businesses he felt had overcharged teams. He claimed that Savannah might not get the races back because of this poor treatment. His tone seemed to be calmer weeks later in his columns with *The New York Times*, but clearly there were many illustrations of resentment simmering beneath the surface in Vanderbilt Cup fans.

Meanwhile, in the western part of the United States, the desire to grow the racing and automobile industry was getting stronger. California had been successfully staging races in and around Santa Monica and San Francisco that were growing in popularity. There was also an increasing curiosity of northeastern automobile interests in the West Coast. East-to-west races were being planned, businesses were moving out west, and the state of California was becoming more attractive to the entire country. There were so many new things to explore, and cities like Savannah may have been forgotten as this phenomenon took hold.

There was also a local effect that may have impacted the loss of the Savannah races—namely, the beginning of a period of political infighting among the city authorities and Savannah Automobile Club members. This stemmed from a disagreement to the city's recent law requiring automobile registration. Eventually, one of the club's most important members, Harvey Granger, would bring suit against the mayor and aldermen, claiming the new law was unconstitutional. The suit went all the way to the Supreme Court of Georgia in 1915 and the city prevailed. But the rift affected the abilities of these parties to be able to work together as they had in prior years to bring the races to Savannah.

Undoubtedly, when people are no longer working well as a team, personal conflicts can prevent progress and thwart the ability to carry out the momentous tasks that were necessary to running a large-scale event. Even the lone presence of Granger in New York, without an entourage of Savannah's city leaders, may have sent a message to the manufacturers and the ACA that things were rocky back in Savannah. Perhaps some felt deterred from getting involved, knowing the city and Savannah Automobile Club members had become antagonistic toward one another. Certainly, the lawsuits and issues were made public in the newspapers and this may have spooked the organizers who needed to rely on whole-hearted cooperation to be successful, especially after the conflicts and splits that had occurred between parties organizing the American Grand Prize and Vanderbilt Cup races in Milwaukee the previous year. As the world had found out in 1912, such problems could lead to someone paying the ultimate price with their life, as David Bruce-Brown had.

There was also the smaller problem after the 1911 Savannah races of the protest of Mulford's record by the National Car Company. The company had massive power in this time and favored the California track in its statements to the press. Could National's resentment

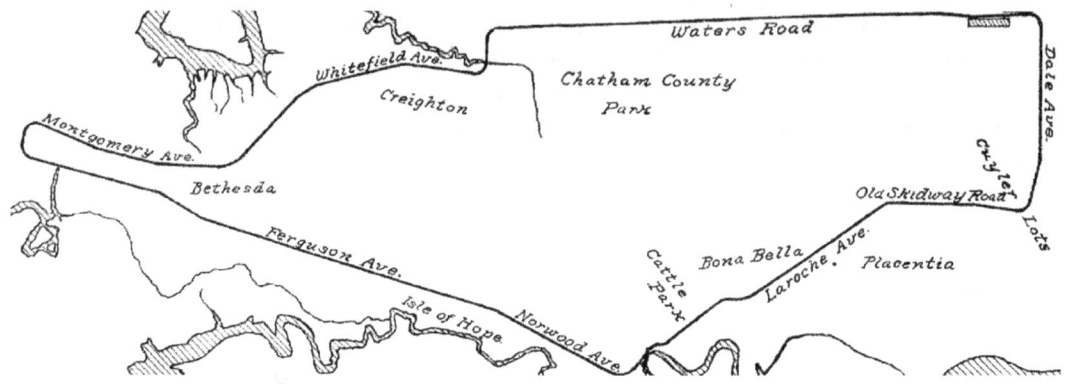

Map of motorcycle course used in 1913 and 1914 for the national championship race, the American Classic in Savannah.

at having its record broken have led to the company trying to suppress further events at Savannah? The protest was widely documented and certainly brought threats with it. Savannah would not have found a champion in this large car manufacturer, but would National's anger over the record have lingered and festered into resentment? We cannot know for sure, but the possibility is there and without manufacturers to support a return to Savannah for the races, all hope was lost.

After the dust settled on the Savannah races of 1911, there would be no more professional automobile racing in the city for decades. However, major motorcycle races were held in 1913 on the course on which the Vanderbilt Cup and American Grand Prize were run. The race was known as the Savannah 300, and it was a national event of great significance to the motorcycle racing world. Savannah held this event through 1914. Most of the 1911 auto course was used. The start-finish line was kept on Waters Avenue just past the last corner from Dale Avenue (now Victory Drive). Riders traveled down Waters to Whitefield Avenue, then the course had a great bend where riders bore right onto Montgomery Avenue. At the bottom was a quick hairpin turn, and then the contestants were on Ferguson Avenue heading toward Isle of Hope, where they rode along Norwood Avenue before turning sharply to the left onto LaRoche Avenue. They would veer right again onto Old Skidaway Road and turn onto the final stretch of Dale Avenue again.

The motorcycle course was 11.25 miles long and the race was 300 miles in total, as the name implies. Over 15,000 spectators watched as the riders took on the many challenges of the five-hour race. The event was organized by the Federation of American Motorcyclists and the Savannah Motorcycle Club. The first race in 1913 was planned for Christmas Day, but had to be postponed until December 27 due to rain.[9] Over 43 motorcycles were entered, including twenty-one Indians, nine Excelsiors, seven Thors, two Yales, three Merkels and one Crane-Atlanta. The race was won by Bob Perry on an Excelsior in 5 hours, 22 minutes and 8 seconds. Perry rode at an average speed of 59 mph. In second place was Maldwyn Jones of Ohio, riding the Flying Merkel V-twin, in 5 hours, 33 minutes and 3 seconds. Famous riders of the period, Herb Camplejohn and Jonathon Yerkes of Jacksonville, Florida, finished third and fourth, respectively. H. Glenn and R.D. Edwards were in fifth and sixth. Two riders, C. Adams and George Porter, suffered broken legs during an accident and retired early.

In 1914, the American Classic Motorcycle Race was again planned for Savannah, only this time it would revert to the Thanksgiving race dates that had proved so popular in the

Maldwyn Jones, motorcycle racer in the American Classic in Savannah.

past with the American Grand Prize and Vanderbilt Cup automobile races. The entrants list was down to 32 motorcycles; however, they were joined by Harley Davidson. Sadly, two of the great early motorcycle racers of the time were killed in accidents: Gray Sloop of Mooresville, North Carolina, was killed instantly early in the race at Waters and Dale Avenue, when he lost control of his motorcycle and crashed into a tree, breaking his neck. Later in the race, Savannah native Z.D. Kelly lost control on a turn and struck a tree as he took a corner in Sandfly. His motorcycle rolled on top of him, crushing his left leg, and he had sustained head and internal injuries from the accident. He was taken to the hospital and eventually died.

The race was won by Ohio racer Lee Taylor in 5 hours, 2 minutes and 32 seconds, breaking the record by 20 minutes. Chicago rider Joe Wolters was second, and third place went to Irving Janke of Milwaukee. Wolters had an excellent race, and if not for a punctured tire toward the end of the race, he likely would have won.[10]

The American Grand Prize and Vanderbilt Cup would continue to be contested together for several years, except in 1913 when the races were supposed to return to Savannah. Santa Monica hosted the two races on February 28, 1914, only three months after the date Savannah was supposed to have the race back. The Santa Monica circuit was also significantly shorter than Savannah's course, measuring 8.4 miles, which gave the contestants a 403.2-mile race. The great races moved once again on February 27, 1915, to San Francisco, which had the smallest circuit of them all: a 3.84-mile course that ran alongside the San Francisco Bay. The race was 400.28 miles in total. The event returned to the Santa Monica circuit on November 18, 1916, and the last race was won by Peugeot. Road racing was over in America. The days of the great Grand Prize and Vanderbilt Cup races of New York and Savannah were barely remembered once speedways and dirt tracks took over.

Racing was not gone forever in Savannah, however. It returned to the Savannah International Raceway (now known as Roebling Road) in 1959. This 2.02-mile track has been used by amateur and professional racing teams for testing and practice, but is not designed

George Cleary, a Savannah native who raced in the American Classic in Savannah in 1913, rode a Thor. He is pictured here in 1914 with the Harley Davidson he rode in the 1914 race. Cleary also opened the Cleary Motorcycle Company in 1912 at 2913 West Broad Street, the first Harley Davidson dealership in the city of Savannah (courtesy Chanel Cleary).

for professional racing, as it lacks grandstands and a tunnel or bridge to reach the infield during races. The designer was John Rueter and the course was built by the Sports Car Club of America with a special endowment from Robert Roebling, a great-grandson of John Roebling and a relative of Washington Roebling, who raced in Savannah in 1910. The first events held by the SCCA were on June 11 and 12, 1960. The venue is owned by the Buccaneer Region of the SCCA and holds amateur racing events for car clubs such as the Porsche and BMW clubs.

Professional racing has been rare in Savannah. Yet, through the amazing efforts of Dr. Rick Timms of Savannah and a group of dedicated business people, civic leaders and race fans, a beautiful new race track was built on Hutchinson Island in downtown Savannah to FIA standards in 1996 and 1997. The track hosted the Indy Lights Series in 1997 and was set to host the larger CART races a year later. However, financial challenges arose, the race became a political pawn in a very ugly year for politics in Savannah and the subsequent races were not run. Like Roebling Road, the track now hosts club, amateur and concours-style events, but many locals hope to see the return of a major professional race. They would certainly welcome the teams who once raced here and now race in Formula One if they chose to return to Savannah for racing.

Epilogue

I am forever thankful to have had the chance to study and relate this exciting and somewhat tragic story of Savannah's racing history. I am not quite sure how I became the voice for this history, but I am very proud and honored to fill that role. Along the way I have met so many wonderful people who felt just as passionately as I do about the significance of the races held here and how the road building techniques used to construct the course became an example to the country.

I was surprised to learn many things as I went along, not the least of which were the stories of the racers and the people who organized the events. It struck me as I researched the drivers that they had highly diverse backgrounds and stories. However, learning about their histories may have been the most difficult part in writing the book. As many of the drivers were new to the sport filled with new technology, they faced the very real danger of death at each match. Likewise, their risk did not end with racing. If they did make it through the perils of a racing career, they had World War I and World War II to contend with. Many of their lives did not end happily, and they are difficult stories to tell. The triumphs and tragedies of these good men are something that I hope readers will consider deeply. Victor Hemery, one of my favorites, may have had the most tragic death of all. He committed suicide while living penniless near Le Mans where he was once a French Grand Prix champion. A road in Paris is named after him, yet few remember his name. I hope this book will bring these men to life again for many people to appreciate and cherish.

My greatest hope is that this book will be enjoyed and that it will educate readers on the early pioneering days of motorsports in Savannah and other cities which are often overlooked. This history was badly in need of being told in modern times on a wider scale, to shine a spotlight on an unlikely little city in the South that just might have made the greatest contribution of all time to American motorsports as we know it today.

Appendix: Specifications and Race Results

• Specifications: Cars of 1911 •

Vanderbilt Cup Race

Car	Driver(s)	Owner	Color	Cylinders	Bore	Stroke	Piston Displacement	Liters
Lozier	Mulford, Grant	Lozier Motor Co.	White	4	5.375 in	6 in	544	8.92
Mercedes	De Palma, Wishart	Mercedes Import	Gray	4	130 mm	180 mm	583	9.78
Pope-Hartford	Disbrow	Disbrow	Vermilion	4	4¾ in	5½ in	389	6.39
Mercer	Hughes	Mercer Auto Co.	Yellow	6	4.36 in	5 in	448	
Fiat	Bruce-Brown, Matson, Parker	Fiat Automobile Co.	Red	4	5 in	7.5 in	589	14.14
Marmon	Dawson, Patschke	Nordyke & Marmon	Yellow and black	4	4¾ in	7 in	496	8.12
Abbott-Detroit	Mitchell, Limberg	Abbott Motor Co.	Blue	4	4½ in	5½ in	349.5	
Jackson	Cobe	Jackson Automobile Co.	Red	4	5 in	5½ in	430	

Car	Wheelbase	Drive	Tires	Magneto	Spark Plugs	Carburetor	Axles	Lubricant
Lozier	124	Shaft	Michelin	Bosch	Bosch	Rayfield	Lozier	Oilzum
Mercedes	116	Chain	Michelin	Bosch	Bosch	Mercedes Special	Mercedes	Monogram
Pope-Hartford	116	Shaft	Michelin	Splitdorf	Bosch	Sundeman	Timken	Oilzum
Mercer	110.5	Shaft	Michelin	Bosch	Bosch	Schebler or Rayfield	Mercer	Monogram
Fiat	116	Chain	Michelin	Bosch	Bosch	Fiat	Fiat	Monogram
Marmon	120	Shaft	Michelin				Marmon	Harris
Abbott-Detroit	120	Shaft	Michelin	Bosch	A.C. Star	Schebler	Timken	
Jackson	105	Shaft	Michelin	Splitdorf	A.C.	Schebler	Lewis	American

American Grand Prize Race

Car	Driver(s)	Owner	Color	Cylinders	Bore	Stroke	Piston Displacement	Liters
Lozier	Mulford, Grant	Lozier Motor Co.	White	4	5.375 in	6 in	544	8.92
Pope-Hartford	Disbrow	Disbrow	Vermilion	4	4¾ in	5½ in	389	6.39
Fiat	Wagner, Bruce-Brown, Bragg	Fiat Automobile Co.	Red	4	5 in	7.5 in	589	14.14
Marmon	Dawson, Patschke	Nordyke & Marmon	Yellow and black	4	4¾ in	7 in	496	8.12
Abbott-Detroit	Mitchell, Limberg	Abbott Motor Co.	Blue	4	4½ in	5½ in	349.5	
Benz	Hemery, Hearne, E. Bergdoll	Benz & Co.	Gray	4	155 mm	200 mm	920	15.2
Marquette-Buick	Basle, Cobe	Buick Motor Co.	Red and white	4	6 in	5¼ in	593	9.73
Mercedes	De Palma, Wishart	Mercedes Import	Gray	4	130 mm	180 mm	583	9.78

Car	Wheelbase	Drive	Tires	Magneto	Spark Plugs	Carburetor	Axles	Lubricant
Lozier	124	Shaft	Michelin	Bosch	Bosch	Rayfield	Lozier	Oilzum
Pope-Hartford	116	Shaft	Michelin	Splitdorf	Bosch	Sundeman	Timken	Oilzum
Fiat	116	Chain	Michelin	Bosch	Bosch	Fiat	Fiat	Monogram
Marmon	120	Shaft	Michelin				Marmon	Monogram
Abbott-Detroit	120	Shaft	Michelin	Bosch	A.C. Star	Schebler	Timken	Harris
Benz	110	Chain	Michelin	Bosch	Bosch	Benz	Benz	Monogram
Marquette-Buick	110	Chain	Michelin	Splitdorf	Splitdorf/A.C.	Schebler	Buick	
Mercedes	116	Chain	Michelin	Bosch	Bosch	Mercedes Special	Mercedes	Monogram

Savannah Challenge Trophy Race

Car	Driver(s)	Owner	Color	Cylinders	Bore	Stroke	Piston Displacement	Liters
Marmon	Patschke, Dawson, Nikrent	Nordyke & Marmon	Yellow and black	4	4²³⁄₆₄ in	5 in	297	
Case	Buckley, Disbrow	J.I. Case Co.	White	4	4⅜ in	5 in	300.7	
Mercer	Hughes, Barnes, Knipper	Mercer Auto Co.	Yellow	4	4⅜ in	5 in	300.6	

Car	Wheelbase	Drive	Tires	Magneto	Spark Plugs	Carburetor	Axles	Lubricant
Marmon	120	Shaft	Michelin	Bosch	Bosch		Marmon	Monogram
Case	96	Shaft	Michelin	Remy	Bosch	Rayfield	Timken	Monogram
Mercer	108	Shaft	Michelin	Bosch	Bosch	Schebler or Rayfield	Mercer	Monogram

Tiedeman Trophy Race

Car	Driver(s)	Owner	Color	Cylinders	Bore	Stroke	Piston Displacement	Liters
Abbott-Detroit	Roberts, Hartman	Abbott Motor Co.	Blue	4	4¼ in	4¾ in	227	
E-M-F	Tower	Simerson	Black and gray	4	4 in	4½ in	226.2	
E-M-F	Evans, Witt	Hanson, Smith	Black and gray	4	4 in	4½ in	226.2	
Ford	Kulick	Ford Motor Co.						

Car	Wheelbase	Drive	Tires	Magneto	Spark Plugs	Carburetor	Axles	Lubricant
Abbott-Detroit	110	Shaft	Michelin	Bosch	A.C. Star	Mayer	Abbott-Detroit	Harris
E-M-F	110	Shaft	Michelin	Splitdorf	A.C.		E-M-F	
E-M-F	110	Shaft	Firestone	Splitdorf	A.C.		E-M-F	
Ford								

Race Results, 1908

American Grand Prize

Car #	Driver	Car	Country	Lap Position 1	2	3	4	5	6	7	8	9	10	11	12	13	14	15	16	Avg. Speed
14	Wagner	Fiat	Italy	2	2	6	4	2	4	4	1	3	2	1	2	3	3	3	1	65.11
8	Hemery	Benz	Germany	8	12	7	6	5	2	2	2	1	1	2	3	2	2	2	2	64.94
6	Nazzarro	Fiat	Italy	6	7	5	3	3	3	3	3	2	3	3	1	1	1	1	3	63.96
15	Hanriot	Benz	Germany	3	3	1	1	1	1	1	5	6	5	4	4	4	4	4	4	62.47
13	Hautvast	Clément-Bayard	France	13	13	11	11	9	9	8	7	7	6	5	5	5	5	5	5	61.22
16	Strang	Renault	France	16	9	8	8	7	7	6	9	9	9	8	8	8	8	6	6	59.77
1	Rigal	Clément-Bayard	France	19	17	15	14	12	11	10	10	10	8	7	7	6	6	6	7	59.47
17	Fournier	Itala	Italy	12	14	12	10	10	10	9	8	8	7	6	6	7	7	8	8	59.34
9	Duray	DeDietrich	France	9	10	14	13	13	14	13	12	12	12	10	10	10	10	Race end		
3	Seymour	Simplex	U.S.	11	11	9	15	14	12	12	13	13	13	11	11	11	11	Race end		
11	Harding	National-6	U.S.	20	20	18	18	16	15	15	14	14	14	12	Out—camshaft					
19	Erle	Benz	Germany	5	5	3	2	6	5	5	4	4	4	Out						
12	Cagno	Itala	Italy	10	6	4	7	8	8	7	6	5	10	Out—rear spring						
2	Mulford	Lozier	U.S.	15	19	17	17	17	17	14	15	15	15	Out						
10	Szisz	Renault	France	4	4	2	5	4	6	Out—front wheel bearing										
7	Zengle	Acme-6	U.S.	17	16	19	19	18	16	Out—front spring										
20	Piacenza	Itala	Italy	14	15	13	9	11	Out											
5	Haupt	Chadwick-6	U.S.	7	8	10	12	Out—bearing												
4	Burman	Buick	U.S.	18	18	Out—mechanical														

Race Results, 1910

American Grand Prix

Car #	Driver	Car	Country	1	2	3	4	5	6	7	8	9	10	11	12	13	14	15	16	17	18	19	20	21	22	23	24	Avg. Speed
15	Bruce-Brown	Benz	Germany	4	4	3	4	5	4	4	2	3	6	3	3	3	3	2	2	2	2	2	2	1	1	1	1	70.55
9	Hemery	Benz	Germany	1	1	1	1	1	1	1	3	5	4	5	5	4	4	5	4	3	3	3	3	2	2	2	2	70.55
17	Burman	Marquette-Buick	U.S.	10	9	9	9	9	7	8	8	7	8	7	7	6	5	5	5	5	4	4	4	4	3	3	3	67.07
4	Mulford	Lozier	U.S.	15	15	15	15	14	14	14	13	10	11	10	10	9	8	7	7	7	6	5	5	5	4	4	4	64.5
12	Horan	Lozier-6	U.S.	11	11	11	11	10	10	10	10	19	9	8	8	7	8	8	8	8	7	7	7	7	6	5	5	63.87
14	Harroun	Marmon	U.S.	12	12	12	12	11	6	9	9	8	10	9	9	8	7	6	6	6	6	6	6	6	5	6		63.82
19	De Palma	Fiat	Italy	8	8	8	7	6	6	6	6	5	6	5	4	2	2	2	1	1	1	1	1	11	Out—cylinder			
10	Nazzarro	Fiat	Italy	6	6	5	4	3	2	2	2	2	2	2	1	1	1	1	2	1	4	Out—chain						
6	Basle	Pope-Hartford	U.S.	13	13	14	14	13	13	14	14	11	12	11	10	9	10	10	9	2	9	Out—piston						
16	Wagner	Fiat	Italy	3	2	2	2	2	3	3	3	3	1	3	3	4	6	9	9	Out								
18	Haupt	Benz	Germany	5	5	5	5	5	4	5	5	4	4	1	1	Out												
7	Grant	Alco-6	U.S.	9	10	10	8	7	8	7	7	6	7	Out—gears														
3	A. Chevrolet	Marquette-Buick	U.S.	2	3	3	10	9	9	11	11	Out—crankshaft																
13	Disbrow	Pope-Hartford	U.S.	14	14	13	13	12	12	12	12	Out—cylinder																
8	Dawson	Marmon	U.S.	7	7	7	6	Out—crankshaft																				

• Race Results, 1911 •

American Grand Prize

Car #	Driver	Car	Country	1	2	3	4	5	6	7	8	9	10	11	12	13	14	15	16	17	18	19	20	21	22	23	24	Avg. Speed
																			LAP POSITION										
48	Bruce-Brown	Fiat	Italy	2	2	2	8	8	6	5	6	5	4	3	3	2	5	4	2	3	3	1	1	1	3	1	1	74.45
47	Hearne	Benz	Germany	7	6	4	2	1	1	2	2	1	1	1	1	1	1	1	1	1	1	3	2	1	2	2	2	74
55	De Palma	Mercedes	Germany	4	5	3	1	5	7	6	7	6	6	4	4	4	3	2	4	4	5	4	4	4	4	3	3	73.75
53	Bragg	Fiat	Italy	1	1	1	5	2	5	3	5	4	3	6	6	6	6	5	5	5	4	5	5	5	5	4	4	70.1
42	Disbrow	Pope-Hartford	U.S.	11	12	10	9	9	8	7	8	7	7	7	7	7	7	6	6	6	6	6	6	7	6	5	5	63.82
44	Mitchell	Abbott-Detroit	U.S.	15	16	13	12	12	11	10	11	10	9	9	8	8	9	8	8	7	7	7	7	7	7	6	Race end	
45	Mulford	Lozier	U.S.	8	9	7	6	3	4	3	3	3	5	5	5	5	4	3	3	2	2	2	2	3	2	Out—driveshaft		
50	Limberg	Abbott-Detroit	U.S.	14	15	12	11	11	10	9	10	9	8	8	9	9	8	7	7	8	8	8	8	8	Out			
41	Wagner	Fiat	Italy	5	3	9	7	6	3	4	4	2	2	2	2	3	2	Out—steering										
43	Basle	Marquette-Buick	U.S.	12	13	11	10	10	9	8	9	8	Out—engine															
54	Wishart	Mercedes	Germany	6	8	14	13	13	13	11	12	Out—cylinder																
51	Patschke	Marmon	U.S.	9	11	8	6	4	2	1	1	Out—engine and chassis separation																
52	L. Bergdoll	Benz	Germany	6	7	5	3	7	12	12	Out—cylinder																	
56	Hemery	Benz	Germany	3	4	15	14	14	14	13	Out—exhaust valve																	
46	Burman	Marmon	U.S.	10	10	6	4	Out—magneto																				
49	Cobe	Marquette-Buick	U.S.	13	14	Out																						

Vanderbilt Cup

Lap Position

Car #	Driver	Car	Country	1	2	3	4	5	6	7	8	9	10	11	12	13	14	15	16	17	Avg. Speed
8	Mulford	Lozier	U.S.	4	4	4	3	1	1	1	1	1	1	1	1	1	1	1	1	1	74.08
10	De Palma	Mercedes	Germany	1	1	1	1	2	3	3	3	3	3	2	2	2	2	2	2	2	73.39
4	Wishart	Mercedes	Germany	3	3	3	2	5	5	4	2	2	2	6	4	4	3	3	3	3	70.97
1	Grant	Lozier	U.S.	7	10	10	9	9	9	8	6	5	4	3	3	3	4	4	4	4	69.82
11	Parker	Fiat	Italy	6	5	9	7	7	7	6	4	6	6	5	5	5	5	5	5	5	68.72
3	Disbrow	Pope-Hartford	U.S.	10	8	8	8	8	8	7	5	4	5	4	6	6	6	6	6	6	67.49
9	Mitchell	Abbott-Detroit	U.S.	13	11	11	11	10	10	9	7	7	7	7	7	7	7	7	Race end		
7	Limberg	Abbott-Detroit	U.S.	14	12	12	12	11	11	10	9	8	8	8	8	8	8	Race end			
12	Patschke	Marmon	U.S.	2	2	2	5	6	6	5	8	Out—pump									
2	Burman	Marmon	U.S.	8	6	5	4	3	2	2	Out—tires										
14	Bruce-Brown	Fiat	Italy	11	7	6	6	4	4	Out—radiator											
15	Matson	Fiat	Italy	5	9	7	10	Out—pump													
6	Hughes	Mercer	U.S.	9	13	13	Out—engine														
5	Cobe	Jackson	U.S.	12	Out—engine																

Notes

Prologue

1. "Dare-Devil Feats at the Casino," *Savannah Morning News*, September 16, 1902, p. 5.
2. U.S. Department of Transportation, "The Road to Civil Rights: Marshall Major Taylor," 2011, www.fhwa.dot.gov/highwayhistory/road/s06.cfm.
3. "The Cyclists Arriving," *Savannah Morning News*, February 20, 1893, p. 8.
4. Ibid.
5. Peter Nye, *Hearts of Lions* (New York: W.W. Norton, 1947), p. 43.
6. "First Day of the Meet," *Savannah Morning News*, February 23, 1893, p. 8.
7. Ibid.
8. Ibid.
9. "With Six Day Race, Men and Motors Now Here," *Savannah Morning News*, September 6, 1902, p. 3
10. Daniel Statenekov, "Chapter 5: Jack Prince," in *Pioneers of American Motorcycle Racing*, November 15, 1996, www.statnekov.com/motorcycles/lives1.html.
11. "With Six Day Race, Men and Motors Now Here," *Savannah Morning News*, September 6, 1902, p. 3.
12. "Six Days Walk Started," *New York Times*, February 10, 1902, p. 10.

Chapter 1

1. Albrecht Durer, "The Great Triumphal Carriage [illustrated work]," *Motor Car Journal 1* (April 14, 1899): 82.
2. Ivor Blashka Hart, *Makers of Science: Mathematics, Physics, Astronomy* (London: Oxford University Press, 1923), p. 63.
3. Thomas T. Solly, *Prestige, Status and Works of Art* (Boston: Racemaker Press, 2008), p. 19.
4. Ibid.
5. Ibid., p. 24.
6. "The Marvelous Growth of Our Automobile Industry [cover]," *Scientific American*, April 9, 1910.
7. Graham Jones, "An Enduring Legacy, Part 2: The Golden Age of Cycling: The World from 1890 to 1914," *Cycling Revealed*, March 2007, www.cyclingrevealed.com/Apr13/EnduringLeg_2.htm, p. 1.
8. Pierre Chany, *La fabuleuse histoire du cyclisme* (Paris: Nathan, 1988).
9. Ivan Rendall, *The Chequered Flag* (London: Wiedenfeld and Nicolson, 1993), p. 12.
10. Ibid., p. 12.
11. Ibid.
12. Peter Helck, *Great Auto Races* (New York: Harry N. Abrams, 1975), p. 26.
13. Rendall, *The Chequered Flag*, p. 15.
14. Ibid.
15. Ibid. p. 26.
16. T. Newcomb, "The Automobile Club of America: Officers and Governors List," *Eighth Annual Automobile Club of America Show* [official souvenir program] (New York, 1907).
17. Jerry Patterson, *The Vanderbilts* (New York: Abrams, 1989), pp. 238–39.
18. Rendall, p. 30.
19. "Club Notes," *Horseless Age*, July 29, 1908, p. 151.
20. Peter Helck, *The Checkered Flag* (New York: Charles Scribner's Sons, 1961), p. 9.
21. "Trail of Blood Is Auto Course," *Indiana Evening Gazette,* October 6, 1906, p. 1.
22. Julian K. Quattlebaum, *The Great Savannah Races of 1908, 1910, 1911* (Columbia, SC: R.L. Bryan, 1957), p. 11.
23. "Speed Craze on Long Island," *Horseless Age,* August 19, 1908, p. 230.
24. "Club Notes," *Horseless Age*, August 19, 1908, p. 230.
25. "Automobilist Cartoon [illustration]," *San Francisco Chronicle*, July 24, 1904.
26. *Gettysburg Compiler*, August 17, 1910, p. 5.
27. "Auto Bill Is Ready," *Oshkosh Daily Northwestern,* March 27, 1907, p. 6.
28. "Residents Threaten to Ask Courts to Stop Vanderbilt Cup Event," *New York Times*, September 29, 1904, p. 7.
29. "No Vanderbilt Race in Jersey," *The News*, July 24, 1907, p. 1.
30. "Speedy Action on Vanderbilt Race," *New York Times*, March 29, 1908, p. 32.

31. Ibid.
32. "Vanderbilt Loyal to A.A.A. Interests," *New York Times*, March 15, 1908, p. 30.
33. Ibid.
34. Ibid.
35. Ibid.
36. Ibid.
37. "Speedy Action on Vanderbilt Race," *New York Times*, March 29, 1908, p. 32.
38. "Foreign Clubs Stand by A.C.A.," *Horseless Age*, July 8, 1908, p. 57.
39. Ibid.
40. "Club Notes," *Horseless Age*, July 15, 1908, p. 91.
41. Ibid., p. 57.
42. Richard J. Hutto, *Their Gilded Cage: The Jekyll Island Club Members* (Macon, GA: Henchard Press, 2006).

Chapter 2

1. "Winton Is After World Records," *Inter-Ocean*, April 5, 1903, p. 14.
2. "Automobile Races at Daytona Beach," *Fort Wayne News*, January 29, 1904, p. 4.
3. "Ormond–Daytona Races," *Chicago Daily Tribune*, December 18, 1904, p. 2.
4. "New 100 Mile Record," *Washington Post*, January 28, 1906, p. 152.
5. "Big Race at Ormond Beach Latest Plan," *Indianapolis News*, January 29, 1907, p. 16.
6. "German Auto Benz Wins Ormond Race," *New York Times*, March 5, 1908, p. 8.
7. "Sensational Time at New Orleans Races," *Atlanta Constitution*, February 21, 1909, p. 4.
8. "No Big Auto Records Made: New Orleans Meeting Very Tame, Even with Oldfield There," *El Paso Herald*, February 7, 1910, p. 3.
9. "Gossip of the Automobilists and Notes of Trade," *New York Times*, March 12, 1911, p. 34.
10. "The First Annual Cotton Carnival," *Galveston Daily News*, August 1, 1909, p. 16.
11. "Fifteen Thousand Viewed Auto Races," *Galveston Daily News*, August 6, 1909, p. 1.
12. "Mulford and Peugeot Are Invincible at Galveston," *Motor Age*, August 6, 1914, p. 14.
13. "Galveston Beach Races Abandoned," *Horseless Age*, March 17, 1915, p. 363.

Chapter 3

1. *America's Greatest Course* [photocard], Foltz Photographics, 1908.
2. Effingham and Chatham County, *Historical and Archaeological Investigations of a Corduroy Road Segment, US 80 Improvements*, n.d., p. 8.
3. Logan Waller Page, "The Motor Car and the Road: The Destructive Effect of High Speed," *Scientific American*, January 15, 1910, p. 46.
4. Peter Helck, *The Checkered Flag* (New York: Charles Scribner's Sons, 1961), p. 47.
5. Ibid., p. 47.
6. Coker F. Clarkson, "History of Good Roads Movements," *New York Times*, May 30, 1909, p. S4.

7. Ibid.
8. Ibid.
9. Joseph Hyde Pratt, "Good Roads Movement in the South," *Annals of the American Academy of Political and Social Science* 35, no. 1 (January 1910): 106.
10. Ibid., 110.
11. "Work Begun on Parkway," *The Automobile*, May 23, 1907, p. 851.
12. "Looks Like a Stock Chassis Race at Savannah in March," *The Automobile*, December 19, 1907, p. 927.
13. "National Interest in Road Congress," *New York Times*, November 12, 1911, p. 46.
14. "Chairman Thompson on European Events," *The Automobile*, October 3, 1907, p. 470.
15. Peter Helck, *The Checkered Flag* (New York: Charles Scribner's Sons, 1961), p. 78.
16. "Long Island Parkway," *Motor*, January 1907, pp. 204–206.
17. "Automobile Track for Indianapolis," *Horseless Age*, January 27, 1909, p. 152.
18. "Indianapolis Speedway Now Ready for its Re-Opening," *The Automobile*, December 9, 1909, p. 987.
19. "Troops for Savannah Race," *New York Times*, November 15, 1908, p. 32.
20. "My Say So," *Automobile Topics*, November 14, 1908, p. 371.
21. "The Construction of Macadam Roads," *Scientific American*, August 1, 1908, pp. 68–70.
22. Ibid.
23. Ibid.
24. "Daylight Practice at Savannah," *Automobile Topics*, October 31, 1908, p. 252.
25. "Two Days Racing at Savannah: March 18/19," *Automobile Topics*, January 25, 1908, p. 1201.
26. "Daylight Practice at Savannah," *Automobile Topics*, October 31, 1908, p. 252.
27. Ibid.
28. "Tomachichi Trophy Valued at $3,000," *Automobile Topics*, February 1, 1908, p. 1276.
29. "Committees Named by Savannah Club," *Automobile Topics*, July 4, 1908, p. 853.
30. City of Savannah Archives, *The Code of the City of Savannah*, Savannah, GA, December 19, 1906.
31. "Presentation of Grand Prize Cup," *The Automobile*, December 17, 1908, p. 870.
32. Liberty County Historical Society, "Completion of U.S. Highway 17," http://www.libertyhistory.org, accessed January 28, 2013.
33. "A.A.A. Contest Board and Technical Committee Appointments for 1910," *Horseless Age*, January 12, 1910, p. 95.
34. *South Eastern Reporter* (St. Paul: West, 1916), p. 690.
35. Andrea Mehrlander, *The Germans of Charleston, Richmond and New Orleans During the Civil War Period, 1850–1870* (Berlin: De Gruyter, 2011), pp. 411–412.
36. W. Harden, *History of Savannah and South Georgia* (Marietta, GA: Cherokee, 1969), pp. 552–553.
37. Ibid.
38. "Carsten Tiedeman to Quit Council; Live in Detroit," *Savannah Morning News*, [Spring] 1928.
39. "Dying with Meningitis: The Little Son of Mr. and Mrs. George Tiedeman," *Savannah Morning News*, February 14, 1901, p. 1.

40. Kenneth E. Palmer, "Foundation Renovation Planned as Memorial," *Savannah Evening Press*, February 7, 1961, p. 1.

Chapter 4

1. "The Stearns Wins Decisive Victories [advertisement]," *Horseless Age*, August 1907, p. 78.
2. "Savannah Challenge," *Automobile Topics*, March 28, 1908, p. 29.
3. "Drivers Who Have Won Their Spurs," *The Automobile*, March 28, 1908.
4. "Fastest Cars Didn't Win at Algonquin," *Automobile Topics*, August 22, 1908, p. 20.
5. "Paderewski's Hands Were Chilled," *Automobile Topics*, May 9, 1908, p. 42.
6. Cy Linder, "Carl Fisher, the Star of Harlem Auto Meet," *Inter Ocean*, October 2, 1904, p. 13.
7. "Auto Crushes Webb Jay," *Chicago Daily Tribune*, August 18, 1905, p. 1.
8. "Driver Robertson Explains Case," *New York Times*, March 15, 1908, p. 30.
9. "By Herbert Lytle," *Savannah Evening Press*, March 18, 1908, p. 1.
10. "One Life Is Paid for Speed Mania," *Atlanta Constitution*, September 30, 1909, p. 2.
11. C.E. Shuart, "Two Accidents Mar Sport," *Indianapolis Star*, May 29, 1910, p. 16.
12. "Youth Autoists Run Races," *Indianapolis Star*, June 5, 1911, p. 4.
13. "News of the Week Condensed," *The Automobile*, February 1, 1912, p. 414.
14. "McCulla a Great Driver," *Savannah Morning News*, March 14, 1908, p. 12.
15. "The Racing Autos Ahead of Record," *New York Times*, September 28, 1907, p. 6.
16. "McCulla Tells of His Accident," *The Automobile*, March 26, 1908, p. 429.
17. "Harrisburg Club Runs 4th Annual Event," *The Automobile*, May 12, 1910, 5.
18. "Fifteen Made Perfect Score, *Automobile Topics*, August 6, 1910, p. 1182.
19. "Packard's Strenuous Midwinter Test," *Horseless Age*, February 26, 1913, 440.
20. "Editorial," *The Automobile*, May 15, 1913, p. 1027.
21. "McCulla Returns to Packard," *The Automobile*, January 27, 1916, p. 205.
22. "Nearly 400,000 People Watch Philadelphia Race," *Automobile Topics*, October 10, 1908, p. 97.
23. Charles Leerhsen, *A Speedway Is Born* (New York: Simon & Schuster, 2011), pp. 82–83.
24. Julian K. Quattlebaum, *Great Savannah Races* (Athens: University of Georgia Press, 1983), pp. 14, 22.
25. "Portola Road Race," *New York Times*, September 12, 1909.
26. "Racing Autos Will Speed Over Oakland Avenue Course Today," *San Francisco Chronicle*, February 22, 1911, p. 11.
27. Herbert Lozier, *Auto Racing Old and New* (New York: Fawcett, 1953), p. 126.
28. "Sport Hill Climbing Contest," *Cycle and Automobile Trade Journal*, July 1908, 58.
29. "Plunge Into Pond," *Washington Post*, August 19, 1905, p. 1.
30. "Glidden Tour," www.vmcca.org/bh/1906.html.
31. Julian Quattlebaum, *The Great Savannah Races* (Athens: University of Georgia Press, 2011), p. xiv.
32. "News Notes," *Automobile Topics*, May 9, 1908, p. 339.
33. Peter Helck, *The Checkered Flag* (New York: Scribner's Sons, 1961), pp. 79–80.
34. "Trade Personals," *Horseless Age*, January 1910, p. 172.
35. "How Strang Met His Death," *Hemmings Blog: Classic and Collectible Cars and Parts*, May 31, 2010, http://blog.hemmings.com/index.php/2010/05/31/how-strang-met-his-death/.
36. "Christie's Hunt for Racing Car," *New York Times*, November 20, 1907, p. 10.
37. "Briarcliffe Trophy Race," *New York Times*, April 25, 1908, p. 1.
38. Doug Nye, *The United States Grand Prix and Grand Prize Races 1908–1977* (New York: Doubleday, 1978), p. 15.
39. "The Hoodoo That Overtook the Mile-a-Minute Man," *Washington Post*, July 10, 1910, p. 8.
40. "World Famous Pilots Reach Motor Speedway," *Indianapolis Star*, May 12, 1911, p. 20
41. Ibid.
42. "Tone Heads New Company," *Automobile Journal*, August 10, 1912, p. 34.
43. "Oldfield Has Narrow Escape in Detroit Race," *Inter Ocean*, August 9, 1905.
44. "Webb Jay Frightfully Injured in Automobile Race," *Fort Wayne Journal-Gazette*, August 19, 1905, p. 1.
45. Quattlebaum, *The Great Savannah Races*, p. xv.
46. "Hoosiers Displays Varied," *Indianapolis Star*, January 15, 1911, p. 18.
47. "Sports News," *Atlanta Constitution*, August 3, 1913, p. 11.
48. "Personal Notes of the Automobile Trade," *Automobile Journal*, August 10, 1912, p. 34.
49. "Personal Notes of the Automobile Trade, *Horseless Age*, July 1, 1917, p. 49.
50. "Autocar Best Performer at Point Breeze," *Automobile Topics*, June 20, 1908, p. 23.
51. "First Hill Climb for Pennsylvania Town," *Automobile Topics*, July 4, 1908, p. 859.
52. Quattlebaum, *The Great Savannah Races*, p. xii.
53. "Locomobile Wins Philadelphia Race," *New York Times*, October 11, 1908, p. 32.
54. "Italy Wins the Grand Prize," *Automobile Topics*, November 28, 1908, p. 507.
55. "Chadwick Sets New Record in Wildwood Meet," *The Automobile*, July 8, 1908, p. 49.
56. "Chadwick 6 Climbed Fastest at Algonquin," *The Automobile*, August 12, 1909, p. 256.
57. "How the Race Was Fought by Laps," *The Automobile*, October 14, 1909, p. 630.
58. Michael J. Seneca, *The Fairmount Park Motor Races* (Jefferson, NC: McFarland, 2003), pp. 118–126.
59. "Zengle Big Winner at Galveston Beach Races," *The Automobile*, August 12, 1911, p. 966.
60. "Zengle Wins Elgin Trophy Race," *Automobile Topics*, September 2, 1911, p. 111.

61. "Sunday Jaunt for Motorists," *Cincinnati Enquirer*, June 1, 1919, p. 57.

Chapter 5

1. "Drivers Named for Racing Cars," *New York Times*, November 12, 1911, p. 46.
2. "Wagner Wins Great Auto Race," *Atlanta Journal*, October 7, 1906, pp. 1–2.
3. Ibid.
4. Ibid.
5. "Secretary Solomon of Auto Meet Board," *Savannah Morning News*, January 11, 1908, p. 12.
6. "First Entry in Chassis Race," *Savannah Morning News*, January 12, 1908, p. 20.
7. "Begin Work on Plans for Meet," *Savannah Morning News*, January 16, 1908, p. 16.
8. "The Automobile Races," *Savannah Morning News*, January 19, 1908, p. 6.
9. City of Savannah, Georgia, *Budget for 1909: Mayor's Annual Report*, 1908.
10. City of Savannah, Georgia, *Mayor's Annual Report*, 1910.
11. City of Savannah, Georgia, *Improvements to Daffin Park by John Nolen*, 1907, Park and Tree Commission Reports, Folder 20A.
12. City of Savannah, Georgia, *Mayor's Annual Report*, 1908, p. 14.
13. City of Savannah, Georgia, *Mayor's Annual Report*, 1908, p. 18.
14. City of Savannah, Georgia, *Mayor's Annual Report*, 1911.
15. "Tomachichi Trophy Valued at $3,000," *Automobile Topics*, February 1, 1908, p. 1276.
16. "Daylight Practice at Savannah," *Automobile Topics*, October 31, 1908, p. 252.
17. "Heavy Betting on These Cars at Savannah Meet," *Atlanta Constitution*, March 11, 1908, p. 111.
18. "Some Record Breaking Speed on Savannah Race Course: Machines in Practice Each Day: Two Accidents," *Reading Times*, March 14, 1908, p. 5.
19. "Tyson Weds, Speeds in Auto," *New York Times*, May 24, 1908, p. 4.
20. "Studebaker Won Out in Endurance Contest," *Savannah Evening Press*, March 19, 1908, p. 8.
21. "Studebaker and Pullman Reach Savannah," *The Automobile*, March 26, 1908, p. 427.
22. "How Soldiers Will Patrol Course," *Savannah Morning News*, March 15, 1908, p. 5.
23. "Savannah Races a Success," *Chicago Daily Tribune*, March 22, 1908, p. 4.
24. "How Soldiers Will Patrol Course," *Savannah Morning News*, March 15, 1908, p. 5.
25. Freg Wagner, *Saga of the Roaring Road* (Los Angeles: Floyd Clymer, 1949).
26. "Is an Ideal Course," *Savannah Morning News*, March 18, 1908, p. 1.
27. "Woman on Course in Racing Auto," *Savannah Morning News*, March 17, 1908, p. 13.
28. "Cost of Auto Racing Game," *Savannah Morning News*, March 17, 1908, p. 13.
29. "Details of Races for Silver Cups," *Savannah Morning News*, March 15, 1908, p. 5.
30. Julian Quattlebaum, *The Great Savannah Races* (Athens: University of Georgia Press, 2011), p. xii.
31. *Savannah Evening Press*, March 18, 1908, p. 1.
32. "Good Going at Savannah," *Cycle and Automobile Trade Journal*, April 1908, p. 41.
33. "Savannah Races a Success," *Chicago Daily Tribune*, March 22, 1908, p. 4.
34. "The Six-Cylinder Candidates for the Southern Cup," *The Automobile*, March 26, 1908, p. 10.
35. Quattlebaum, *The Great Savannah Races*, p. xiv.
36. "Savannah Races a Success," *Chicago Daily Tribune*, March 22, 1908, p. 4.
37. "Difficulties Met and Overcome," *The Automobile*, March 26, 1908, pp. 10–11.
38. Ibid., p. 11.
39. *Savannah Evening Press*, March 19, 1908, p. 1.
40. Quattlebaum, *The Great Savannah Races*, p. xv.
41. "At the Festive Board with Georgia's Governor," *The Automobile*, March 26, 1908, p. 428.

Chapter 6

1. "German Auto Benz Wins Ormond Race," *New York Times*, March 5, 1908, p. 8.
2. Michael Seneca, *The Fairmount Park Motor Races* (Jefferson, NC: McFarland, 1973), p. 24.
3. Peter Helck, *Great Auto Races* (New York: Harry Abrams, 1975), pp. 122–124.
4. "1908 Jericho Starting Line Up," November 25, 2010, www.vanderbiltcupraces.com/blog/article/Friday_november_26_2010_starting_lineup_of_the_6_j_cars_of_the_1908_jericho_s.
5. Julian Quattlebaum, *The Great Savannah Race* (Athens: University of Georgia Press, 2011), p. 34.
6. www.historicracing.com/drivers, n.d.
7. "Cagno and Itala Win Targa Trophy," *The Automobile*, May 10, 1906, p. 777.
8. Peter Helck, *Great Auto Races* (New York: Harry Abrams, 1975), pp. 230–233.
9. Bosch advertisement, *The Automobile*, October 3, 1907, p. 102.
10. "Going Some," *Cincinnati Enquirer*, November 24, 1908, p. 4.
11. "Spectators Stop Hill Climb Contest," *New York Times*, December 5, 1909, p. 34.
12. "Some of the Trouble of the Light Cars," *The Automobile*, December 3, 1908, p. 778.
13. "A Great Day for the Little Fellows," *The Automobile*, September 9, 1909, p. 427.
14. Gary Doyle, *Ralph De Palma: Gentleman Champion* (Oceanside, CA: Golden Age, 2005), p. 54
15. "Indoor Cycle Races," *New York Times*, September 27, 1901, p. 8.
16. Doyle, *Ralph De Palma*, p. 54.
17. "Souvenir of the Grand Prize Race Over the Savannah Course," Indian Refining Co., 1910.
18. Quattlebaum, *The Great Savannah Races*, p. 119.
19. "Racing Drivers and Their Past Performances," *Motor Age*, May 29, 1919, p. 22.
20. Helck, *Great Auto Races*, p. 83.
21. Fred Wagner, *Saga of the Roaring Road: A Story of Early Auto Racing in America* (Los Angeles: Floyd Clymer, 1949).

22. http://www.motorsportshalloffame.com/halloffame/1991/Ralph_Depalma_main.htm, n.d.
23. "Concerning Those Who Will Drive: Arthur Duray," *The Automobile*, October 4, 1906, p. 423.
24. www.historicracing.com/drivers.cfm?type=drivers_alpha&tStart+Row=139&AlphaIndex=D, n.d.
25. "Motor Specialists Find Niche in Service," *Motor Age*, June 17, 1917, p. 15.
26. "Rivista illustrata mensile," *Fiat Journal*, 1914, 9.
27. "The Open Air Show at Empire Track," *Horseless Age*, May 1906, p. 149.
28. "How the Lancia–Hilliard Driving Won the Light Car Race," *The Automobile*, December 3, 1908, p. 774.
29. "The Light Car Race," *Automobile Topics*, November 28, 1908, p. 512.
30. "Two Bodies Are Found," *Daily Mail*, September 23, 1936, p. 3.
31. "Obituaries: Charles Ewing Easter," *Daily Times* (Salisbury, MD), July 14, 1962, p. 10.
32. "The Herkomer Trophy Contest," *Motor Car Journal*, June 16, 1906, p. 339.
33. "Approves New Prince Henry Tour," *Automobile Topics*, February 18, 1911, p. 1253.
34. "Peugeot and Benz Break Climb Record," *The Automobile*, June 15, 1913, p. 1157.
35. "Unconscious Man Drives Benz Car," *Savannah Morning News*, November 27, 1908, p. 1.
36. "Race and Competition at Charles River Track," *Horseless Age*, October 1898, p. 50.
37. Ivan Rendall, *The Chequered Flag* (London: Weidenfeld and Nicolson, 1993), p. 27.
38. Hans Etzrodt, "Grand Prix Winners 1895–1945, Part I," www.kolumbus.fi/leif.snellman/gpw1.htm, n.d.
39. "Auto Record," *Indianapolis News*, September 16, 1901, p. 11.
40. *Daily Review* (Decatur, IL), November 17, 1901, p. 1.
41. "Wildcat Engine Wrecks an Auto," *Chicago Daily Tribune*, October 31, 1901, p. 1.
42. "Harking Back a Decade," *The Automobile*, November 28, 1902, p. 137.
43. "Fournier to Try Air," *Inter Ocean*, November 20, 1908, p. 4.
44. "Successful Evening Flights," *London Times*, August 23, 1909, p. 6.
45. Rendall, *The Chequered Flag*, p. 39.
46. Quattlebaum, *The Great Savannah Races*, p. 45.
47. "Willie Haupt," www.champcarstats.com/drivers/HauptWillie.htm, n.d.
48. Helck, *Great Auto Races*, pp. 176–179.
49. "How the Autos Climbed Skippack Hill," *The Automobile*, July 2, 1908, p. 7.
50. "Souvenir of the American Grand Prize: How the Race Was Won and Fun," Indian Refining Co., 1911.
51. Seneca, *Fairmount Park Motor Races*, pp. 194–199.
52. Claude Yvens, *Lucien Hautvast: Sportsman, Gentleman-Driver et tutoyer de legends* (Neufchatel: Weyrich, 2005).
53. Helck, *Great Auto Races*, p. 178.
54. "Nazzaro Replaced by Wagner for Savannah," *Automobile Topics*, October 21, 1911, p. 103.
55. *Club Journal*, October 1, 1910, p. 503.
56. "Eddie Hearne Indianapolis 500 Racing Statistics," www.racing-reference.info/driver/Eddie_Hearne, n.d.
57. "Victor Hemery Biography," www.vanderbiltcupraces.com/bio/hemery, n.d.
58. "Chevrolet's Opinion of the Big Race," *The Automobile*, June 24, 1909, p. 1014.
59. www.carsablanca.de/Magazin/rennsport/beruehmte-rennfahrer-victor-hemery, n.d.
60. "The Story of the Winner," *The Automobile*, October 11, 1906, p. 8.
61. Quattlebaum, *The Great Savannah Races*, p. 18.
62. "Grand Prix of France," *Horseless Age*, July 26, 1911, p. 139.
63. "L'accident de M. Fournier," *La vie au Grand Air*, July 29, 1911, p. 503.
64. "Harry Payne and Family Among Those at Course," *New York Times*, October 11, 1908, p. 31.
65. "White Mountain Tour Ends Successfully," *Automobile Topics*, July 29, 1905, p. 1140.
66. "Baltimore's First Show," *The Automobile*, April 12, 1906, p. 653.
67. "Gossip of the Race," *The Automobile*, December 3, 1908, p. 795.
68. "International Light Car Race at Savannah, GA: November 25, 1908," *The Automobile*, December 3, 1908, p. 775.
69. Curt McConnell, *A Reliable Car and a Woman Who Knows It* (Jefferson, NC: McFarland, 2000), p. 23.
70. "Lozier Advertisement," *New York Times*, July 17, 1907, p. 7.
71. "Lozier Wins Race," *Inter Ocean*, September 13, 1908, p. 17.
72. Quattlebaum, *The Great Savannah Races*, pp. 39, 42.
73. "Make 1196 Miles in 24 Hours," *Daily Review*, October 17, 1909, p. 1.
74. "Mulford Wins Elgin Race," *Oshkosh Daily Northwestern*, August 29, 1910, p. 6.
75. Charles Leerhsen, *Blood and Smoke* (New York: Simon & Schuster, 2011), p. 192.
76. Allen Brown, www.oldracingcars.com/driver/Ralph_Mulford, 2000.
77. Leerhsen, *Blood and Smoke*, p. 246.
78. Quattlebaum, *The Great Savannah Races*, p. 121.
79. www.racing-reference.info/driver/Ralph_Mulford, n.d.
80. http://www.grandprixhistory.org/nazzaro_bio.htm, n.d.
81. "Versatile Driver-Constructor," *World of Speed*, 1972, pp. 1511–1514.
82. Ibid.
83. "The Man Who Can Drive Two Miles a Minute," *Illustrated London News*, June 13, 1908, p. 1.
84. Helck, *The Checkered Flag*, pp. 119–120.
85. http://www.grandprixhistory.org/nazzaro_bio.htm, n.d.
86. National Records and Archives Administration, New York Passenger Lists: 1820–1957.
87. "Itala Grand Prix Car," *Classic Car Weekly*, classiccarweekly.wordpress.com/2012/06/21/itala-grand-prix-car/, June 21, 2012.
88. driverdb.com/drivers/victor-rigal, February 12, 2011.
89. "Grand Prix Event at Amien," *Indianapolis Star*, March 23, 1913, p. 30.

90. "French Grand Prix," *The Automobile*, February 19, 1914, p. 478.
91. "Duray on Special Work," *The Automobile*, November 25, 1915, p. 991.
92. www.grandprixhistory.org/mille-miglia-history.htm, n.d.
93. Mauthasen Gusen Concentration Camp records, Austria.
94. "Drivers of the American Grand Prize and Course Over Which They'll Race," *New York Times*, November 22, 1908, p. 1.
95. "Simplex Advertisement," *Automobile Topics*, June 25, 1908, p. 213.
96. Seneca, *The Fairmount Park Motor Races*, pp. 80–81.
97. Jow Saward, "Ferenc Szisz: The Hungarian Railway Engineer," www.grandprix.com/ft/ftjs032.html, October 31, 2001.
98. Ferenc Szisz, www.historicracing.com/drivers.cfm?type=rivers_alpha&tStartRow=139&AlphaIndex==S, n.d.
99. Cyril Posthumus, *The 1906–1908 Grand Prix Renaults* 79 (Surrey: Profile, 1969), p. 4.
100. Remy Paolozzi, "The Long Reign of Louis Wagner," Autosport.com, October 28, 2008.
101. Rendall, *The Chequered Flag*, p. 57.
102. Helck, *The Checkered Flag*, p. 116.
103. "Wagner Wins Great Auto Race," *Atlanta Journal*, October 7, 1906, p. 1.
104. "Wagner Won a Vanderbilt," *New York Times*, November 27, 1908, p. 6
105. "Wagner en vol [cover]," *La Vie au Grand Air*, June 4, 1910.
106. Remy Paolozzi, "The Long Reign of Louis Wagner," Autosport.com, October 28, 2008.

Chapter 7

1. "The Grand Prize Race at Savannah," *The Automobile*, August 1, 1908, p. 1145.
2. Ibid.
3. Ibid.
4. "Small Car Race, Too, for Savannah," *Automobile Topics*, August 15, 1908, p. 1272.
5. Ibid.
6. "Light Car Race Decided Upon," *Automobile Topics*, August 29, 1908, p. 1410.
7. Ibid.
8. "More Entries for Savannah Races," *Automobile Topics*, October 13, 1908, p. 251.
9. "Concerning the Light Car Races," *The Automobile*, November 12, 1908, p. 668.
10. "Buick Enthusiasm at Savannah," *Washington Post*, December 7, 1908, p. 11.
11. "What the Grand Prize Cost," *New York Times*, November 8, 1908, p. 32.
12. "Speed Practice at Savannah Begins Monday," *Automobile Topics*, November 14, 1908, p. 365.
13. "One Killed in Auto Crash," *Inter Ocean*, November 22, 1908, p. 9.
14. "Savannah Race Gets First Victim," *New York Times*, November 22, 1908, p. 29.
15. Julian Quattlebaum, *The Great Savannah Races* (Athens: University of Georgia Press, 2011), p. 28.
16. "List of Manifest of Alien Passengers for the United States," Record 190, 1907.
17. "Ellis Island: Passenger List," Marius De Rosa, ID #102109140151, October 17, 1907.
18. Savannah Health Officer's Department, *Record of Marriages and Deaths*, November 20, 1908.
19. Quattlebaum, *The Great Savannah Races*, p. 31.
20. "Some Troubles of the Light Cars," *The Automobile*, December 3, 1908, p. 778.
21. Ibid.
22. Ibid., p. 777.
23. Ibid., p. 778.
24. Quattlebaum, *The Great Savannah Races*, p. 31.
25. "Italian Car, American Driver Was the Winning Combination in International Race," *Cincinnati Enquirer*, November 26, 1908, p. 10.
26. "Italian Auto in Front," *Washington Post*, November 26, 1908, p. 8.
27. "International Light Car Race of the A.C.A. at Savannah, GA," *The Automobile*, December 3, 1908, p. 775.
28. Quattlebaum, *The Great Savannah Races*, p. 35.
29. "The Light Car Race: Order of Finish," *Automobile Topics*, November 28, 1908, p. 510.

Chapter 8

1. Cyril Posthumus, *The 1906–1908 Grand Prix Renaults* 79 (Surrey: Profile, 1969), p. 11.
2. http://www.seriouswheels.com/cars/top-1908-Benz-150-hp-Racing-Car.htm, n.d.
3. http://www.ultimatecarpage.com/car/5215/Itala-100hp-Grand-Prix.html, n.d.
4. "What the Grand Prize Cost," *New York Times*, November 8, 1908, p. 32.
5. "Michelin's Prize Offers," *New York Times*, November 15, 1908, p. 32.
6. "All Roads Lead to Grand Prize Race," *New York Times*, November 18, 1908, p. 11.
7. "By Road to Savannah," *New York Times*, November 15, 1908, p. 32.
8. "Additions and Withdrawals for Savannah Races," *The Automobile*, November 7, 1908, p. 294.
9. "The Automobile Races," *Palestine Daily Herald*, November 25, 1908.
10. "Auto Races at Savannah Start," *Brisbee Daily Review*, November 26, 1908, p. 8.
11. Julian Quattlebaum, *The Great Savannah Races* (Athens: University of Georgia Press, 2011), p. 39.
12. Ibid.
13. Ibid.
14. Doug Nye, *The United States Grand Prix and Grand Prize Races* (New York: Doubleday, 1978), p. 13.
15. Quattlebaum, *The Great Savannah Races*, p. 40.
16. Ibid.
17. "Wagner Stops for Wine," *New York Times*, November 27, 1908, p. 6.
18. Peter Helck, *Great Auto Races* (New York: Harry N. Abrams, 1975), p. 78.
19. "Wagner's Winnings," *New York Times*, November 27, 1908, p. 6.
20. Quattlebaum, *The Great Savannah Races*, p. 44.
21. "Savannah as It Was and Is," *Automobile Topics*, July 18, 1908, p. 904.

22. Ibid.
23. Ibid.
24. "Annual Report of the American Automobile Association," *Horseless Age*, December 2, 1908, p. 819.
25. "Savannah as It Was and Is," *Automobile Topics*, July 18, 1908, p. 904.
26. "A.A.A. Membership," *Horseless Age*, December 9, 1908, p. 842.
27. "A Blow to Racing," *Horseless Age*, December 2, 1908, pp. 812–813.

Chapter 9

1. "Boston Meet," *Horseless Age*, May 31, 1905, p. 619.
2. "Simplex Scores in Brighton's Brutal 24 Hours," *The Automobile*, October 8, 1908, p. 492.
3. Julian Quattlebaum, *The Great Savannah Races* (Athens: University of Georgia Press, 2011), p. 116.
4. Paul Fearnley, "America's First Racing Legend," *Racer*, February 2010, 57–59.
5. "Daytona Beach Races," *Horseless Age*, March 1909, p. 442.
6. "Cold Gray Dawn Start for Vanderbilt," *Horseless Age*, July 27, 1910, p. 143.
7. Helck, *The Checkered Flag*, p. 127.
8. Souvenir of the American Grand Prize, How the Race Was Won and Run, Indian Refining Co., 1911.
9. "Bruce Brown Is Tendered a Banquet," *Automobile Topics*, December 17, 1910, p. 681.
10. "Bruce-Brown Will Drive Fiat Among Foreign Talent," *Horseless Age*, January 31, 1912, p. 277.
11. "Bruce-Brown Mets Death in Practice," *Automobile Topics*, October 5, 1912, p. 508.
12. Fred Wagner, *Saga of the Roaring Road* (Los Angeles: Floyd Clymber, 1949), p. 72.
13. Helck, *The Checkered Flag*, p. 125.
14. "Simplex Scores in Brighton's Brutal 24 Hour," *The Automobile*, October 8, 1908, p. 492.
15. Helck, *The Checkered Flag*, pp. 88–89.
16. Ibid.
17. "Louis Disbrow Held," *Sioux Valley News*, July 17, 1902, p. 3.
18. Helck, *Great Auto Races*, p. 80.
19. Louis Disbrow, www.vanderbiltcupraces.com/drivers, n.d.
20. Harry Grant, www.vanderbiltcupraces.com/drivers, n.d.
21. Charles Leersen, *Blood and Smoke* (New York: Simon & Schuster, 2011), pp. 163–172.
Joe Horan
22. "What Happened in 1910," *Motor*, December 1910, p. 66.
23. Helck, *The Checkered Flag*, p. 127.
24. Leerhsen, *Blood and Smoke*, p. 220.
25. Tim Considine, *American Grand Prix Racing: A Century of Drivers and Cars* (Osceola, WI: MBI, 1997), p. 186.
26. "Limberg Killed in Metropolitan Event," *The Automobile*, May 18, 1916, p. 887.
27. "Vanderbilt Cup Race by Laps," *Automobile Topics*, December 2, 1911, p. 140.
28. "Entry Blanks for Elgin," *The Automobile*, May 13, 1915, p. 872.
29. Michael Seneca, *The Fairmount Park Motor Races* (Jefferson, NC: McFarland, 2003), p. 107.
30. http://www.oldracingcars.com/driver/Joe_Matson, n.d.
31. www.champcarstats.com/drivers/ParkerEdward.htm, n.d.
32. www.vanderbiltcup.com/drivers/Patschke Cyrus.htm, n.d.
33. "Preparing for Vanderbilt and Grand Prize Races," *Automobile Topics*, September 3, 1910, p. 1441.
34. Tim Considine, *American Grand Prix Racing: A Century of Drivers and Cars* (Osceloa, WI: MBI, 1997), p. 19.
35. "Hearne Is the Only One Left of the Millionaire Drivers," *Muskogee Times Democrat*, September 30, 1914, p. 9.
36. www.firstsuperspeedway.com/photo-gallery/spencer-wishart-elgin, n.d.
37. "Wishart to Sell Truck," *Horseless Age*, December 6, 1911, p. 868.
38. "Hearne Is the Only One Left of the Millionaire Drivers," *Muskogee Times Democrat*, September 30, 1914, p. 9.

Chapter 10

1. Julian Quattlebaum, *The Great Savannah Races* (Athens: University of Georgia Press, 2011), p. 67.
2. "How They Ran the Second Grand Prize," *Motor*, December 1910, p. 136.
3. "Dawson Always in the Lead," *Chicago Daily Tribune*, November 12, 1910, p. 9.
4. Quattlebaum, *The Great Savannah Races*, p. 70.
5. Ibid., p. 68.
6. "Record-Breaking Time," *Atlanta Constitution*, November 12, 1910, p. 3.
7. "Local Car and Driver Finish Second in Race for the Tiedeman Trophy," November 12, 1910). *Atlanta Constitution*, p. 3.
8. Quattlebaum, *The Great Savannah Races*, p. 71.
9. "Grand Prize Was a Decidedly Modern Race," *Horseless Age*, November 30, 1910, p. 11.
10. Doug Nye, *The United States Grand Prix and Grand Prize Races* (New York: Doubleday, 1978), p. 16.
11. Tim Considine, *American Grand Prix racing* (Osceola, WI: MBI, 1997), p. 19.
12. Quattlebaum, *The Great Savannah Races*, p. 82.
13. Helck, *Great Auto Races*, p. 80.
14. Helck, *The Checkered Flag*, p. 170.
15. Souvenir of the Grand Prize Race Over the Savannah Course: Savannah, Georgia, November 11–12, 1910, Indian Refining Co., 1911.
16. Quattlebaum, *The Great Savannah Races*, p. 76.
17. Helck, *The Checkered Flag*, p. 81.
18. Ibid.
19. "American Wins Grand Prize," *Automobile Topics*, November 19, 1910, p. 5.
20. "Way They Finished," *Atlanta Constitution*, November 13, 1910, p. 4.
21. "American Wins Grand Prize," *Automobile Topics*, November 19, 1910, p. 5.
22. "David Bruce-Brown Wins Grand Prize in New Time," *Inter Ocean*, November 13, 1910, p. 27.

23. "Grand Prize Was a Decidedly Modern Race," *Horseless Age*, November 30, 1910, p. 11.
24. "Way They Finished," *Atlanta Constitution*, November 13, 1910, p. 4.

Chapter 11

1. Julian K. Quattlebaum, *The Great Savannah Races of 1908, 1910 and 1911* (Columbia, SC: R.L. Bryan, 1957), p. 99.
2. "The Curtain Raisers," *Horseless Age*, November 29, 1911, p. 827.
3. Quattlebaum, *The Great Savannah Races of 1908, 1910 and 1911*, p. 98.
4. "The Curtain Raisers," *Horseless Age*, November 29, 1911, p. 826.
5. "All Eyes Now Turned on Savannah Races," *Washington Herald*, November 26, 1911, p.
6. "World's Most Famous Will Be at Savannah," *Watchman and Southron*, November 15, 1911.
7. "Oldfield Barred from Vanderbilt Press Stand," *Horseless Age*, November 29, 1911, p. 827.
8. Quattlebaum, *The Great Savannah Races of 1908, 1910 and 1911*, p. 103.
9. Ibid., pp. 105–106.
10. "Mulford in Lozier Wins Classic Vanderbilt Race," *Horseless Age*, November 29, 1911, p. 826.
11. Peter Helck and Ralph Mulford, Foreword to the Vanderbilt Cup race 1911. *The checkered flag*. New York: Charles Scribner's Sons, p. 90.
12. "That Record Question at Savannah," *Horseless Age*, December 6, 1911, p. 843.
13. "Everything But Speed Is Forgotten in the Vanderbilt Cup Race, Won by Ralph Mulford," *Cincinnati Enquirer*, November 29, 1911, p. 9.
14. "Abbott-Detroit's Good Work in Race," *Harrisburg Telegraph*, December 6, 1911, p. 6.
15. "Ralph Mulford in Lozier Drives in Victorious Style for Whole Race," *San Francisco Chronicle*, November 28, 1911, p. 10.
16. "Wagner on Savannah Races," *New York Times*, November 26, 1911, p. 34.
17. "Sports," *El Paso Herald*, November 30, 1911, p. 5.

Chapter 12

1. Julian K. Quattlebaum, *The Great Savannah Races of 1908, 1910 and 1911* (Columbia, SC: R.L. Bryan, 1957), p. 92.
2. Quattlebaum, *The Great Savannah Races of 1908, 1910 and 1911*, p. 111.
3. Doug Nye, *The United States Grand Prix and Grand Prize Races 1908–1977* (New York: Doubleday, 1978), pp. 20–25.
4. Peter Helck, *The Checkered Flag* (New York: Charles Scribner's Sons, 1971), p. 127.
5. Peter Helck, *Great Auto Races* (New York: Harry N. Abrams, 1975), p. 85.
6. Helck, *The Checkered Flag*, p. 127.
7. "Brown Wins Grand Prize," *Gettysburg Times*, December 1, 1911, p. 3.
8. "Hemery's Benz Scored Fastest Lap," *Horseless Age*, December 6, 1911, p. 837.
9. Helck, *The Checkered Flag*, p. 119.
10. "New Mark for Road Racing," *Indiana Gazette*, December 2, 1911, p. 6.
11. "New Record for Auto: Bruce-Brown Wins the Grand Prize Race at Savannah," *Washington Post*, December 1, 1911, p. 3.
12. "Grand Prize Won by David Bruce-Brown," *Chicago Daily Tribune*, December 1, 1911, p. 13.
13. "Fighting for Second Place," *Horseless Age*, December 6, 1911, p. 842.
14. "New Mark for Road Racing," *Indiana Gazette*, December 2, 1911, p. 6.

Chapter 13

1. Julian K. Quattlebaum, *The Great Savannah Races of 1908, 1910 and 1911* (Columbia, SC: R.L. Bryan, 1957), p. 125.
2. "New Mark for Road Racing," *Indiana Gazette*, December 2, 1911, p. 6.
3. "Savannah Men Coming for Races," *Automobile Topics*, January 4, 1913, p. 531.
4. "Some Impressions of a Former Grand Prix Manager by Victor Breyer," *The Automobile*, December 3, 1908, p. 771.
5. Ibid., p. 772.
6. "Little Hope for Savannah Races," *Automobile Topics*, October 4, 1913, p. 580.
7. Ivan Rendall, *The Chequered Flag* (London: Weidenfeld and Nicolson, 1993), p. 70.
8. Peter Helck, *Great Auto Races* (New York: Harry N. Abrams, 1975), p. 65.
9. "Bob Perry Wins Motorcycle Race," *Atlanta Constitution*, December 27, 1913, p. 1.
10. "Killed in Cycle Race," *New York Times*, November 26, 1914, p. 1.

Bibliography

Books

Chany, Pierre. *La fabuleuse histoire du cyclisme.* Paris: Nathan, 1988.
Doyle, Gary. *Ralph De Palma: Gentleman Champion.* Oceanside, CA: Golden Books, 2005.
Harden, W. *History of Savannah and South Georgia.* Marietta, GA: Cherokee, 1969.
Hart, Ivor Blashka. *Makers of Science: Mathematics, Physics, Astronomy.* London: Oxford University Press, 1923.
Helck, Peter. *The Checkered Flag.* New York: Charles Scribner's Sons, 1961.
_____. *Great Auto Races.* New York: Harry N. Abrams, 1975.
Hutto, Richard J. *Their Gilded Cage: The Jekyll Island Club Members.* Macon, GA: Henchard Press, 2006.
Leerhsen, Charles. *Blood and Smoke: A True Tale of Mystery, Mayhem and the Birth of the Indy 500.* New York: Simon & Schuster, 2011.
_____. *A Speedway Is Born.* New York: Simon & Schuster, 2011.
Lozier, Herbert. *Auto Racing Old and New.* New York: Fawcett, 1953
McConnell, Curt. *A Reliable Car and a Woman Who Knows It.* Jefferson, NC: McFarland, 2000.
Mehrlander, Andrea. *The Germans of Charleston, Richmond and New Orleans During the Civil War Period, 1850–1870.* Berlin: De Gruyter, 2011.
Nye, Doug. *The United States Grand Prix and Grand Prize Races 1908–1977.* New York: Doubleday, 1978.
Nye, Peter. *Hearts of Lions.* New York: W.W. Norton, 1947.
Patterson, Jerry. *The Vanderbilts.* New York: Abrams 1989.
Posthumus, Cyril. *The 1906–1908 Grand Prix Renaults.* No. 79. Surrey: Profile, 1967.
Quattlebaum, Julian K. *The Great Savannah Races.* Athens: University of Georgia Press, 2011.
_____. *Savannah races of 1908, 1910, 1911.* Columbia, SC: R.L. Bryan, 1957.
Rendall, Ivan. *The Chequered Flag.* London: Wiedenfeld and Nicolson, 1993.
Seneca, Michael J. *The Fairmount Park Motor Races.* Jefferson, NC: McFarland, 2003.
Solly, Thomas T. *Prestige, Status and Works of Art.* Boston: Racemaker Press, 2008.
South Eastern Reporter. St. Paul, MN: West, 1916.
Wagner, Fred. *Saga of the Roaring Road.* Los Angeles: Floyd Clymer, 1949.
Yvens, Claude. *Lucien Hautvast: Sportsman, Gentleman-Driver et tutoyer de legendes.* Neufchatel: Weyrich, 2005.

Periodicals

Atlanta Constitution
Annals of the American Academy of Political and Social Science
The Automobile
Automobile Topics
Automobile Journal
Brisbee Daily Review
Chicago Daily Tribune
Cincinnati Enquirer
The Club Journal
Cycle and Automobile Trade Journal
Daily Mail
Daily Review
El Paso Herald
Fort Wayne Journal Gazette
Gettysburg Compiler
Harrisburg Telegraph
Horseless Age
Illustrated London News
Indiana Evening Gazette
Indiana Gazette
Indianapolis News
Indianapolis Star
Inter Ocean
London Times
Motor
Motor Age
Motor Car Journal
Muskogee Times Democrat
New York Times
The News
Oshkosh Daily Northwestern
Palestine Daily Herald
Racer
Reading Times
Rivista Illustrata Mensile

San Francisco Chronicle
Savannah Evening Press
Savannah Morning News
Scientific American

Sioux Valley News
La Vie au Grand Air
Washington Herald
Washington Post

Watchman and Southron
World of Speed

Websites

www.autosport.com
www.blog.hemmings.com/index.php
www.carsablanca.de
www.champcarstats.com
www.classiccarweekly.wordpress.com
www.cyclingrevealed.com

www.driverdb.com
www.fhwa.dot.gov
www.firstsuperspeedway.com
www.grandprix.com
www.historicracing.com
www.kolumbus.fi
www.motorsportshalloffame.com

www.oldracingcars.com
www.racing-reference.info
www.seriouswheels.com
www.statnekov.com
www.ultimatecarpage.com
www.vanderbiltcupraces.com
www.vmcca.org

Index

Page numbers in ***bold italics*** indicate pages with illustrations.

AAA *see* American Automobile Association
Abbott-Detroit 143, 168–169, 172–178, 179–196
Abercorn Street 40
ACA *see* Automobile Club of America
ACB *see* Automobile Club de Brussels
ACF *see* Automobile Club de France
ACG *see* Automobile Club of Germany
Acme 47, 54, 58, 120–134, 145
Acme Sextuplet 52, 65, 74, 75, 77, ***79***
Adams, C. 202
Ainsley 156
Air Show 89
Ajax tires 119
Albright 156
Alco 140, 141, 148, 153–166, ***159***
Alcyon 87
Alda 108
Alfa Romeo 106, 110, 111
Algeria 108
Algonquin Cup 47, 59, 97
Allison 37
ALMS *see* American Le Mans Series
Amarillo, Texas 25
America 91
American Aristocrat 114, 117
American Automobile Association (AAA) 12, 17, 18, 19, 21, 23, 24, 26, 28, 29, 34, 35, 37, 44, 46, 49, 55, 61, 62, 71, 79, 99, 112, 133, 134, 146, 167, 170–178, 199–202
American Classic Savannah 300 motorcycle race 202, ***203***, ***204***
American Grand Prize 120–134, 153–166, 179–196, 197, 200–203; *see also* Grand Prize of the Automobile Club of America
American Le Mans Series (ALMS) 2
American Locomotive 81, 149

American Motor League 17
American Underslung 47, 50, 54, ***57***, 58, 65, ***66***, ***67***, 68, 74, ***75***, ***76***, ***77***, ***78***, 93
"America's Greatest Automobile Course" 31, ***32***, ***33***
Amiens race 106
Amilcar 88
Amplex 143
Amsterdam, New York 55
Anderson, John 25
Annesberger, W. 148
Antoinette (aircraft) 92
"The Appendix" 125
Apperson 47, 50, 62, 68, 73, 74, 75, 76, 77; Jackrabbit 49, 58, 62, 65, 66, 71, 72, 73
Apperson, Edgar 5, 66, 67
Aries 88
Arles Salon, France 98
Ascot 28, 144
Astor 17, 24, 142, 144
Athletic Park 7, 167
Athy, Ireland 95
Atlanta, Georgia 50, 54, 55, 64, 74, 79, 123, 142
Atlanta Constitution 102, 166
Atlantic Avenue 44, 63
Atlantic City 51
Atlantic Coast Highway 43–44
Atlantic Ocean 31, 36, 41, 43
Atlas 114
Auffargis, France 108
Augusta 62
Augusta gravel 39, 40
Austria 107
Autocar 114
The Automobile 25, 94
Automobile Club de Brussels (ACB) 95
Automobile Club de France (ACF) 23, 24
Automobile Club of America (ACA) 12, ***17***, 18, 19, ***21***, ***22***, 23, 24, 43,

46, 61, 71, 112, 113, 122, 133, 134, 141, 153–166, 167, 200–202
Automobile Club of Germany (ACG) 23, 24
automobile hearse 116
automobile industry growth 15
automobile registration 44
"The Automobile Speed King of the World" 176
Automobile Topics 106, 133, 165
Auvergne 83, 86
aviation inventions 5

Bablot 144
Baby Peugeot 87
Bacon, Judge Oliver T. ***43***
Bacon, Roger 15
Baily Carriage Company 51
Baird, Isaac 6, 10
Baird, John 6, 7
Baker, D'Arcy 104
Baldwin, George J. 43
Baldwin, Ralph 61
Ballot 97, 110
Baltimore 64, 81, 88
Barber, Tom 41
Barber Asphalt Paving Company 63
Barnes 169–170
baseball 7, 12
Basle, Charles 101, 135, 153–166, 179–196
Basle, M. 153–166
Batchelder, A.E. 23, 133
Bates, James 49
Battey, Frank C. ***43***, 44, 61, 62, 70, 79, 100, 116
Baxter 12
beach races 18, 25
Beasley, Abraham 9
Beecroft 101
Belgian Grand Prix 88, 96
Belgium 95, 96
Benz 17, 23, 27, 28, 52, 69, 81, ***89***, 90, 92, 93, 94, 97–99, 110, 120–

222

Index

134, *127*, 136, *137*, 138, 143, 147, 153–166, *157*, *158*, *159*, *160*, *164*, *165*, *166*, 171–178, 179–196, *182*, *185*
Bergdoll, Erwin 59, 80, 179–196, *185*
Bergdoll, Louis 27, 80–81, 94, 118, 143
Berliet 106
Berlin 89
Bête Noir, Alco 141
Bétheny 92
Beverly Hills 86
bicycle racing 2, 6
bicycle technology 5
Bigio, Guido 105
Birmingham, Alabama 25, 55
"Birthplace of Speed" 25
Blandford 35
Blériot (aircraft) 92
Blitzen Benz 81, 90, 99
B.L.M. 124
BNC 88
Boillot, Andre 106
Bollée 90, 97, 108
Bologna, Italy 37, 96, 199
Bona Bella 76, 149, *188*
Bonaventure Cemetery 46
Bonaventure Shell Road *8*
Books, John 61
Bordeaux, France 95, 106
Bordino, Pietro 105, 183
Bosch magneto 120, 122, 131; *see also* Simms-Bosch magneto
Boston 64, 99, 100, 101, 107
Bostwick, A.L. 91
Boulogne, France 93
Bowden 26
Boyd, William J. 70
Bragg, Caleb 28, 137, 138, 146, 179–196, 197
Brescia 83, 86, 106
Brescia to Mantua to Verona race 106
Breugeot Aircraft Company 108
Briarcliffe 55, 56, 57, 68, 81, 99, 106, 136
Briarcliffe Model Stearns 52
Bridgeport hill climb 53
Briggs, Ernest 151
Brighton, Massachusetts 144
Brighton Beach 52, 53, 86, 101, 125, 135, 143, 145, 146
Broad Street 71
Broadway 44, *132*
Bronx, New York 50
Brooklands 36, 41, *57*, 88, 104, 111, 134
Brooklyn 84, 101, 145
Brooklyn Polytechnic 84
Broughton Street 71, *113*, 123, 167
Brown, Gov. (Georgia) 150–151
Brown, W.F. 38
Bruce-Brown, David 2, 85, 94, 97, 98, 99, 105, 109, 110, 136–138, *137*, 146, 147, 153–166, *164*, *165*, *166*, 171–178, 179–196, 197, 201
Brunswick, Georgia (bicycle racers from) 10

Brussels 95
Bryson, T.A. 12, 82, 84, 116, 117, 154
Buckley 169–170
Budapest 107
Buffalo 49, 54
Buffalo Derby 53, 54, *73*
Buffalo Velodrome 7
Buick 52, 55, 81, 89, 92, 97, 107, 114, 115, 117, 118, 119, 120–134, 139, 140, 142, 153–166, *163*; *see also* Marquette Buick
Buick Bug 28
Buick Phenomenon 114–115
Bull Street 42, 62, 63, 64, 84, 123
Bullet 25
Burman, Bob 28, 53, *81*, 94, 118, 119, 120–134, 143, 153–166, *163*, 171–178, 179–196
Burns, John 3, 118
Burns, William R. 81–82

Cagno, Alessandro *82*, 83, 91, 105, 120–134, *125*
California 44, 139, 177
California Arrow dirigible 167, *168*
Callahan, *Daredevil* 12
Cambridge, Massachusetts 141
Cameron, Everett 83
Cameron, Forrest 83, 117, 118, 119
Cameron Car 83, 117, 118
Camplejohn, Herb 202
Canada 54
Candler, Asa 167
Cape Martin 92
Carsten Hall 46
Case, J.I. 39, 56, 180
Case car 56, 97, 141, 142, 168–169
Castaneta, Renzo 106
Cedrino, Emanuel 136
Ceirano brothers 103, 105
cement bicycle track 11
Cesso 105
Chadwick 29, 59, 60, *94*, 120–134, *125*
Chalmers, Hugh 48
Chalmers-Detroit 81, 82, 114, 118, 119, 143, 144
champagne, first poured in winner's circle 99, 136, 137, 165, 183
Champcar 2
Chandler, Billy 102, 153–166
Chapin, Roy 45, 46, 58
Chapple, A.G. 50
Charles River race 90
Charleston, South Carolina 10, 31, 45
Charlton Street 64
Charron, Fernand 90
Chase, Judge 19
Château-Thierry hill climb 86
Chatham County 38, 44, 63, 133, 167
Chathams 70
The Checkered Flag 3, 109, 137
Cherbourg 116
Chevrolet, Arthur 138–139, 153–166
Chevrolet, Gaston 139
Chevrolet, Louis 37, 53, 55, 98, 107, 139, 140, 155
Chevrolet Brothers Aircraft Co. 139

Chicago 3, 17, 47, 51, 93, 142, 143
Chicago Automobile Club 18, 19, 47, 59, 91
Chicago Daily Tribune 26
Chicago Times-Herald 17
Christie, Walter 25, 55, 71, 106, 142
Christie Car 27, 55, 106
Cincinnati 185
Circuit d'Auvergne 103, 107
Circuit des Ardennes 82, 86, 87, 92, 95–98, 108
Circuit du Nord (Paris) 97
City Hall Savannah 62, 133
City Market Savannah *112*
Cleary, George *204*
Cleary Motorcycle Company 204
Cleborne, A.B. 70
Clément, Albert 92
Clément-Bayard 92, 95, 96, 101, 106, 120–134
Clermont-Ferrand 103, 107
Cleveland, Ohio 47, 54
Cleveland News–Cleveland Automobile Club Reliability Run 51
Clifton, William 50
Climb to the Clouds 99
Coastal Highway 17, 44
coastal plain 31
Cobe, Harry 101, 139, 171–178, 179–196
Cobe Cup 97, 98
Cody, Lew 70
Cohen, Harry 151–153
Cole 135, 147, 151
Coliseum at Wheelmen's Park 7, 9, 10, 11, 12, 13
Cologne 95
Columbia 26
Columbia Yachting Club 68
Columbus 146
Coney Island 91
Connerat, R.V. 6, 10
Connors, Herbert P. 84, 116, 118, 119
Continental tires 115, 118, 122
convict labor *39*, *41*
Coppa della Velocita 83
Coppa Florio 2, 87, 98, 103, 122, 177, 199
Coppa Velocita Brescia 87
Corbin 144
Corona 146
Corsa (Fiat) 120
Corson, J.G. 70
Costello, Thomas 84, 118, 119, 147, 151–153
Cotton Carnival (Galveston) 28–30, 199
Coupe de la Sarthe 87
Coupe de l'Autodrome 88
Coupe des Voiturettes 87
Coupe d'Evreux 98
La Coupe Internationale 90
course building 21
Coventry, England 11
Crane-Atlanta 202
Criterium des Entranuers 106
Criterium International Belgium 95
Croker, Frank 26
crowd control 19

Crown Point 49
Crowter, J.G. 70
Cugnot 15
Cuneo, Joan 27, 28
Curtiss Airplane 58, 102; *see also* Curtiss Flyers
Curtiss Flyers 102, 175; *see also* Curtiss Airplane
Cuyler *9*
cycle classes 114

Daffin Park 46, 62, 63
Dale Avenue 42, *159*, *161*, *162*, *164*, *184*, 187, 202, 203
Daley, A. 70
Dallas, Texas 24
Dancy, William 70
D'Aoust Hispano-Suiza 88
Darracq 26, 27, 28, 50, 51, 61, 86, 92, 97, 98, 108, 109
D'Auvergne, Christian 106
Davant, Captain 93, 132
Davis, George 73
Dawson, Joseph Crook 140, 142, 145, 147–151, *150*, 153–166
Dayton, Ohio 5
Daytona Beach races 18, 25, 26, 29, 136
Decauville 26
De Dietrich 27, 86, 87, 122
De Dion 95, 106, 114, 139
De Dion, Count Jules 16, 17, 95
Delage 87, 106, 111, 144
Delauney-Belleville 88
demise of road racing 2, 197–204
Demogeot, Victor 26
De Palma, Ralph 27, 28, 53, 84–86, 105, 120, 141, 146, 153–166, *162*, 171–178, 179–196
De Rosa, Marius 63, 84, 115–117
DeSoto Hotel 10, 70, *123*
Detroit 3, 51, 57, 58
Dewar, Sir Thomas R. 26, 136
Diamond tires 65
Dieppe, France 23, 24, 87, 96, 137, 199
diminutive rider 10
Dingley, Bert 143
dirigible 22; *see also* California Arrow
Disbrow, Louis 140–141, 153–166, 168–169, 171–178, 179–196
Dixie Overland Highway 44
Doorley, Martin 147, 151–153
Dorian 28
Dourdan, France 86
Doyles Race Track 5, 7, *8*, 85
Duesenberg 29, 93, 97, 103
Dugdale hill climb 143
Duke of Marlborough 17
Duray, Arthur *86*, 86–88, 96, 120–134, 144
Dürer, Albrecht 15
Duryea 106
Duryea Brothers 5, 17, 71

East Cameron, Pennsylvania 93
East Huntington Street 46
Easter, Charles Ewing 88–89, 118, 119

Eastwood, Clint 46
Eaton, Jay 12
Eck 8
Economaki, Chris 2
Edge, S.F. 104
Edwards, R.D. 202
egg race (with bicycles) 10
electric-powered vehicle 15, 17
Elgin Trophy 60, 81, 86, 93, 97, 101, 143, 146
Eliminations Française de la Coupe International 92
Elkwood Park, New Jersey 53
Ellis, Charles 62
Ellis Island 117
Elmore 114
Emden 93
E-M-F 52, 147, 151–153, 168–169
Empire Track at Yonkers 89, 136
Endicott, Harry 29, 102, 151
Endicott, William 151
endurance 16, 51
Erle, Fritz 89–90, *89*, 120–134
Estill 40, 41, 42, 62, 63, 71, 72, 119, 125
Europe 19, 68, 90, 91, 105, 115, 117, 119, 136, 155, 183, 185, 196, 199
European aristocracy 16
European Grand Prix Circuit 86
Evans 168–169
Evanston, Illinois 17
Everall, H.J. 91
Excelsior 87, 202
Exiner, Rose Budd 69
Eyck, Robert 61

Fabry, Maurizio 105
Fagnano 156
Fairmount Park Motor Races 54, 59, 81, 94, 97, 101, 107, 134, 135, 139, 142, 144, 146
Falcar 148, *149*
Fariss, Seaton 68
Farman, Henry 92
"Fastest Race Ever Run" 183
fatalities 19, 37, 61, 99, 180, 197
fear of the automobile *16*, 19, 20, 88
Federal Highway Administration 5
Federation of American Motorcyclists 202
Ferguson Avenue 42, *164*, *181*, *186*
Ferrari, Enzo 103
Ferro 131, 153–166
Feyhl 156
Fiat 7, 23, 27, 28, 44, 50, 52, 55, 69, 82, 83, 85, 88, 98, 99, 103, *104*, 105, 109, 110, 120–134, *121*, *127*, *130*, *132*, 136, 137, 141, 144, 145, 148, 153–166, *159*, *161*, *162*, 171–178, 179–196, *198*
54th Street and Broadway *17*, *22*
Firestone, Harvey 25
Firestone tires 59, 168
first female driver 17
Fisher, Carl 30, 36, 200
flag 72, 194
Flagler, Henry 25, 26, 29
Floretta 105
Florida 25, 26, 27, 30, 98, 171, 173

Florio, Count Vincenzo 103
Flying Death 68
Flying Dutchman II 135
Flying Merkel 202
Foltz 32, 33
football 7
Ford 52, 114, 168–169
Ford, Henry 25, 70, 155
Formula One 2, 5, 204
Forsyth Park 116
Fort Erie 91
Fort George hill climb, New York 47, 48
Fort Lee–Edgewater hill climb 83
Foster, Charles 140
Fournier, Achille 92
Fournier, Henri 90–92, 99, 105, 120–134
Fournier, Maurice 92, 99
Fournier Searchmount Company 92
France 15, 17, 32, 53, 55, 83, 88, 92, 116, 122, 155, 199
Frankfort 89
Franklin 114
French Grand Prix 2, 53, 83, 86, 87, 90, 91, 92, 93, 98, 99, 103, 105, 106, 108, 110, 111, 129, 137, 144, 183, 199
Frieberg 59
Frontenac 103, 139

Gaillon hill climb 90
Galveston, Texas 25, 29–30, 59, 60, 199, 200
gas-powered vehicle 17
gasoline-fueled internal combustion 15
Gearless 69
Gelnaw (or Gelnau), Frank 148–151
General Automobile Reserve 87–88
Georgia Historical Society 3
Georgia State Savings Association 45
German Army 88
German Club 160, *161*, 162
German Volunteers 70
Germany 15, 45, 87, 103, 110, 155
Geschevanter, Felix 148
Giant's Despair hill climb 93, 94, 97, 136
Gilbert 81, 106
Gilette, P.T. 70
Gingerbread architecture 46
Giro d'Italia 103
Glencoe, Illinois 18, 19
Glenn, H. 202
Glidden, Charles Jasper 54
Glidden Tour 54, 71, 73
Goetz 156
Golden Era of Road Racing 1, 135, 166
Good Roads Movement 5, 34, 35, 57
Gordon Bennett Cup 19, 53, 68, 82, 86, 90, 91, 92, 95–97, 103, 107, 108
Gould, W. 26
Grand Central Palace 22
Grand Prix at Lyon 108
Grand Prix of Verona 106
Grand Prize of America Avenue 1

Grand Prize of the Automobile Club of America 120–134, *126*, 153–166, 179–196; *see also* American Grand Prize
Granger, Harvey *43*, 44, 61, 62, 199, 201
Grant, Harry 120–134, 140–142, 144, 153–166, *159*, 172–178
Great Auto Races 94, 200
Great Depression 86
The Great Savannah Races 2, 197
The Great Triumphal Carriage 15
"Greatest Race in America" 200
Green Dragon 26, 171
Greenfield 138
Gregoire 114, 117
Grey Ghost 103
Grimm *8*
Gross, W.W. 10
Gruner, Bert 61
Guardian Detroit Trust 46
Gueard, Ross 73
Guggenheim Trophy 53
Gunderson, Olaf 68
Guyot 144
Gyroscope 114

Habersham 41, 43
Hall (mechanician) 156
Hall, Ethel 83
Hamilton, C.M. 53
Hanriot, René 52, 92–93, 120–134, 194
Hanriot et Cie monoplane 110
Hanson, George 152
Harding 50, 68, 120–134
Harkness, Harry 144
Harlem 48
Harley Davidson 203, 204
Harris, R.V. 70
Harrisburg, Pennsylvania 177
Harroun, Ray 27, 140, 145, 147, 153–166
Hartman, Harry 143, 168–169
Harvard 17
Hathaway, J.F. 25
Haupt, Willie *94*, 93–95, 120–134, *125*, 147, 153–166, *158*, *159*
Hautvast, Lucien 95–96, 106, 120–134
Havens, Beckwith 102, 167, 175
Hayners Bridge 153, *187*
Hearne, Eddie 85, 96–97, 120–134, 144, 146, 179–196
Heim (mechanician) 156
Heinemann 147, 148–151, 169–170
Helck, Peter 3, 94, 109, 111, 137, 183, 196, 200
Hemery, Victor 27, 52, 94, 97–99, *98*, 109, 110, 120–134, 136, 137, 153–166, *159*, 179–196
Henry, Ernest 110
Herkomer Trophy 89
Herr, Don 60
Herrick, Harvey 177, 178
Herring-Burgess 100
hill-climbing capabilities 16
Hilliard, William M. 99–100, 118, 119

Hol-Tan 100
Horan, Joseph 29, 147, 153–166, *164*
horse races 12
The Horseless Age 29, 54, 153, 166
Hotchkiss 21, 27, 49, 61, 73, 81
Hotchkiss, President 61, 133, 134
Houpt-Rockwell 143
Houston 2
How the Race Was Run and Won 38
Hudson Motor Car Company 45, 51, 58, 103
Hudson (ship) 117
Hughes, Hughie 148–151, 169–170, *170*
Hull, R.M. 43, 199
Hungary 107
Hunter Army Airfield 38
Hussars 70
Hutchinson Island 1, 204
hydraulic vehicles 16

Imlay City, Michigan 81
Indian motorcycle 50, 202
Indian Refining Co. Inc. 38, *42*, 43
Indianapolis 500 25, 28, 29, 36, 37, 50, 56, 60, 65, 71, 85, 86, 93, 97, 103, 110, 135, 138–141, 143, 144–146, 197, 200, 201
Indy Lights 1, 204
Innsbruck, Austria 89, 95
International Association of Recognized Automobile Clubs 24
International Light Car Race 41, 42, 112–119
international race sanctioning 17, 19, 21, 23
International Sweepstakes 139
Interstate 52
Irish Jasper Green 70
Isle of Hope 42, 46, 74, 75, 76, *78*, 105, 130
Isotta-Fraschini 28, 47, 50, 51, 53, 55, 58, 65, 68, 69, 75, 77, 85, 107, 114, 141
Itala *82*, 83, 91, 105, 106, 120–134, *125*
Italian Grand Prix 110, 111
Italy 17, 65, 82, 84, 86, 104, 116, 119, 155

Jackson 28, 114, 139, 172–178
Jacksonville, Florida 26, 31, 44, 202
Jamaica Speed Trials 107, 136
Janke, Irving 203
Jeffers, Earl 118
Jekyll Island Club 24
Jericho Sweepstakes 81, 82
Johnson, G.H. 70
Johnson, Hiram 52
Johnson, J.L. 7, 10, 148, 151
Jones, Jabez 70
Jones, Maldwyn 203
Juhasz, Jean 84, 116

Kaiserpreis 87, 96, 103, 129
Kansas 96
Kaufman, A.G. 199
Keene (or Keane), Bruce 148–151, *150*, 156

Keene, Foxhall 91
Kellogg, Stanley 50
Kelly, Z.D. 203
Kelsey, Carl 100, 118, 119
Kelsey, R.G. 27
Kenilworth Park, Buffalo 58
Kiev 98
Kirscher 28
Kiser, Mr. John F., and Mrs. 74
Kjedlsen, S. 115
Klagenfort 89
Klaw and Erlanger Trophy 28
Klaxton Trophy 28
Kline Kar 51
Knickerbobcker Crisis 20; *see also* Panic of 1907
Knight, Harry 151
Knipper, William 48, 68, 103, 151–153, *153*, 169–170
Knox 28, 51
Kohlsaat, H.H. 17
Kramer (mechanician) 156
Kulick, Frank 28, 168–169

La Chaux de Fonds, Switzerland 138
La Consuma hill climb 87
La Roche 42, 73, *125*, 150, 160, *161*, *180*, *188*
La Sarthe 97
Labrousse, Madame 17
Lambert, Percy 88
Lancia 44, 100, 103, 114, 118, 119, 147, 151–153, *153*
Lands End to John D. Groats race 50
Lanza, Gaetano 90
Las Vegas 2
Lattimore, Ralston 70
Laurel Grove Cemetery 116
Laurence, Virginia 69
Lawrence, Sarah Dimpie 140
Lawson, Gus the Terrible Swede 12
Le Mans 87, 88, 90, 97, 199
Le Pré-Saint-Gervais, France 108
League of American Wheelmen 5, *6*, 7
Lebanon, Pennsylvania 145
Lee (mechanician) 156
Lee, Lawrence 70
Leland, Frank 47–48, 54, 58, 73, 74
Lemaître, Alain 16
Leningrad to Tiblisi to Moscow race 83
Leonardo da Vinci 15
Levey (or Levy), Harry 27, 73
Liberty Street 10, *123*
Liège 95
Light, Oliver 72
Lightning Benz 99
Limberg, Carl 143–144, 172–178, 179–196
Lincoln Street 10
Lindsay, W.J. 7
Linn, Joseph 67
Linz 89
liquid vehicles 16
Locomobile 53, 57
Locomotive 91
Long Island, New York 12, 20, 24,

27, 36, 37, 44, 46, 70, 83, 89, 91, 109, 139, 199
Long Island Automobile Derby 49, 50, 84, 93
Long Island Parkway 18, 19, 20, 34, 36, 37
Longaker, V.A. 66
Lorimer, J.B. 48, 49, 59, 72, 73, 119
Lorraine-Dietrich 87, 93, 108, 120–134
Los Angeles 97, 135
Louisville Road 10, 11
Lowell Road Race 49, 53, 57, 141, 143, 144
Loxley Trophy 26
Lozier 47, 51, 52, 65, 66, 75, 77, 101, 102, 107, 120–134, 141, 146, 153–166, 171–178, 179–196
Lozier, H.A. 101, 125, 129, 147
Lynch 52
Lyon, France 87, 95
Lytle, Herbert 48, 49, 51, 54, 57, 58, 59, 68, 71, 72, 74, 77, 79, 102

M & M Land Co. **8**
Macadam 32–39, 74
Macadam, John L. 35
MacAlpin, Henry 7
Macon, Oliver T. 199
Madison Square Gardens 143
Madonian Mountains 83
Maggi, Comte Aymo 106
Malsher, David 2
Manchester hill climb 50
Manker, Billy 59
Mannheim 89
Mardi Gras 27
Marion 55, 57
Marmon 81, 89, 145, 147, 148–151, 153–166, 169–170, 171–178, 179–196
Marquette Buick 81, 135, 139, 147, 153–166, **163**, 179–196; *see also* Buick
Marriott, Fred 27
Marseilles, France 116
Martin, Stanley 143
Massachusetts 83, 144
Massapequa 84, 143, 144
Massuero, Pilade 105
Match des Champions 88
Matheson 54, 73, 124
Matson, Joseph 144, 155, 172–178
Mauthasen Gusen 107
Maxwell (mechanician) 180
Maxwell 52, 84, 100, 114, 119, 147, 151–153
Mazotti, Franco 106
McCormick 69
McCulla 50, 51, 58, 68, 74, 75, 76
McDonald 26
McFarland, George 177
McNay, Jay 180
Meadowbrook Hunt Club 171
Mechanics Road **8**
Mercedes 23, 50, 53, 85, **103**, 110, 122, 135, 141, 146, 171–178, 179–196
Mercer 52, **125**, 145, 146, 148–151, 169–170, **170**, 171–178

Merkelbeek, Belgium 95
Merrimimack 84
Merz, Charley 60
Metropolitan Opera House 101
Metropolitan Trophy 144
Michelin 115, 120, 122, 162
Michener, Harry 51, 52, 74, 75, 77, 101
Midnight in the Garden of Good and Evil 46
Milan 106
"Mile a Minute Man" 55
military 92
military role 38, 63, 64, 70, 132, 150, **155**, 171, **182**, 183
Mille Miglia 106
Miller car 97
Milwaukee 143, 146, 197, **198**, 199
Minneapolis 93
Mitchell, John M. 71
Mitchell, Julian 56
Mitchell, Leland 172–178, 179–196
Model T 28
Moline 114
Monaco 31
"Monaco of the South" 2
monopolies 29, 30
Monte Carlo Casino 91
Montgomery Cross Roads 42, 73, 94, 158, 173, **174, 175**, 186, 189
Monti, Flaminio 106
Montreal 139
Monweiler 100–101, 118, 119; *see also* Muntwyler
Moore, James 16
Mora 69
Morgan, William 25
Morris, David Hennen 17, 21, 23
Morris, Gaston 143
Morris Park 24-hour race 50, 68
Mors 90, 91, 95, 106
Morton, Bob 70
Moscow 98
Moscow to St. Petersburg race 87
The Motor 54
motor bicycles 12
Motor Club of Harrisburg 51
Motor Cups Holding Company 199, 201
motor-paced racing 11
Motor Parkway Sweepstakes 135
Motor Sports Hall of Fame 86
motorcycle racing 2, 202
Motte, J. Ward 43, 199
Mount Auburn, Iowa 143
Mount Ventoux hill climb 83, 86
Mount Washington, New Hampshire, hill climb 99
Mudd, Frank X. 25
Mulford, Ralph 29, 52, 53, 60, 85, 101–103, **102**, 120–134, 125, 141, 145–147, 153–166, **164**, 172–178, **177**, 179–196
Muller 131
Munich 89
Munn, Capt. J.W. 29
Munsey magazine 24
Muntwyler 100–101; *see also* Monweiler

Napier 26, 27, 99, 104, 105
National 29, 120–134, 138, 139, 140, 155, 177–178
National Circuit Meet of Cleveland 100
Naval Reserves 70
Nazzaro & C. Fabbrica di Automobili 105
Nazzaro, Felice 52, 85, 96, 103–105, **104**, 120–134, **124, 130**, 153–166, 183
New Hampshire 54
New Haven, Connecticut 136
New Jersey 20, 87
New Orleans, Louisiana 25, 27–29, 55, 56
New York 3, 17, 22, 23, 26, 46, 49, 54, 55, 58, 61, 62, 64, 76, 84, 87, 115, 117, 122, 123, 136, 139, 140, 144, 146, 162, 199, 201
New York Court of Appeals 19
New York State Automobile Association 21, 23
New York Stock Exchange 20
New York Times 23, 56, 85, 109, 178, 201
New York to Paris race 74
New York to Seattle race 54
Newby 37
Newsetter (or Neustetter), Malcolm 52, 53, 74, 75, 77, **79**
Newton 105
Nice, France 86
Nikrent 169–170
Nolen, John 63
Norristown, Pennsylvania 94
North Carolina 171
Northern 114
Norwalk, Connecticut 83
Norwood Avenue 150, 169, 193, 202
Nostradamus 15
Notre Dame University 96
NSU motorcycle 50

Oakley, Cincinnati 91
O'Brien, F. 148
O'Byrne, W.C. 10
Ocean Parkway 91
Odon, Indiana 140
Oglethorpe Drive 154
oiling **42**
Old Skidaway Road 202
Oldfield, Barney 26–29, 56, 57, 71, 84, 85, 168, 171
Olds Pirate 25
Oldsmobile 114
Omaha 93
Opel 108
Ormond Beach 25, 26, 69, 71, 80, 135, 136
Oshkosh, Wisconsin 20
Ostend 88

Pablo Beach 26
Packard 27, 28, 51, 52, 81, 85
Paderewski, Ignacy Jan 48
Padua 82
Padua to Vicenzo race 103
Palermo 83

Pamlico Formation 31
Panhard-Levassor 16, 90, 95, 103
Panic of 1907 20; *see also* Knickerbocker Crisis
Pardington, A.R. 35
Paris 7, 63, 88, 92, 106, 107, 135
Paris to Berlin race 90
Paris to Bordeaux race 90, 106
Paris to Lyon race 90
Paris to Madrid race 86, 92, 106, 107, 108
Paris to Marseille race 17
Paris to Rouen race 16
Paris to Spa race 17
Paris to Vienna race 86, 91, 97, 107
Parker, Edward H. 144, 172–178
Passaic, New Jersey 85
Patschke, Cyrus 53, 101, 120–134, 145, 172–178, 179–196
Patton, Harry 148
Pennsylvania 49, 58, 60, 72, 73, 145
Penske, Roger 1
Pepparday 53, 106
Perry, Bob 202
Perry Hill 47, 59
Le Petit Journal 16
petitions and lawsuits 20
petrol power 16
Peugeot 16, 29, 87, 103, 106, 110, 111, 199, 200, 203
Philadelphia 27, 50, 52, 54, 64, 69, 70, 80, 92, 93, 123, 141, 146
Phillips Hill 47, 59
Piacenza, Giovanni 105, 120–134
Pierce bicycles 84
Pipe 95, 96
Pittsburgh, Pennsylvania 50
Point Breeze Race of Philadelphia 58, 81, 101
police 18
Polk, R.H. 7
Pollotti, Roxie 144
Poole, Al 53, 54, 58, 74, 75, 76, 101, 119, 145
Pope, Alexander 5
Pope-Hartford 135, 140, 141, 148, 153–166, 172, 178, 179–196
Pope-Hummer 5, 141, 168–169, 172–178
Pope-Toledo 26, 48, 49, 68
Pordenone 82
port city 13, 34
Porter, George 202
Portola Road Race, California 52
Potter, Alice 28
Pozzo (mechanician) 156
Prest-O-Lite 30
Price, Joseph 25
Prince, Jack (aka, John Shillington) 6, 11, 12
Providence, Rhode Island 93
Pulitzer 24
Pullman automobile 69, 70, 148
Pullman train car 171

Quattlebaum, Julian 2, 197

Raceabout 84
Racer magazine 2

Ragdale, A.H. 151
Rainey Brothers 12
Rambler 114
Ramsay, Alice 100
Rauers, J.J. 61
Reber Manufacturing 58
Reims 92
Renault 23, 26, 50, 52, 55, 56, 65, 69, 107, 108, 110, 120–134, *127*, 135, 139
Renault brothers 107
Rhode Island 83
Richmond, C.S. 7
Rickenbacker, Eddie 29
Rigal, Victor 96, 101, 106–107, 110, 120–134
Riverside, Connecticut 69
"Road Race Meet of the Century" 61, 170
Roberts, Mortimer 168–169
Robertson, George 28, 47, 50, 52, 53, 59, 67, 68, 117
Robinson, Pete 93
Rochester, New York 143
Rockefeller 24, 25, 29, 62
Roebling Road 203, 204
Roebling, Charles 146
Roebling, John 146, 204
Roebling, Washington Augustus, II 146, 148–151, 204
Roebling-Planche car 148, 155
Rolland-Pillain 99, 106, 110
Rome 106
Rothmans Porsche Series 1
Round-the-State-Tour (Georgia) 167
Royal Automobile Club 134
Rules of the International Recognized Clubs at Ostend 23

safety 19, 23
Saga of the Roaring Road 71, 86
St. Cloud, Paris 16
Saint-Hadelin de Vise College 95
St. Johns Cathedral 116
St. Louis, Missouri 21, 63
St. Patrick's Day 63, 70
St. Petersburg 98
Salsman (also Salzman), George 47, 49, 53, 54, 73, 74
Saluzzo 82
San Antonio, Texas 25, 28
San Francisco, California 52, 141, 203
Sandfly 203
Santa Monica, California 103, 138, 146, 201, 203
Savannah, Mayor of 32, 43–46, *45*, 46
Savannah Automobile Club 24, 32, 46, 61, 70, 79, 113, 133, 167, 171, 179, 201
Savannah Automobile Club Car *11*
Savannah Challenge 47–59, 63, 66, *78*, *79*, 147–151, 168–170, *170*, 171, 173
Savannah Electric Company 5, 6
Savannah Electrics (baseball team) 9
Savannah Evening Press 49, 72
Savannah Gray Brick 46
Savannah Morning News 71, 90

Savannah Motorcycle Club 202
Savannah Volunteer Guard 70
Savannah Volunteer Guard Armory *64*
Savannah Wheelmen 6, 10
La Savoie (ship) 115
Scarritt, Winthrop E. 17
Schroeder, E.J. 103, 183
Schuman, R.E. 10
Scudelari, Anthony 138
Sealed Bonnett contest 101
Searchmount Automobile Company 92
Senna, Ayrton 80
Seraye (mechanician) 156
Seymour, Joseph Morton 107, 120–134
Shaft, F.B. 81
Shapiro, Mrs. A.H. 71
Sharpe-Arrow 155
Shawmut 99
Sheepshead Bay 85, 93, 144
Shepherd, Elliott 49, 61
Sheppard, L.D. 48
Sheppard Auto Co. 48
Sherman Antitrust Act 30
Shubenacadie, Nova Scotia 83
Sillé le Guillaume, France 97
Simms-Bosch magneto 120
Simplex 28, 69, 85, 107, 120–134, 141, 143, 155
Sioux City 145, 146
Skidaway Road 5, *9*, 42
Skippack Hill 94
Slidell, Louisiana 139
Sloop, Gray 203
Smith (bicycle racer) 7
Smith, Coker F. 35
Smith, F.L. 115
Smith, Hoke 61, 64, 70, 167
Société Française de Petite Outillage (S.P.O.) 84, 115, 116, *117*, 119
Society of Automobile Engineers (SAE) 100
Solomon, Arthur W. *43*, 61, 62, 171, 199
Soukhanoff, Prince Boris 88
South Carolina 171
Souther, Henry Engineering 113, 114
Southern High-Powered Cup 48–59, 63, 64, 73
Southern Runabout Cup 71
Spa 31, 88, 95
Spa Criterium 86
Spanish American War 142
Spartanburg, Pennsylvania 142
Spaulding, Jeanne (aka, Louise Alexander) 56
speed 16
"the Speed King" 103, *104*, 129, 130
speeding 18
Speedwell 52
S.P.O. *see* Société Française de Petite Outillage
Sports Car Club of America (SCCA) 204
Sprint cars 139
Standard Oil 29
Stanley Steamer 26, 27

Starr, Grace Ethel 69
steam-powered vehicles 15, 16
Stearns 47, 48, 49, 52, 54, 58, 65, 73, 74, 75, 101, 145
Steensen, H.R. 10
Stevens-Duryea 52, 93
Stevens Technical Institute 84
Stiles *8*
Stillwell, W.B. 62
Stoddard-Dayton 155
stoker 16
Strang, Louis Putnam Christie 28, 32, 47, 51, *55*, 55–58, 74, 75, 79, 120–134, *128*, 136, 142
street car line 7
Studebaker 29, 69, 70, 144
Sturges motorcycle 17
Stutz, Harry 57, 60
Sunbeam 106, 144
Supreme Court 44, 201
"the Surly One" 98, 129
Susa Mont Cenis hill climb 82
Switzerland 100
Sydney to Melbourne Cup 50
Szisz, Ferenc 52, 56, *86*, 107–108, 120–134

Talbot 111
Targa Florio 83, 87, 90, 92, 103, 105, 106, 109, 111, 120, 129
Taunus Mountains, Germany 95
Taylor, Lee 203
Taylor, Major Marshall 10, 84
Texas State Automobile Association 29
Thomas, E.R. 53, **73**
Thomas, Frank 89, 119
Thomas, H.T. 25
Thomas Car *34*, 73, 93, 94
Thomas-Detroit Bluebird 48, 59, 72, 73
Thomas-Detroit Flyer 49, 54, 65, 72, 73, 74
Thompson, Jefferson De Mont 21, 23, 36
Thor motorcycle 202, 204
Thorne, William 142
Thunder at Sunrise 3
Thunderbolt 5, 6, 7, 10, 12, 42, 71, 74, 85, 125, *156*, 167
Thunderbolt Casino 5, *7*, 79, 100, 113
Thunderbolt Shell Road 7
Tiedeman, George W. *43*, 44, 61, 62, 72, 79, 112, 116, *150*, 167, 171, 199; children of 46
Tiedeman, Irvin 45, 46
Tiedeman, Otto 45
Tiedeman Mortgage and Finance 46
Tiedeman Trophy 84, 143, 147, 151–153, *153*, 167–170, 171
Tiffany and Gorham 79, 100
Timms, Rick 1, 204

Tipo 105
Titanic 145, 146
Tomochichi Trophy 63, 64
Tone, Fred 47, *57*, 57–58, *66*, *67*, 74, *75*, *76*, *77*, *78*
total value of manufactured automobiles 15, 16
Tracey, Joseph 53, 61
Tracy, Paul 1
Train, J.K. 70
Trésaguet 32
trick riding 6
Trinidad Lake Asphalt 38, 62, 123
Tsar Nicholas Rally 98
Turin 82, 83, 103, 105, 137
Turville, Charles 12
Tyson, John H. 55, 68

U.S. Navy 142
U.S. Office of Road Inquiry 5
U.S. Steel 30
University of Toronto 1

Van Sicklen, N.H. 43
Vanderbilt, Consuelo 17
Vanderbilt, Cornelius, III 17, 21; family 12
Vanderbilt, William Kissam, Jr. (aka, Willie K) *17*, 19, 20, 21, 23, 26, 35, 70, 91, 106, 122, 133, 136
Vanderbilt, William Kissam, Sr. 17
Vanderbilt Cup 2, 5, 12, 19, 21, *24*, 26, 27, 29, 34, 35, 36, 37, 46, 49, 50, 53, 54, 55, 61, 62, 65, 67, 71, 79, 83, 85, 87, 98, 99, 100, 101, 102, 107, 108, 109, 133, 134, 136–142, 144–146, 150, 153, 155, 166, 168, 170–178, *173*, *177*, *179*, 191, 197, 199, 200–203
Veil, Duster and Tire Iron 100
Velocitas Sine Periculo 21
Vernon River 42
Victorian District 46
Victory Drive 5, 6, *9*, 31, 40, 62, 63, 72, 125, 202
La Vie au Grand Air 99, 110
Vienna 89, 107
Vigilance League 69
Virginia 70
Voisin brothers 92

Waco, Texas 25
Wagner, Fred *71*, 72, 73, 85, 94, 117, 118, 127, 138, 148, 151, 172, 178, 201
Wagner, Louis 52, 61, 85, 92, 98, 99, 105, 106, 108–111, *110*, 120–134, *159*, *161*, 179–196, 192
Waldorf-Astoria 199
Walker 54
Wall Street 146
Wallie, William 151
Walthour, Bobby 12
War Cruiser 76

Warsaw 5, 7, 42
Warsaw River 5, 7
Washington, D.C. 70
Washington Park 91
Watchman and Southron 171
Waters Avenue 42, 119, 149, *159*, *161*, *163*, *164*, *184*, 202
Watson, William 107
Wauwatosa 138
Webb, Jay 49, 54
weight specifications 114
Welsh, Steve 10
West, T. Newell 38
Whaley, T.P. 10
Wheeler 37
Wheeler, H.C. 6, 10
Wheelmen's Park 5, 7, 8, *9*, 10, 63, 84
Whitaker 6
White, G.R. 70
White Bluff Drive 38, 42, 72, 73, 101, 118, 127, 131, 175, *190*
White Mountains, New Hampshire, to New York City race 100
The White Riders 10
Whitefield Avenue 42, *195*, 202
Whitesides, S.M. 7
Wichita Falls, Texas 25
Wilkes-Barre hill climb 93, 97, 136
Williams, Charles L. 6, 10
Williams, F.W. 6
Williamson, W. 62
Willys 145
Willys-Overland 58
Wilmington Island 12
Wilmington River *6*, *7*, 42, 85
Wilson, M. Ed 10
Winton, Alexander 25, 91
Wisconsin 56
Wishart, Spencer 141, 146, 172–178, 179–196
Wishart-Dayton Auto Truck Company 146
Witt, Frank 151–153, 168–169
Wolters, Joe 203
wooden bicycle racing tracks 11
World of Wheels 1
World War I 63, 80, 83, 87, 90, 92, 96, 105, 106, 108, 110, 144
World War II 96, 139
Wray, William 76
Wright, Ellery 147, 151–153
Wright, Orville, and Wilbur 5, 92

yacht races 7, 12
Yale 195
Yale motorcycle 202
Yamacraw 64
Yerkes, Jonathan 202

Zengle, Len 47, 49, 58–59, 60, 72, 73, 120–134
Zimmerman, August 7, 9, 10

www.ingramcontent.com/pod-product-compliance
Lightning Source LLC
Chambersburg PA
CBHW081552300426
44116CB00015B/2858